Flying for the Air Service

Flying for the Air Service:
The Hughes Brothers in World War I

David K. Vaughan

Bowling Green State University Popular Press
Bowling Green, OH 43403

Copyright © 1998 Bowling Green State University Popular Press

Library of Congress Cataloging-in-Publication Data
Vaughan, David Kirk.
    Flying for the air service : the Hughes brothers in World War I /
David K.
        p.   cm.
    Includes bibliographical references and index.
    ISBN 0-87972-761-6. -- ISBN 0-87972-762-4 (pbk.)
    1. Hughes, George Forbes, 1892-1971--Correspondence. 2. Hughes,
Gerard Hastings, 1895-1996--Correspondence. 3. World War, 1914-1918--
Aerial operations, American. 4. United States. Army Air Forces--
Biographies. 5. World War, 1914-1918--Personal narratives, American.
6. Air pilots--United States--Correspondence. I. Title.
D606.V38   1998
940.4'4973--dc21
                                                                98-15414
                                                                CIP

Cover design by Dumm Art

Contents

List of Illustrations

Introduction

This book describes the flying activities of two brothers who began and completed their aviation careers together in the United States Air Service during World War I. George and Gerard ("Jerry") Hughes entered pilot training together prior to the onset of World War I and completed training within one week of one another. As the war ended, they briefly flew together once again in the same aero squadron in France. Although they began and ended their careers in one another's company, they followed separate paths during a fifteen-month period between the beginning and the end of their wartime odysseys. George, the older brother, saw service over the front during much of that fifteen-month period, while the younger brother, Jerry, spent most of the war as an instructor pilot in the United States.

They were among the first to fly in the United States Air Service, and the descriptions of their experiences in their parallel careers, as provided in the letters they wrote during the war, and the narratives they prepared after the war ended, present a complete picture of Air Service activities at home and abroad from the earliest days of American involvement to the end of the war. The two Hughes brothers were in constant contact with each other and with their mother, and their letters illustrate with great clarity the personal impact of the American war in the air. In addition to providing many technical details and operational insights, their narrative offers a glimpse of the attitudes and experiences of two reasonably typical American young men as they developed from neophyte aviators to seasoned flying veterans. Their remarks show how they and many others like them viewed the challenge presented by the war in France. Through their comments we can sense how the national mood evolved from the time of the American entry into the war in France until its conclusion.

Historical Background

When America entered the war in 1917, aviation as an instrument of war was an unknown quantity. The Air Service was the newest branch of the United States Army; it was not officially established until America had been at war for a year, in May of 1918. The first Army unit associated with flying activities had been the Aeronautical Division of the U.S.

Army Signal Corps; it was established in 1907 at the request of President Teddy Roosevelt. Roosevelt believed that the Army should be prepared to accommodate the potential represented in the wonderful new flying machine that had been invented and demonstrated by Wilbur and Orville Wright, who first flew in December of 1903 and who sold their first flying machine to the Army in the fall of 1907. Initially, the Aeronautical Division was concerned more with balloons than with flying machines, for the division was primarily interested in developing its reconnaissance capabilities and increasing the speed and reliability of the messages it was responsible for transmitting.

However, the reliability and capability of flying machines increased dramatically, and the Army formed the Aviation Section of the Signal Corps in July of 1914, one month before the war in Europe began. In spite of the rapid development of aviation in Europe, largely as a result of the war in the air, American aircraft were slow to evolve. By the time America entered the war, in April of 1917, it had produced only a few training aircraft, built primarily by the Burgess, Curtiss, and Standard aircraft companies.

Although the American leadership entered the war with optimistic visions of the numbers of aviators and aircraft it hoped to commit to the war effort, the reality was that in April of 1917 America had very few pilots and no aircraft capable of enduring the rigors of combat. A massive training program was begun, but before pilots could be trained, airfields had to be built and training aircraft had to be produced.

Although a large aviation appropriations bill had been passed in July of 1917 for the unprecedented amount of $640 million, it took time to build airfields and aircraft, and aircraft production reached desired levels only in October and November of 1918, just as the war ended. In the meantime, student pilots had to be trained slowly and in relatively small numbers, in aircraft that were fragile and unreliable, and on airfields that had just been constructed.

The Military Careers of the Hughes Brothers

George and Gerard Hughes were among the vanguard of these early fliers. Students at Harvard University during the winter of 1916-1917, they volunteered when the call went out for young men to join the Aviation Section of the Signal Corps, as it was called then. Along with many of their Harvard classmates, they were accepted into the Army's training program at Mineola, New York, on Long Island near Garden City. There, on two large grass pastures, they learned how to fly.

They had just reported for duty at Mineola when America officially entered the war in April of 1917. They completed their training at Mineola in July. Among the very first of the new American pilots, they were initially tasked not to travel to the front and fight the war, as they had hoped, but to stay in the United States and instruct other pilots. George, the older of the two, was sent to Wilbur Wright Field, at Dayton, Ohio. Jerry was sent to Chanute Field, at Rantoul, Illinois.

Then, in October of 1917, George was notified that he had been placed in command of a new unit, the 12th Aero Squadron, and was given the job of taking the new squadron across the Atlantic to France. George guided the squadron successfully across the Atlantic, arriving in France at the end of December. By February of 1918 the squadron had been designated as an observation squadron, and was declared combat-ready by May. George flew with the squadron until the middle of July, when he was placed in charge of a new unit, the 258th Aero Squadron. For two months, George trained his men and obtained the necessary aircraft and support equipment. Finally, just as the 258th was about to be declared combat-ready, the war ended.

In the meantime, Jerry Hughes was involved in training novice pilots at two locations in the United States. He remained at Chanute Field until December of 1917, and then was assigned as an instructor at Rich Field, near Waco, Texas. He instructed at Waco until August of 1918, when he was finally sent to France. Bad weather delayed his progress through the advanced American flying school at Issoudun, where he spent the entire month of October. He then moved to the American gunnery school at St. Jean de Monts, which he completed in a week's time. He was cleared for reassignment to a combat unit, but arrived at the assignment station in Toul, France, just as the war ended.

Even though the war was over, the Hughes brothers anticipated flying together in the 258th as part of the occupation forces entering Germany. However, a few days after the Armistice George suffered an emotional breakdown that caused them to change their plans and return to the United States with the bulk of the returning veterans. They arrived in New York City late in January and were released from the service early in February 1919. Between the two of them, however, their experiences encompassed practically the full range of adventures that befell American aviators in World War I. George had flown in combat and been shot at, and he had commanded a squadron that was becoming combat-ready as the war ended. Jerry, meanwhile, had flown as an instructor at two fields in the United States and had escaped death a number of times, narrowly avoiding catastrophe as a flight instructor. Amazingly, although both experienced numerous flying accidents, neither received serious physical injury. Flying in combat, however, took its toll on George, whose illness clearly resulted from the strain of flying during the war.

In addition to providing insight into the typical experiences of American Air Service pilots at home and abroad in World War I, the written accounts of the two Hughes brothers explain the details of the flying activities of Air Service pilots at home and abroad. Although the records of many of the men who flew in combat have been partly documented, details relating to their daily training and noncombat activities are often missing. The name of George Hughes, for instance, appears in two accounts of American airmen flying in the war (Hudson 291; Sloan 147). Brief illustrated biographies of both brothers appeared shortly after the war in the comprehensive *New England Aviators 1914-1918: Their Portraits and Their Records* (Lowell 1, 206-10) (Figs. 1 and 2). These works mention only a few positions and dates. Information about the activities of men who conducted training in the United States is even more sketchy and incomplete. In the comments made by both George and Jerry during their periods as instructor pilots, we learn of the hazards faced by those who trained the pilots as well as those who received the training.

For American pilots the chances of injury or death were much greater in training than in combat; American participation in the war was much less extensive than that of the British or French (Vaughan 9-10). American-led and -equipped squadrons were involved in the war for only the final six months of a conflict that lasted more than four years. The relative brevity of the American participation does not diminish the effects of the rugged conditions and hazardous experiences that had to be endured by American aviators, conditions and experiences that are well documented in the letters of the Hughes brothers.

During the time that the two Hughes brothers matured from apprentices to masters of the flying trade, they came in contact with many notable people of the period, including Quentin Roosevelt, youngest son of former President Teddy Roosevelt, fated to fall in combat over France; Bert Acosta, famed civilian flight instructor; Victor Pagé, one of the earliest authors of aeronautical engineering texts; Rudolph "Shorty" Schroeder, one of the first and best test pilots, who set an altitude record over Dayton, Ohio, after the war; Frank Coffyn, one of the first pilots trained by the Wright brothers; Major Harry Brown, who gained infamy by landing by mistake with a flight of 96th Aero Squadron bombing aircraft at the German-held town of Metz; Elmer Haslett, colorful operations officer of the 12th Aero Squadron, who eventually became a prisoner of war and wrote a book about his experiences; Guy Gilpatric, later well-known author of the "Glencannon" stories, which appeared in

Fig. 1. Captain George Forbes Hughes, United States Air Service. Photograph made after Captain Hughes returned to America. The pin shown below the pilot's wings on the left breast is the Lion of Belfort, a landmark of the town near which the men in the 258th Aero Squadron trained; it was adopted as the squadron insignia. The strain of flying in combat is evident.

Fig. 2. Lieutenant Gerard (Jerry) Hastings Hughes, United States Air Service. This photograph was taken after the war. Jerry also wears the pin of the Lion of Belfort, the insignia of the 258th Aero Squadron. The Sam Browne belt Jerry is wearing (the leather belt-shoulder strap combination) was the hallmark of aviators who flew in France.

the *Saturday Evening Post;* General William "Billy" Mitchell himself; and many officers who later rose to the rank of general, including Clinton Russell, Lewis Brereton, Ralph Royce, and Thomas Hanley.

Family Background

Like so many other American aviators in the Air Service, the Hughes brothers came to the war as products of the relatively upper-class environment of the east coast college system. Both George and Jerry were students at Harvard when they joined the Air Service. Before moving to New England, they had been raised in the rugged environs of the south Texas farming regions. Their father, William George Hughes, had come to Texas from England in 1878 at the age of eighteen. A man of determination and independent outlook, William Hughes was a product of a distinguished British heritage.

His great-grandfather, the Reverend Thomas Hughes, was the vicar of Uffington Church and one of three canons of St. Paul's Cathedral, London. His wife, Mary Ann Watts Hughes, was an outgoing hostess and a scholar as well, authoring a biography of Sir Walter Scott, who was a visitor in their household (Perry 3). William's grandfather, John Hughes, an only child, was an author and artist. He and his wife, Margaret Elizabeth Wilkinson, raised six children, five boys and a girl: George, Thomas, William Hastings, Walter Scott, Arthur, and Elizabeth. The girl, Elizabeth, a talented singer, was a friend of Jenny Lind, Alfred Tennyson, George Eliot, and George Frederick Watts. Her brother Thomas Hughes, a scholar and writer, gained lasting fame by writing the classic work, *Tom Brown's School Days* and other works based on his experiences at the Rugby school for boys. Later, in 1880, he helped to found a "Christian Socialist-oriented community for middle to upper class British immigrants," at Rugby, Tennessee, located 35 miles northwest of Knoxville (Perry 4).

William's father was William Hastings Hughes, the middle son, who established a successful wine importing business. One of four children, William received a good education for a while at Marlborough until his father's reduced circumstances forced him to leave school. Seeing that the family fortunes were diminishing, William decided to move to America. His determination to travel to Texas may have resulted from a meeting with a Dr. W. G. Kingsbury of San Antonio and Boerne, Texas, who had traveled to England to promote English immigration to Texas (Perry 7).

William landed in America in the fall of 1878 and by March of 1879 he had bought a 160-acre parcel of land near Boerne, Texas, which he stocked with two rams his father had shipped from England. For the next four years he increased the size of his sheep herd and the size of his ranch. He persuaded his two brothers, Gerard and Henry, to work the ranch with him. In the meantime, his father had come to New York and his grandmother, uncle Thomas Hughes, and sister had come to live at the utopian community in Rugby, Tennessee. William married a girl from a nearby family, Lucy Caroline Stephenson, in 1888. Three children were born of the marriage: Jeanie Elizabeth, 1889; George Forbes, 1892; and Gerard Hastings, 1895. George and Gerard were constant companions, sharing the adventure of Texas ranch life together.

By 1902 the Hughes ranch amounted to over 7000 acres. However, just when it seemed that William Hughes's fortune was about to become fully established, he died tragically, on November 26, 1902, just outside Belleville, Illinois. He was accompanying a load of goats he intended to sell to a buyer in Kentucky when the freight train in which he was riding was struck by another train in rainy weather. William, who was sleeping in the caboose, was instantly killed. After untangling the legal details of the Hughes estate, Lucy and her three children moved to Boston early in 1904. Her father-in-law, William Hastings Hughes, convinced her that she and her children should move to New England. For the next twelve years the boys were raised in the Boston area. Both attended the Milton Academy before entering Harvard. The older brother, George, attended Dartmouth College briefly before dropping out to travel to Oregon for a while, and then joined his younger brother at Harvard. In the fall of 1916 they applied for Air Service training, and in March of 1917 they were accepted.

The Evolution of This Book

Long after the Hughes brothers returned from the war, Jerry Hughes retyped the old letters that he and George had written to their mother and to each other. In addition, he provided an accompanying narrative that clarified gaps in the letters or explained some incidents that were omitted or covered quickly in the letters. Jerry originally intended this account to be read primarily by the two daughters of his older brother George, who had died in 1971, and by his own son and three daughters and the members of their families. Knowing that members of his family might not be familiar with the technical terminology and organizational peculiarities of Air Service operations, he explained these details carefully and provided additional historical information. Jerry sorted through photographs that he and his brother had taken during the war, identifying the people in them to the best of his ability, and providing additional commentary.

Jerry worked on his project for many years, placing his comments and accompanying photographs in loose-leaf notebooks. In the meantime, both his brother's children and his own had grown and formed families of their own. One day, after reading a copy of the book of letters of another Air Service pilot that I had edited (*An American Pilot in the Skies of France: The Diaries and Letters of Lt. Percival T. Gates, 1917-1918*), he asked his daughter Jean to contact me to see if I would be interested in helping him organize the materials he had gathered. Once I learned his story, I readily agreed.

Narrative Materials

The narrative that follows consists of a number of speaking voices. The source of each is identified at the beginning of each segment within each section. As editor, I have supplied in italics introductions and occasional additional commentary for each of the sections; my comments are intended to establish the historical framework against which to view the experiences of the Hughes brothers. At the heart of the narrative are the letters written by George and Jerry Hughes during 1917 and 1918. Most often the recipient is the boys' mother, Lucy Hughes. Several of George's letters are addressed to Jerry. Jerry also wrote to his brother, but these letters do not seem to have survived. Less frequent addressees are Jeanie Hughes, the boys' older sister; Mrs. Morgan Brooks, a friend of the family whom Jerry often visited in Rantoul, Illinois; and two youthful acquaintances of Jerry's Boston upbringing, the De Boutillier sisters.

Interspersed throughout the letters is the voice of Jerry Hughes, in the explanatory narrative he prepared after his brother's death. This narrative is insightful not only for the additional information it provides, but for the later, more mature perspective it gives of the youthful attitudes and actions, primarily of Jerry himself, but also, on occasion, of comments George made in his letters to their mother. An additional voice is that of Jerry's brother, George. Although George never wrote an extended narrative after the war, as Jerry did, he wrote a brief commentary in his photo album identifying the contexts of some of the pictures. He included a chronological account of the travels of the 12th Aero Squadron as it moved from Dayton, Ohio, to Amanty, France, and then to the front. These comments were especially helpful in identifying the evolution of the unit's leadership and training activities. George's album also included various documents that provide factual milestones at times when there are no letters to give an indication of important events in George's career in the 12th and 258th Aero Squadrons.

The overall effect is a chorus of voices, mine as editor, Jerry's looking back on events at a distance of some sixty years, George's postwar comments, and at the heart of all of these, the letters themselves, written by George at the age of 24 (in 1917) to 26 (in 1919) and Jerry at the age of 22 to 24. But without the lifelong efforts of Jerry Hughes to maintain and develop his and his brother's stories as Air Service pilots, this document would not have come to fruition. Jerry served as caretaker of the facts and documents that constituted the history of an important period of time in their lives and in the American military's century of growth. That is the story that is presented here.

The narrative is divided into nine main sections. Although such division might appear to be artificial or unrealistic, focusing on each person's activities in separate packages, in fact the logic of the narrative is scarcely interrupted, for two reasons. When they were together in training or in France, they shared the duties of writing to their mother, and so the information provided in their letters is sequential. When they were apart, living in different locations, there was a delay in the transmittal of their mail. When Jerry was in Illinois and George was in Ohio, there was often a delay of two to three weeks. Trans-Atlantic mail took six weeks; thus, when George was in France, it might take as much as three months for the communication loop to be closed: six weeks for a letter to reach the States, and another six weeks for the reply to reach France. George's sense of isolation while he was in France can clearly be attributed to the delay in receiving mail. The slowness of the mail and the lack of rapid communication explain why Jerry was in France for almost two months before George learned about it. It is also not surprising to discover that mail to the men in France was slow to reach them, because a man might move about irregularly during training or while in combat, as the squadron moved from one field to another as combat requirements dictated.

In the material that follows, I have silently eliminated comments pertaining to minor family affairs and have standardized spelling and punctuation. I have inserted clarifying remarks, shown in brackets, whenever I thought terms or concepts required further explanation. In addition, whenever unusual or historically significant people are mentioned in the narrative, I have placed an asterisk [*] after their names, indicating that further clarifying comments about them can be found in an appendix. The identities and activities of many people are explained in the narrative; other names, however, have been impossible to identify with any certainty. A bibliography lists source works I have cited in this Introduction and elsewhere and which provide informative reading pertaining to flying activities of the World War I era. The bibliography also lists other works pertaining to the units and people described in the narrative.

Finally, I would like to thank several people who helped with the preparation of this narrative. Stephen Wright, great-grand-nephew of

Wilbur and Orville Wright, and a professional photographer in the Dayton area, provided invaluable assistance in preparing the photographs used in this book. Barbara Solosy, Pat Browne, and other readers for the Popular Press at Bowling Green, Ohio, gave me useful feedback on the narrative's form and content. Jerry and Charlotte Hughes provided energetic support to my wife and me, especially when we visited the Hughes family in New Hampshire in November of 1994. Their daughters, Jean and Marion, also provided assistance in preparing and sending materials through the mail. Other members of their families have also been helpful and supportive of this project. But this narrative would never have seen print without the lifelong efforts of Jerry Hughes, who diligently kept this record of his and his brother's World War I activities alive for many years. Through this narrative, not only do the experiences of those two World War I fliers live again, so do the experiences of every other person they mention, and by extension, all those Americans who flew for the cause of the Allies in the skies of America and France in 1917 and 1918.

1

In Training at Mineola

George and Jerry Hughes learned how to fly at Mineola Field, located in Garden City, Long Island, New York. George and Jerry were attending Harvard University when they volunteered together to serve in the United States Air Service. As their earliest letters show, they traveled to New York to pass the necessary tests. Eventually they were accepted into the Air Service. George arrived at Mineola by the fifteenth of April 1917, and Jerry arrived a few days later. When they began, there were so few military pilots that civilian instructors were hired to provide training. George Hughes was assigned one of the best—Bert Acosta.* Jerry Hughes was assigned to Wil Wheaton, a new civilian instructor who was understandably nervous about his responsibilities. George and Jerry Hughes spent the first month or so settling in to camp routine and attending ground school—classes on aircraft rigging and engines, Morse code, drill. On the first of May they began their flight training; Jerry's records show that on that day he received ten minutes of flying time with Instructor Manning. He received an additional 45 minutes later that week. Partly because their instructors were still involved in training, and partly due to rainy weather, their class was slow in starting.

There were three main phases of flying training. First the student had to demonstrate the ability to take the aircraft off and land it safely. Then after soloing the aircraft in the landing pattern, the student was required to practice solo maneuvers in the air. Finally, the student was required to fly a solo cross-country flight with thirty-mile legs to a distant field and then to return to the home field. Around the first of June George demonstrated progress in his flying, but that progress was inconsistent. After learning what he needed to do to correct his problems, he soloed on June 5 Jerry soloed over a week later, on June 16. Once George and Jerry passed the crucial hurdle of solo status, their letters to their mother reflect increased animation and confidence.

Especially in the letters he wrote home after he soloed, George demonstrates a real ability to describe flying experiences and his reaction to them in clear and direct language. Having passed his solo test,

George began to demonstrate the "take-charge" attitude that becomes increasingly evident in his subsequent letters. George's style in his letters home is controlled and structured, while Jerry's style is more spontaneous, more emotional, and more succinct. These distinctive characteristics of the two Hughes brothers remain evident in their subsequent letters.

For the next month they practiced their landings and then flew the necessary cross-country flight that signaled completion of the course and the awarding of their wings—the reserve military aviator (RMA) ranking. George won his RMA on July 7, while Jerry passed his on July 11. According to his flight log, at the time he completed the program at Mineola, Jerry had flown for a total of just over twenty hours of flying time. Their training was relatively accident-free; only one classmate died in training, though they saw two enlisted men fall to their deaths when they took off in an aircraft they did not know how to fly.

JERRY'S COMMENTS

In the fall of 1916, my older brother, George, and I were at Harvard University, living together at 42 Matthews Hall, in the "yard." A notice was posted which stated that the Aviation Section of the Signal Corps (the Army Air Corps of those days) wanted a group of volunteers to enlist for the purpose of learning to fly and becoming Reserve Military Aviators (RMAs). Only college men should apply. The same notice was posted in practically all the big Eastern colleges.

George and I had been interested in flying for four years. When George was at Dartmouth in 1911-1912, he joined the flying club up there and participated in the first flying competition between schools, going with other members over to Cornell to vie with their glider team. I told George that I was going to get a form and apply. He said that if I did, so would he. We obtained the necessary papers. In due course, we received word from the Signal Corps in December of 1916 that we should report to Governor's Island, in New York City, for physical examinations.

We journeyed down to the big city full of hope that we could pass the tests. They examined us in various ways, especially checking our eyes. Because the program was new, the requirements were not as exacting and severe as they were later, after war was declared in April of 1917. Then, thousands of young men were drawn into the Corps. I am sure that would never have passed if I had gone in later, because of my eyes [Jerry wore glasses throughout his flying career]. We sat up at Harvard through that winter waiting for word. Late in February we were told to travel to Mineola for one last series of tests.

GEORGE HUGHES TO LUCY HUGHES
Saturday, 3 March 1917
Dear Mother:

I was very sorry to hear that you are worried about us. It's the worst thing you can do, for several reasons. In the first place, we are not in the Corps as yet. Don't waste your good money by coming down here to talk to us about it, as we are in too deep to turn back. It is impossible for us to pull out now, and the only thing that can keep us out is some unfitness—which will be determined by the examiners.

We go down to New York again tomorrow and will have the examination on Wednesday. The die will be cast then. Don't be too sure about our not getting into the war, and anyway, we should be actively preparing. If preparation is postponed until time for action actually arrives, we will be in a pretty fix, all right. These fool pacifists are doing more harm by voicing their imbicilic opinions through the papers than the devil and all his imps could possibly do—with the Kaiser as his campaign manager.

What's more, even if I do start training now, it will not affect my graduation with my class, as I am a half year ahead anyway. As far as I can see, I am not taking a very foolish step. Gerard and I will probably be back by Thursday—Friday at the very latest.
Affectionately,
George

GEORGE HUGHES TO LUCY HUGHES
Wednesday, 14 March 1917:
Dear Mother:

I guess we passed those tests all right. It was the simplest affair imaginable; so simple in fact that it was provoking to think we had to go all the way down there for it. The examination consisted of answering a few simple questions as to schools attended, occupation during the last four years, general capabilities—such as knowledge of autos and engines. The only test for mentality that I could see was a written quiz on what the phrase "armed neutrality" conferred to our minds. We were expecting a question on the submarine affair and were crammed to the gills with dope. But we got fooled. It had been the question they had been asking but evidently they decided that a little change was in order. We are to be notified in due time from Washington as to when we will be called and where sent.
Affectionately,
George

GERARD HUGHES TO LUCY HUGHES
Thursday, 22 March 1917
Dear Mother:

It begins to look like war now; not that things are any worse than they have been for some time. Every edition of the papers has more startling developments. Today Russia is torn to pieces by new outbreaks, and Germany offers to mediate. Here at college no one seems to know what a declaration of war will mean for us. We don't know whether the college will be shut down or not. I expect to hear at any time about going to Mineola. You need not get worried about us and our going to war. This country could not send any forces to Europe for a year at the least, and there is no doubt that the war over there will be over by then.
Affectionately,
Gerard

JERRY'S COMMENTS

Finally we were notified that we had passed the physicals and would soon receive orders to report to the Army Headquarters in Boston for enlistment. George received his orders first and immediately enlisted. I took the oath on April 6th, the day war was declared. Soon after, we received orders to report to the Army flying field at Mineola, Long Island [Figs. 3 and 4].

GEORGE HUGHES TO LUCY HUGHES
Tuesday, 17 April 1917
Dear Mother:

No need to worry about us for some time to come. They won't let us fly before the first of May anyway. The men who have been here all winter are using the machines all the time to finish up as soon as possible. We are doing machine shop work and getting acquainted generally. We rise at 5:15; breakfast at 6:10; go on duty on the flying field around the hangars 7 to 12, getting to know the aviators, the machines, etc.

Managed to get a "taxi" ride this morning. That is a ride across the field without rising from the ground, but there doesn't seem to be any chance of bumming a "joy ride" aloft from any of the pilots. You have to have a special permit before they will take you. Have dinner at 12 and from 1 to 3 instruction in military junk, such as guard duty. We will probably be put to drilling in a few days. From 3 to 5, work down in the machine shop on motors. After supper, supposed to work until dark on wireless, semaphore, and all methods of signaling. Wish you would get me three heavy towels and send them parcel post. If Gerard hasn't

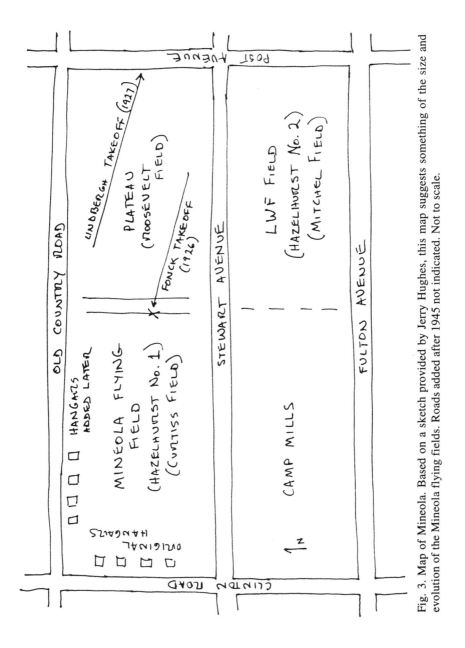

Fig. 3. Map of Mineola. Based on a sketch provided by Jerry Hughes, this map suggests something of the size and evolution of the Mineola flying fields. Roads added after 1945 not indicated. Not to scale.

Fig. 4. Mineola Field. Taken in the spring of 1917, this is a view of the northeast corner of the field, with Clinton Road out of sight to the left and Old Country Road running from left to right behind the hangars in the background. The buildings at the right provided housing for the flying students.

left yet, ask him to bring my shoe trees—if he hasn't packed them
already
Affectionately,
George

GERARD HUGHES TO LUCY HUGHES
Undated, April 1917
Dear Mother:
   It has been foggy every morning for several days, and so we have
not been able to fly. A big thundershower came up this afternoon and it
will probably clear things up considerably. We are getting more and
more work. From now on in the afternoon we have the following schedule: 12:20-12:50, Non-Comm School [Military Customs and Courte-
sies]; 1:00-2:00, Military Law Lecture; 2:00-3:00, Drill; 3:00-4:00,
Motor Lecture; 4:00-5:00, Machine Shop.
   Besides this we have to read our book on motors and study Infantry
Drill Regulations and Map Reading. It is hard to study at night because
one is tired and the light is poor. In the morning it is hard too—because
we are busy all the time in the hangars. We have just received our first of
three inoculations for paratyphoid. It made several pretty sick—especially those who keep late hours.
   George and I automatically "hit the hay" at eight every night. The
bunch kidded us a bit at first, but they are beginning to do the same thing
now. When you wake up at 4:30 you have to get to bed before midnight.
Every day discipline stiffens up. Fellows are getting hit right and left.
One got called down today for falling asleep in the Military Law Lecture. Over a week ago, one student was flying alone. He was very sleepy,
because of staying out late the night before. His machine got in a side
slip near the ground when coming down with the motor off. He shot on
the motor again and saved himself from a spill. Just shows that aviation
is something which must be taken seriously.
   In all the exams we have had since we came here, George and I
have got over 90 except one, when we both got 75. George topped the
list in the last one. All these tests go down on your record and are sent to
Washington when you are recommended for a commission. I wouldn't
be surprised if we were sent to France before the end of July. Perhaps
inside of thirty days. They must have men in Europe to prepare for the
great number of aviators to be sent later on.
Affectionately,
Gerard

GERARD HUGHES TO LUCY HUGHES
Undated, April 1917
Dear Mother:

Sanitary conditions here are all right. As good as you will find in any army camp. There are few flies because there are only trucks and aeroplanes around—no horses or mules. I don't know whether we will have any furloughs between now and September. We know very little about our future. Apparently the administration is bent on making aviation a telling factor in the war. The more developments that go on in that branch of the service the better off we are. If we do well we are in direct line for promotions because we are in the advance guard. We become First Lieutenants when first commissioned and the next step is Captaincy. If luck is with us we may get that high some day.
Affectionately,
Gerard

JERRY'S COMMENTS:

Because we were the first to be trained at Mineola, we had an unusual situation. There were about fifty men in our class. Eight or ten different colleges must have been represented—or even more. There were fellows from Princeton, Yale, Columbia, Syracuse, Union, and of course Harvard. I particularly remember John Baker, Duncan Fuller, Roderick Tower (his father had been ambassador to Russia at one time), and Quentin Roosevelt,* youngest son of former president Theodore Roosevelt.

We were enlisted as sergeants and the Signal Corps didn't know how to handle us. This business of training a group of young college boys in the art of flying was a new experience for the old Army. As sergeants, we would have a little more prestige and a bit more money than the regular private's pay. And so they settled on the idea of making us sergeants. Of course, they knew that if and when we passed the flying course of instruction, we would be commissioned as lieutenants. The regular enlisted men on the post were not too happy about us having that rank because they looked upon us as a bunch of pampered college brats.

While we were in training at Mineola in the spring of 1917, our commanding officer was Captain [Walter] Kilner.* But the man in direct charge of our class was Sergeant Vine. He was a veteran of the Signal Corps with many years of service. He was the over-lord of our quarters and laid down strict rules; he went strictly "by the book." Under his tough and hard-boiled exterior we found a man with a warm and tender heart. In a way, he was like a mother hen with a brood of little chicks. Because he was accustomed to being in charge of regular enlisted men,

he didn't know quite what to make of us college boys. We were different somehow; but I am sure that he liked us really, and by and large we
got along well together.

Some months after leaving Mineola, we heard of Sergeant Vino
again. He was sailing overseas and was the Top Sergeant of a new
squadron. His convoy was attacked by a submarine and his ship was
struck by a torpedo. As it was sinking, good old Sarge, true to his training as a soldier, rushed down into the depths of the foundering vessel
and gathered up his company's records. He emerged just in time to jump
into the water. He was picked up by a rescue vessel—clutching his
squadron papers! We cheered when we heard the news.

GEORGE HUGHES TO LUCY HUGHES
Saturday, 28 April 1917:
Dear Mother:

I am on guard duty again. The bums had the nerve to slap me on
two Saturday nights in succession, but I don't care much, though it is
such a fine day for going on a trip somewhere I am going to have my
bicycle sent down by the college proctor, who can go into any of our
rooms for us. The roads down here are wonderful and I hope to be able
to travel around on them a little. Last night was uneventful, save for
some night flying done by Instructor Bert Acosta.* He went up and flew
around for half an hour or so. We could follow him very easily as he had
small lights on his wing tips, and whenever he shut them off a search-
light was turned on him. Finally he mounted into the air until his lights
looked like stars. Then he looped the loop and volplaned [coasted;
glided] down to ground again. Acosta is the best aviator here at Mineola
and the only one who is allowed to do stunts with a machine. Men are
cheap enough, but these airplanes cost eight thousand and up—so stunts
in general are forbidden.
Affectionately,
George

JERRY'S COMMENTS

Most of our flight instructors at Mineola were civilian pilots,
because the Army had trained too few pilots to have enough military
instructors for us all. There were about six of them for the fifty of us. A
French pilot came over later as an instructor; he had been sent by the
French government. The planes were some old Curtiss Jennies that had
been kicking around the Signal Corps at various posts. The repair shops
and ground crews were hard pressed to keep enough of the craft in flying
condition so that we could get the necessary time in the air.

GERARD HUGHES TO LUCY HUGHES
Thursday, 30 April 1917
Dear Mother:

I have been on guard duty since 5 PM last night. I get off at 5 today. We have two hours on guard and four off. My post is a mile long. I patrolled it twice last night—between nine and eleven and between one and three AM. There was no excitement. A bird jumped up and scared me but that was all. The grub is about what we got at Plattsburg [a New York state military training camp Jerry attended in the summer of 1916]: a little better in some respects and a little worse in others.

The other reserve sergeants with us are a pretty good lot of fellows. A lad [Carroll D. Weatherly] who sleeps next to me was a first lieutenant in the Canadian Army. He commanded a machine gun section and was at the front for about nine months. He was severely wounded in the back, and was in the hospital for five months. He just obtained his discharge from the Canadian Army and enlisted in aviation for excitement. [Quentin] Roosevelt is not particularly interesting looking. He is big and heavy and looks very young [Fig. 5].

We have done no flying as yet; don't know when we will. You needn't worry about us. The accidents are few and far between, and those that have occurred have not proved serious as far as the aviators are concerned. It is strange how cut off from the sentiment of the country you are when in the Army. We get an occasional paper, but the "regulars" are poorly informed as to what is really going on in the outside world.
Affectionately,
Gerard

According to Jerry's flight records, he flew for the first time on May 1, airborne for a total of ten minutes, probably two or three quick circuits of the landing pattern above the field. He flew five more times during the next week with three different instructors, averaging a little over fifteen minutes per ride. Finally, on May 9, he flew with his permanent flying instructor, Wil Wheaton. Wheaton flew with Jerry fifteen times before clearing Jerry to fly solo on June 16. Jerry flew eighteen solo flights before completing his flying program. When he finished, Jerry had a total of 19 hours and 22 minutes of flying time, half of which he had flown solo and half with his instructors.

JERRY'S COMMENTS

Quentin Roosevelt was probably the youngest member of our flying class. Quentin had his bunk next to mine in the barracks at Mineola. His bunk at first was one of those old canvas cots. He soon came to me and

Fig. 5. Quentin Roosevelt. George Hughes took this picture near the Mineola train station during the time they were in training at Mineola.

said, "Last summer, I was out in Wyoming and was thrown by a horse. It gave me a bad back, and this old cot is killing me! Would you swap beds with me?" My bunk was a sturdier iron bed. I felt sorry for him and said okay. I always believed he was telling the truth and not just pulling my leg.

The equipment we flew was often in rough shape and we had to wait for it to be repaired before we could go up for our rides. Our flying clothes were of a mixed breed, too. Our group photograph [Fig. 6] shows what a varied combination of clothes we flew in. Most of us flew in leather coats to keep the cold out; sometimes we had to buy them ourselves, as the Army had not yet decided what constituted an official flying uniform [Fig. 7].

GEORGE HUGHES TO LUCY HUGHES
Thursday, 17 May 1917
Dear Mother:

I suppose you are beginning to wonder what has become of us down here. Well, we are alive and kicking, but haven't been able to do much flying during the last week or so. I got up today for the first time in the last six days. The days have been clear, but as soon as the sun begins to heat things up, the air gets too puffy [turbulent] for us fledglings and only the first, and sometimes the second man assigned to each machine is able to get up before it gets too rough.

Gerard and I are still quite satisfied with our lot. This business is getting to be exceedingly interesting for we have just about reached the point where the learner feels that he is a hopeless case. They say that nearly everyone comes to that point sooner or later, and all you can do is keep on until you get past that stage. I guess some of our bunch will be dropping out for one cause or another in the future. A considerable number are becoming discouraged because they aren't progressing as fast and easily as they thought they would. But it's just like anything else, you always strike a certain stage in most any new game where you seem to get worse instead of better. Then, if you keep on, you get to where you are on solid ground, so to speak.

The last two lessons I have had were mostly on landings. It's quite a stunt to bring one of these birds softly to the ground. I can see how Merritt lost control of the LWF [Lowe, Willard, and Fowler—makers of an unsuccessful training aircraft] easily enough. Things look considerably different when you start coming down and the ground comes up to meet you by leaps and bounds—in a way that is highly interesting. If the weather will just calm down a bit so that we can go up several days in succession, I guess I will get on to the hang of it all right, though up until now it has been a little too deep for me. Today is the first real Spring weather we have had. It is quite hot, in fact, and I have spent most of my time since sunrise just sitting outside the guardhouse door basking myself in the good old summer heat.

Fig. 6. The Flying Men of Mineola. Front row, left to right: Murray McConnell, Duncan Fuller, John Baker, Ira Hibbin, David Lindsay, Austin Quick, Corporal O'Connor (not a flying student), Dudley Norton, unidentified, Gerard Hughes, Smith. Second row, left to right: Torrey Webb (one of the pilots to fly the air mail in the summer of 1918), Junius Richards, Henry Lindsley, Jr., George Church, Philip Epyer, William Carruthers (the only man in the class to die during training), Roderick Tower, Logan McMenemy, Charles Trowbridge, Henry Drayton, Walter Jacob, Francis McDonald, Willis Boggs, Lorenzo Snow. Back row, left to right: Robert Bartholomew, Potter Trainor, Paul Goldsborough, Frank McCreery, Ray Dunn, Hallam Peters, T. E. Tillinghast, Edward "Lem" Killgore, Cyrus Smythe, Shiras Blair. Not pictured: Reynolds Benson, Spenser Brainard, "Hop" Carr, Gordon Dodge, Geoff Dwyer, C. O. Lowe, "Pappy" Gaines, Guard, H. H. George, George Hughes, Walter King, Sid Murphy, George Palmer, Quentin Roosevelt, Herb Tiffany, Carol Weatherley.

I was on guard again last night as Corporal of the Guard of the 3rd relief, the third time running. The 3rd relief is the worst of the whole bunch. The night passed very quietly indeed; no excitement of any sort, though one of the reserve men didn't get back until 1:30 this morning. Everyone is supposed to be in by one o'clock, so the sentinel refused to admit the poor cuss and he had to wait for four hours before he could gain admittance to the post. I suppose he will be restricted for two or three weeks for not getting back on time.

Affectionately,

George

Fig. 7. George Hughes and his Jenny. The Curtiss JN-4 aircraft was the best-known of the American training aircraft used during the war. Here George Hughes stands by his aircraft in typical flying gear: a leather jacket, leather helmet, goggles, scarf, gloves. Even in May the weather could be cool. It was windy and noisy in the cockpit in any kind of weather.

JERRY'S COMMENTS

The incident that George refers to—about Merritt losing control of his LWF aircraft—was a tragic one. It was a spectacular incident involving two enlisted men, Merritt and Spalino. The Lowe, Williard, and Fowler (LWF) Corporation, of College Point, Long Island, had built a few two-place airplanes, hoping to sell them to the Signal Corps for training purposes. The Army had found these ships poorly constructed in some ways and had declared them unsafe to fly. It almost takes an act of Congress for one of the services to dispose of something, and so when these LWFs were condemned, the two assigned to our field were just sitting there waiting for some sort of disposition.

One day an order came from headquarters for two enlisted men to look over those two jobs and police them up a bit. No particular reason, probably. Just the business of giving a couple of men something to do. Merritt and Spalino were working in the shop when they got the order to take on this little job. Spalino was a good-natured little Italian who had entered the Signal Corps with the vague idea that he might get a chance to learn to fly. Merritt had more than a vague plan to learn the art; he was determined to fly. As time went by, and these two fellows saw college boys taken in and given a chance to fly while they stood around and watched, they were a bit unhappy. Merritt was more than unhappy, he was bitter.

They took the canvas coverings off the motors of the LWFs and cleaned away some oil and fussed around generally. Then Merritt got in the back seat, where the controls were located. He sat a moment and then called out, "Hey, Spalino! Swing the prop!" The little Italian, used to taking orders, obediently gave the propeller a twirl. He did it a couple more times and then the motor started. Merritt sat for a little while longer, letting the motor idle and warm up. Then he yelled again, "Hey, Spalino! Pull out the chocks—and get in the front seat!" And again the little lad did as he was told.

I was standing out on the field at the time and all of a sudden I saw this LWF starting out across the grass, saw it gathering speed and then jumping like a jack rabbit as it dashed out toward the plateau in the distance. Merritt had been up for a few rides with instructor Allen but had never handled the controls. It was natural that he would over-control, at least in the beginning. Finally, he was airborne and started to climb. He seemed to calm down and began to handle the plane with some skill. After he made it into the air over the plateau, he swung off to the right and headed in the direction of Freeport.

All hell broke loose on the field. Sirens screamed and men dashed out to lay canvas strips on the grass as a signal for all aircraft to land without delay. In short, it was an emergency! I can still see Bert Acosta bringing in his Jennie in tight S-turns as he came in fast over the corner of the field. It wasn't long before everybody on the post had gathered in a large crowd at the northwest corner of the field, where headquarters was located. There were at least two hundred men standing around, and we were all asking the same questions: Can Merritt fly that plane back? Where has he gone? If he gets back, can he make a landing? The ambulance was parked in the middle of the field.

In about ten or fifteen minutes a speck appeared in the sky. It was the LWF heading for home. Finally Merritt came over the southwest corner at an altitude of about 1200 feet. As he approached, he throttled down and started to glide, losing altitude. Then, when he was well over the field and just south of us, he gave her the gun again. Instead of pulling up and leveling off again, as he should have done, he nosed the plane down further and further until he was heading straight down. Jet black smoke streamed out of the exhausts and then, after a plunge of about five hundred feet, the wings snapped off and the heavy laminated fuselage roared headlong until it struck the ground with terrific impact.

As the ship came down and wings fluttered away, and it was obvious that the two boys were doomed, there arose from that crowd of men an agonizing moan, the like of which I had never heard, and hope never to hear again. It was a spontaneous cry of anguish. That incident left a marked impression on us and let us know, in no uncertain terms, that flying has its dangers. As for those two unfortunate boys, Spalino was obviously the victim of his own good nature. Some said Merritt had intentionally committed suicide. There was no evidence that the plane malfunctioned in any way—until the wings came off.

GEORGE HUGHES TO LUCY HUGHES
Thursday, 24 May 1917
Dear Mother:

The bread arrived this afternoon and was a very welcome surprise; thank you very much. I am having a deuce of a time with this flying business, and am almost afraid that I will get kicked out with the first cut; but you can never tell. I may be able to come back strong enough to stick. Two of our fellows made their first solo flights this morning. They are the first to get away alone, but others will be following in the next few days—and then the grand sorting out will occur. Day before yesterday, four of the bunch were called up on the carpet and informed that they aren't up to par and that unless they show marked improvements, they will not stay on the flying list. No announcement has been made as

to what will be done with men who are dropped from the program. Presumably they will be transferred to some other branch of [Army] service.
Affectionately,
George

GEORGE HUGHES TO LUCY HUGHES
Wednesday, 30 May 1917
Dear Mother:

Last Monday a company of the New York 47th National Guard came in and camped along the edge of the flying field. They are to do all the guard duty for us. We won't have to act as watchmen at all. They are a tough-looking bunch and have an unsavory reputation. They stand guard with Springfield rifles and fixed bayonets, so I guess there won't be many fellows trying to sneak home through the lines in the early hours of the morning, the way they have up until now.

Today is a holiday [Memorial Day]; no flying or work of any sort, but it is cloudy and chilly, so I doubt if I will go anywhere. I am writing this in bed. We don't have to get up on Sundays and holidays until 7:30, two hours later than usual. It was cloudy and foggy yesterday, but we managed to get in some flying. Acosta took his class up in a new Burgess machine that has the seats side by side, instead of tandem [front and back] as in the Curtiss. The Burgess is also heavier and rides like a Pullman car. You can hardly realize you are up in the air, it goes along so steadily. It was a cinch to run it, in comparison to the Curtiss JNs. I was only up 13 minutes, but got along fairly well. I seem to be getting along fairly well in general, and if I don't have a relapse, I ought to be alone [solo] soon.
Affectionately,
George

GEORGE HUGHES TO LUCY HUGHES
Wednesday, 6 June 1917
Dear Mother:

Monday I was so punk at landing that Acosta said he would have to look up my time to see if he would be justified in continuing my instruction. I went out to the field where the soloists fly and watched them for about an hour and a half, and then it suddenly dawned on me why I couldn't bring the old kite to the ground. I haven't been keeping my head out to one side and consequently couldn't judge my distances. Added to that, I have been coming down too steep and not gliding far enough. The correct way for the beginner is to make a gentle descent with a long glide and a soft settle at the end, though it generally happens that you hit a bump and bound ten or fifteen feet into the air, whereupon you "give her the gun" and take another trip around the field. I saw two students do it while I was on the Plateau (that's the name of the field you use when you're flying solo). Well, having seen how it should be done and a good many examples of how it shouldn't be done—which were even more instructive—I came back feeling that I could do it just as well as the bunch already loose.

I got up the next day feeling ready for anything and told Acosta that if I didn't come through with the goods he could take me up 5000 feet and throw me overboard. He made the first three landings for me, then I took hold and made a couple of darned good ones, even if I do say it myself, whereupon he climbed out of the seat and told me to go to it, and that I was to have the privilege of learning a few facts about flying at first hand. I didn't feel a bit nervous and asked him to buckle up his belt so it wouldn't get tangled in the controls, which rather tickled him. Then I opened up the throttle and climbed some five or six hundred feet into the air, circled the field and landed as smooth as ice. I made four more landings, then Acosta got in and we returned to the hangars. Strange to say, I didn't feel nervous a single instant that I was alone. The old bird is much easier to handle when you are alone.

It climbs faster and seems to travel better in all ways, although I guess later one gets good at it, and an extra person doesn't make any difference. Though just at present it's a great relief to be alone and not have someone ready to give you the devil all the time; knowing it's up to you, you do your best and take more interest in what's going on. Those of us who are alone [flying solo] have to rise at 4:00 AM, go to the hangars, and get out our machines, and as soon as the mist clears away, we start in. Long Island seems to have an inexhaustible supply of fog. At least we get a generous supply every night.

So far we haven't been able to get up [take off] before six o'clock, but we keep it up, turn and turn about, until eleven. About five men are assigned to each machine, so we get about an hour apiece when the weather holds good. This morning was my maiden [solo] trip, so to speak, and I got the bunch up on their tiptoes. Those on the waiting list stood in a bunch in the middle of the Plateau and watched us land. Well, my first two landings were okay, but evidently no one took note of that fact, so when I came around for my third, and seeing I wasn't going to make a perfect landing, I pushed on the power and rose again. Then I proceeded to do this same little stunt twice more—making it three times running.

The bunch on the ground began to get highly excited, thinking I was scared to come to earth. But on the fourth lap I got the old kite into the place and glide I wanted and made a good landing, much to the relief of those on the ground. The thing that worried them the most was that the other ones would have been all right if I had let her glide long enough to settle, but I was taking no chances—which is the only way anyhow, so why should I worry about those on terra firma?

Gerard is coming along better now. He is in the back seat and will probably be alone [solo] by next week. Once he does [go solo], he will be all right. You ought to see some of the nuts flying alone and you wouldn't worry about him. The extra time with the instructor won't hurt him—even though Wheaton isn't any too good. Flying is much like shooting. Anyone can show you the principles, an expert can give you a few pointers, but the practical experience is what counts—and I think that Gerard could get away with a solo flight right now.

Affectionately,
George

JERRY'S COMMENTS

My instructor was a young fellow named Wil Wheaton. This lad probably didn't have much more than fifteen total hours in the air when he started with us, and he was perhaps more afraid of flying than his students. There were six of us who flew with him—Willis Boggs, Sid Murphy, David Lindsay, Shiras Blair and Mike Dunn. And me, of course. Mike Dunn had the distinction of being the only member of the entire outfit to crack up a plane. I remember how Wheaton kept a tight grip on the controls all the while I was with him. It was only when he soloed me, and I was alone in the air that I felt that I was flying the ship. This experience with Wheaton taught me a lesson because later, when I was instructing, I put myself in the place of my cadets and after a short time with them I held up my hands so that they could see they were flying—not me. The one flight control on those craft which could get you into real trouble was the rudder. You worked that with your feet, of course, and so for awhile I kept my shoes close to the rudder bar—just in case. When the student had overcome his initial nervousness, he was in complete control.

GERARD HUGHES TO LUCY HUGHES
Sunday, 10 June 1917
Dear Mother:

This has been a quiet Sunday. George was in charge of quarters, so we didn't go anywhere. He spent most of his time writing letters. He feels that now he is flying alone [solo], he can tell people he is here. I'm not flying alone yet, but if luck is with me, I may get loose this week.

But one can never tell. I feel perfectly able to handle a machine. However, a person doesn't really learn how to fly until he goes up by himself; for then he has only his own wits and nerve to depend upon, and is naturally on the jump all the time. Time down here is beginning to fly. At the same time things are putting on a much more systematic appearance. We now have an engine expert called Lieutenant Pagé* who instructs us in aeroplane design and in the care and troubles of motors. He is fine, extremely well-liked. He is a first lieutenant and weighs about 300 pounds.

It may be two months before we get our commissions—if we get them. Yet again, we may be in France inside of a month. You always seem anxious about whether we will like aviation. You may rest easy on that score. We like it as much as ever, and even more now that we are flying alone. Flying is something that everybody cannot do, and something which comparatively few people have indulged in to date. Add to that prestige the pleasure of flying—the thrill and excitement which it is possible to get—and you can easily see that the average young animal (like ourselves) will not soon tire of it all.

They are coming down hard on our bunch now. Some of the fellows have been going out a good deal, staying out late, and since flying and liquor and late hours don't jibe, they are keeping an eye on them. Seven got restricted the other day for being late for reveille. Must close now.
Affectionately,
Gerard

JERRY'S COMMENTS
One of our instructors was a rotund lieutenant named Victor Pagé.* He was our engineering officer and lectured to our class on mechanics and aerodynamics. He was a very likable fellow. As I remember, he spoke with a slight lisp and the class laughed at some of his pronunciations, but liked him very much. He was later promoted to captain and wrote many books about aircraft construction and operation.

GERARD HUGHES TO LUCY HUGHES
Tuesday, 12 June 1917
Dear Mother:
George is flying alone, as you know, but hasn't gone up in the last couple of days because of fog and repairs. I am not flying alone yet and haven't any idea when I will be. Yesterday five of our machines flew over New York and dropped Liberty Bond circulars. It must have taken the papers some time to come down as they were dropped from an altitude of over 5000 feet. Some of the birds went up as high as 8500 feet. The lucky

ones from our crowd who went with the pilots and did the distributing said they had a wonderful experience—and I guess they did at that.
Affectionately,
Gerard

GERARD HUGHES TO LUCY HUGHES
Sunday, 17 June 1917
Dear Mother:

Yesterday was a bit hazy but we flew. At least some of us did. A fellow named Lindsley and I were turned loose yesterday by Wheaton—our instructor. I thought that Lindsley and I were the worst of our group, but we beat the rest to it. Old Wheaton was tickled to death at our showing. He was pretty nervous about turning us loose, but when we both flew away and came back, landing nicely, he was ready to yell for joy. He turned two of our class loose in the middle of the week. They had flown a lot before. One did very well. The other [Dunn] smashed his landing gear on one of his landings and was put back under instruction for two more hours. Lindsley and I are the first in our class to get loose [fly solo] who have never flown before, and we get quite a bit of satisfaction out of the fact. George and I went in to New York yesterday afternoon with another fellow. He took us to an Italian restaurant on West 11th street, between 5th and 6th avenues. We got a wonderful five-course dinner for 70 cents.
Affectionately,
Gerard

JERRY'S COMMENTS

Each member of our class eventually soloed. This was the dramatic moment when the instructor climbed out of the plane and said, "Take her away! You are on your own!" Needless to say, that is one of the great emotional experiences of a lifetime. At last, you are flying! Each man had about five or six hours of dual instruction, and then, flying solo, we practiced take-offs and landings over and over again. To this phase we devoted about ten hours.

Finally we were ready for the reserve military aviator (RMA) tests. First we had to make a cross-country flight to a point thirty or forty miles distant and back. In our case, we flew down Long Island and landed on a little grassy meadow at Smith's point. Next we had to do proper figure eights. After that it was precision tests seeing if we could land close to a given mark, first with the motor running, then with a dead stick. All this business took place over at a great grass-covered stretch of land which lay south of the main field. This area later became known as Mitchel Field.

We were initially told that nobody was sure how to get out of a tail-spin. Acrobatics were taboo, of course. Captain Ralph Taylor, one of our Officers in Charge of Flying (OCFs) told us that so far as he knew, if you got into a spin the best thing you could do was place the controls in neutral and hope the aircraft would fly out of the spin. The only problem with this advice was that you had to react more quickly if you were close to the ground.

GERARD HUGHES TO LUCY HUGHES
Thursday, 28 June 1917
Dear Mother:

I notice in your letters that you show signs of weakness in regard to our going to France. Undoubtedly we will go, and instead of wishing it were otherwise, you should be glad. To have two sons in this war—both first lieutenants and both in a service which requires fellows a good deal above the average, both physically and mentally, is surely enough for one mother.

We can't live forever and if we get killed in France we will have done our duty, and you will have done yours—which is what we live for anyway. It would be better than getting run over by a jitney, with no glory and no satisfaction of having died in as good a cause as has ever been fought for. Yes sir! You have every reason to be proud of your sons—if I do say so—and how much better for us to go abroad as officers, marked as men of nerve and ability, than to stay at home to be drafted like common cattle, later to be shipped to Europe, like drops in the ocean, there to be slaughtered in a hole under the ground.

The harder this country goes into the war, the sooner it ill be over and the fewer men will be killed. The way things are going right now, it seems that Germany is going to catch hell all right. We may survive it and we may not. There is nothing like being a fatalist—and that's the attitude which you get in aviation. All that the people who stay at home can do is to get into as heroic a mood as possible, get a broad point of view and let come what may. Well, we haven't finished our training yet and our commissions are still in the distant future. Go ahead and get that Chevrolet.
Affectionately,
Gerard

JERRY'S COMMENTS

Oh youth! Where is thy wisdom? What a way to allay the fears of an anxious mother! This letter may have been the result of certain unfortunate incidents that occurred at Mineola. Only one of our class was killed in training. His name was Carruthers. During one flight lesson he and his instructor landed their Jennie out on the field and then for some reason or other, Carruthers got out of the plane and went to the front of the aircraft. Probably the motor had stalled and the student was swinging the prop to start it again. Whatever the reason, he accidentally walked or fell into the propeller, was struck on the head, and killed. This saddened us all because the man was a very nice, likable fellow, older than the rest of us, and very quiet.

GEORGE HUGHES TO LUCY HUGHES
Monday, 2 July 1917
Dear Mother:

Gerard and I are getting along pretty well now. We have got so that we can make reasonably safe landings almost every time, and I guess our air work is okay. I was up with an instructor the other day for a lesson in making an "S"—a maneuver that is used to slow up one's speed when too close to the ground to make a spiral turn—and he said my air work was exceptionally good. I expect that by the end of this coming week we will be ready to take our reserve military aviator (RMA) test, after which we should receive our commissions, and then we will find out what they intend to do with us.
Affectionately,
George

GERARD HUGHES TO LUCY HUGHES
Sunday, 8 July 1917
Dear Mother:

It is good and warm down here and we are having fine flying weather, which means that we are making quite a bit of progress. On the 4th we went to Coney Island and watched the natives in bathing suits. We tried one of the roller-coasters in order to get some thrills. I lost my hat on one of the turns. We tried the "Chute," where you dash down in a fold boat, hit the water with a smack, and then leap wildly through the air for about twenty feet. It is terrible to watch, but there is nothing to it when you are actually in the boat. There was a huge crowd there despite the muggy weather.
Affectionately,
Gerard

GERARD HUGHES TO LUCY HUGHES
Monday, 9 July 1917:
Dear Mother:

Today was rather cloudy and it rained a bit. I flew around in the clouds this morning. You can't see a thing when you plunge into the mist. You have to drive the machine from the feel and the sound of your wires. George and I went to Long Beach Sunday morning. Fine bathing beach—society place—had a nice swim in the big surf. We went to New York in the afternoon and saw movies at the Rialto Theater. We have to beat it off to town to break up the monotony of this place.

Affectionately,
Gerard

GEORGE HUGHES TO LUCY HUGHES
Wednesday, 11 July 1917
Dear Mother:

Last Saturday I went on a little cross-country trip in one of the birds. Left Mineola at eleven o'clock, but had hardly taken off when my engine went dead and I had to come down. After considerable investigation, it turned out that the gas had shut off while I was taxiing for my get-away. The engine was perfectly okay, so I started out again and climbed to an altitude of about 3500 feet. I set out down the Island for a place called Smith's point, some 35 miles distant. The weather was slightly hazy, and couldn't get a very extended range of vision—probably about ten miles.

But the country below was as plain as could be and made a picture quite beautiful to behold. There are just hundreds and hundreds of big ploughed fields. I never saw a place equal to this Long Island for ideal farms. The ground is just as smooth and as flat as can be. There wasn't a moment when I didn't have a good landing place in plain view. The things that stand out the boldest when you are high up are the ploughed fields and the roads. The roads are the plainest of all, and the higher you go, the more pronounced they become. There are some wonderful roads around here. I saw one that was as straight as a ruler for at least ten miles, not the slightest sign of a curve or turn. All the way down I could see the two shore lines of the Island and was able to track my location all the time.

About seven miles from my destination, I cut off the engine and coasted down to earth, opening up the throttle every now and then to keep the gas from choking up the cylinders. It's wonderful how far you can glide one of these machines. I was somewhat afraid I had cut off my engine too soon, but when I arrived at the field, I had more altitude than I knew what to do with, and had to make a couple of spirals. And even then I overshot, so that I was forced to make a circle around the field and then land. The Smith's Point field is a very easy place to find, as all you have to do is to follow the shoreline of Great South Bay until Smith's Point butts in and blocks it up.

The field doesn't belong to the Government, but is owned by a couple of ladies who live there in a farm house, and they are always tickled to death to have the machines come and land in their front yard. Whenever they hear the buzz of a JN they run out and hoist up an American flag so that the pilot can get the direction of the wind. One day—for some reason or other—the flag wasn't hoisted and one of our fellows made a landing with, instead of into, the breeze, and came blamed close to ending up in a clump of trees before the machine stopped. It was his own fault, however, as he should have been able to get his wind direction from the ripples in the water.

The day I blew in, the flag was up and when I finally landed the old bird didn't roll more than fifty yards after the wheels touched ground. I didn't linger very long but took off again almost immediately, being behind time on account of my delay at the start. I made very good time on the return trip, overtaking a couple of planes that had the start of me by at least ten minutes. I like this cross-country work. It's great to sail along and watch the ground unfold below you. It's so far off that you don't feel as though you could possibly fall. It looks like another world, just as soft and nice to look at as you could wish for. You can hang your head right over the edge of the fuselage and stare straight down without getting the slightest sensation of dizziness.

When I was on top of the Woolworth Building—only seven hundred feet up—it made my fingers tingle to look over the edge. But in a bird you don't realize how far you are from the ground. The buildings just blend into the general view and people are so little you don't notice them; and you begin to feel that you are the biggest thing on the landscape and you simply feel great. That's the dangerous part of this game. You begin to feel so much at home that you are apt to get caught napping. Old grandpa gravity is always on the job looking for you and you don't stand much chance of slipping anything over on him, so it behooves you to always bear in mind that the ground is as hard as ever.

It won't be long now before we finish up here, but as yet nothing definite has been decided as to our future. No one seems to know. The high moguls at Washington haven't found it convenient to open up. But I guess they will have to before long. we may be able to get a day or so off, but you never can tell.

Affectionately,

George

JERRY' S COMMENTS

As I recall, every member of our class passed the tests and received his RMA rating and his commission as a First Lieutenant. It was then we got the bad news. No overseas activity for us! No heroics in France fighting the Boche! Because we were so far ahead of the others, we were confident we would soon be on our way to the front and, as "knights of the air" would soon be tangling with the "Red Baron." No such thing happened. Because of the tremendous demand for any kind of pilot who could teach flying, only a handful of us ever got overseas. Instead, we were scattered all over the United States, sent to new fields which were appearing everywhere. Some went to Houston, some to Dallas and Fort Worth, some to Mt. Clemens, Michigan, and many other places. George completed his flying on July 6th and was sent to Wilbur Wright Field in Dayton, Ohio, an enormous complex with two flying units. Most other fields had only one. I completed my flying on July 11th, and after a little delay, was sent to Chanute Field, in Rantoul, Illinois.

2

George Hughes, Flight Instructor, Wilbur Wright Field

George Hughes was assigned to Wilbur Wright Field, at Dayton, Ohio, even before he received his commission as a lieutenant in the Air Service. He was one of the first flying officers to be assigned to the field, which was still under construction when he arrived. Wilbur Wright Field was approved and prepared in record time. Authorization to commence construction at Wright Field was given on May 16, 1917; construction began on May 27 with the goal of completion by July 14, just over six weeks later (Sweetser 56-57). This activity included leveling the field, and building hangars, maintenance facilities, and housing. George Hughes arrived in Dayton, Ohio, on July 17, even as the dust raised by construction activities was still in the air. He lived in temporary residence until the officers' housing was completed. At Wright Field he flew three new (for him) aircraft, the Curtiss Jenny JN-4A, the JN-4D, and the "Baby" Standard. He disliked the Standard; he thought it was too slow and tame.

In his letters to Jerry, George provides advice on how to fly the training aircraft, and we can almost hear what it would be like to be a student of his as he gives these instructions. George quickly adopts a stance in his letters that becomes standard, that of the old-timer, giving his younger brother the "inside dope" on how to fly aircraft and how to survive generally in the flying business. George's style develops a hard edge of confidence bordering on cynicism. In his letters to Gerry he indulges in mild profanity and service vernacular that add impact and color to the information he is conveying. This pattern becomes more pronounced later, when George leaves for France. As a result of George's crisp style, his letters speak to us many years later with a unique tone of voice as well as a wealth of detail.

Over time, George developed proficiency and confidence as a flight instructor. Flying regularly, he amassed over 100 hours of flying time by the end of September, an impressive record for someone who had flown for the first time in June. He soloed two of his students about the first of October, one of whom was Charles S. "Casey" Jones,* who later *became a legendary pilot and entrepreneur. The hazards of flight instruction are everywhere evident in his letters. He mentions at least ten accidents that occur at Wright Field in a four-month period, including one in which he is involved. Surprisingly, the casualties were light and only one person was killed, a visiting Navy pilot candidate.*

JERRY'S COMMENTS

Wilbur Wright Field must have received more planes than any other field, except Kelly Field in San Antonio, perhaps, because George started right out instructing and rolling up time in the air when he first arrived in July of 1917. This was what we all wanted, of course—time in the air—because when we graduated at Mineola we had a total of only twenty to twenty-five hours of flight time. That was mighty little flight time and hardly enough to qualify us as first-rate instructors.

When I visited George in October, he took me up in his Jenny, and I had a good look at Wilbur Wright Field—it was twice the size of Chanute Field, where I was assigned. And how the wind blew over that place! And the dust storms! The field was built right on the bank of the river and the surface had no grass on it—just sand and dirt. When it rained, the field was a sea of mud, and if they tried to fly, they were cursed with broken propellers.

GEORGE HUGHES TO LUCY HUGHES
Sunday, 20 July 1917
Dear Mother:

We left Mineola Monday noon and arrived at Dayton at ten the next morning. Had a very peaceful and uneventful trip. The night was fairly cool, but the Lord help us if it wasn't hotter than blazes when we arrived here. We hired an automobile and drove out in style. The field is about five miles from Dayton. Fairfield is a mile or so further on. This is the most monstrous establishment imaginable. The report claims that the buildings cover sixteen acres, and I believe that is a very conservative estimate. The barracks in which we are quartered are fully one-half mile from Headquarters and the Main Gate is a good mile and one-half from Headquarters. I believe the total acreage of the post is 2500 acres.

Everything is brand new. We are among the very first to arrive. There are only about three companies of soldiers, some twenty flying pupils and three Mineola instructors. We felt at home from the very first. The chief instructor here [Norton] was at Mineola and he is fixing everything up for us. He put us on the flying list this afternoon and all but two of us got twenty minutes flying. I believe that Norton is only acting chief, but Allen, the man reported to be taking his place, is also a Mineolaite.

The place is so big I hardly know how to describe it. It must have originally been a lot of small farms. You approach the field from Dayton over the Springfield Pike, and when about two miles away you see what looks like a lot of strips of ploughed land, but on closer inspection they turn out to be the roofs of hangars. I haven't had the opportunity to count the hangars in full, but there are about thirty strung out in one row, and still others are going up [Fig. 8].

Before you reach the hangars, you pass along one side of the landing field. The Pike Road runs right through the post and alongside the pike is a trolley line with fast inter-urban cars. It takes about thirty-five minutes to get to Dayton by car. The fare is twenty cents. The cars run every hour, so we are pretty well fixed.

To return to the landing field—I should judge, from what I have seen of it, that it must contain well over four hundred acres. It's by far the busiest spot around; it simply swarms with trams and men who are busy leveling off the ground. I haven't been able to estimate the number of horses, but I did count six steam rollers puffing along. The ground is so level it almost makes you dizzy to look at it. The only bad part of is that whenever a bird takes off, the propeller stirs up a tremendous amount of dust. I suppose, however, that in time it will be seeded down. The field is down in a sort of valley, though the surrounding country is but slightly higher. The ridge on which our barracks are situated may be some fifty to seventy-five feet higher. The Headquarters building is among the first to which you come and it looks like an old farm house; it is composed of brick and is certainly more ancient than the surrounding structures.

The first person we ran into was Manning, a Mineola instructor. He seemed to like it here, except for the heat. At Headquarters we met Wheaton, Gerard's instructor. He is fairly disgusted with the diggings; said he would give all he has in the world to get back to Mineola. The heat is laying him out. The place is so big it takes him half a day to walk to his hangar. The birds are all different from the ones we had on Long Island. Here we have "Baby" Standards and Curtiss JN-4As and they fly quite differently from the ones we had at Mineola. Wheaton doesn't enjoy himself over-much in the air anyhow.

After an hour or so of fussing around at Headquarters, we were assigned to Barracks B-3. Each building is composed of two long rooms—or one long room divided in the middle, according to they way you want to look at it. On the east side is a piazza [porch] running the full length, about 300 feet long I should judge. Running out from the center on the west side is a little L containing showers and a lavatory—with the best of porcelain basins. This is the most wonderfully equipped

Fig. 8. Wilbur Wright Field, Dayton, Ohio. Photo shows the long line of over twenty hangars running north and south along the east side of the flying field. Photo taken looking to the north, toward the town of Fairfield. The diagonal line is in the interurban rail line that connected the towns of Dayton and Springfield. The Wright brothers' first flying field is located approximately beneath the aircraft from which George Hughes is taking the picture.

place I have run into for some little time. You feel as though you were in a hotel. The showers are the saving feature of the place. I fall into them thrcc timcs a day. At least I did today. We haven't any hot water as yet, but that's no hardship. The barracks are fitted for hot water heating and couldn't be any more convenient. We have lights of course. In back of each barracks is a mess hall, just a few steps away.

We have been assigned to mess with the 12th Aero Squadron, and they certainly set a wonderful table. They have just been transferred here from Texas and have some $2000 in the mess fund. The food is far above what we had at Mineola. It's almost fit for a human being to eat. At present we are supposed to sleep and eat on the post. I suppose, after we get our commissions, we will be allowed to put up in Dayton. We are mighty well fixed for the time being; we have half of B-3 to ourselves, with so much room to spare that we hardly know what to do with ourselves. At Mineola the beds were so close together that you had to crawl over the end to get in, but here we are so far apart that we seem lonesome.

It seems quite likely that we will get our commissions. If mine comes to you, please forward as soon as possible in order that I can get fixed up [off the post] without delay. We had one whale of a thunderstorm this afternoon. It cleared the atmosphere but surrounded us with a lake of mud. I doubt we will be able to fly tomorrow on account of the softness of the ground.

I had my first trip in a Standard machine. I don't like them as well as the JNs [Curtiss "Jennies"] we had at Mineola. These Standards are sluggish, slow to answer the controls, and are about ten miles per hour slower; but they will probably do very well as training machines. At present we have only about fifteen machines but in a week or so we ought to have a perfect swarm of them. They have all kinds of them up in the storehouse, and they are putting them together as fast as possible. I believe each of us is to be in charge of a gang to assemble machines for awhile. After we have become thoroughly familiar with these machines, we are to be used as instructors. At least, those are the plans at present—but they are liable to be changed overnight.

I went into Dayton this morning and did some shopping for the gang. One of the bunch went in yesterday and got some shirts for 65 cents and everyone else wanted some. But unfortunately the bum couldn't remember the name of the store. All the directions he could give me were that the store was on the corner of two streets—about one block off Third Street. It took me about two hours to find the place. I went into about every store in the old burg and finally came to one on Fourth and Main, where they had khaki shirts for 65 cents. So I suppose it was the same place, since at all the other stores, shirts were one dollar or better. Well, it's time for me to ring off.

Affectionately,

George

GEORGE HUGHES TO GERARD HUGHES

Tuesday, 6 August 1917

Dear Gerard:

I suppose you saw in the paper that Captain Taylor and Pell fell [in an accident at Mineola] last Thursday. Henry Lindsley, who arrived yesterday, said they hit not 100 yards from his house. He was in the automobile at the time and hearing someone shout an order up above, he looked up and saw the machine coming down in mad gyrations, sweeping first to the left and then the right. He immediately started running for the field where it was evident the machine would land. His father and mother also came out and they were all the first to arrive at the spot.

Captain Taylor was dead. He bore no external bruises but his neck seemed to have been broken by the shock. Pell was still conscious and even tried to help when they lifted him out, but he was so badly smashed and bruised that Lindsley didn't even recognize who he was. It is expected that Pell will live. We don't know what the machine was but Lindsley said it was a new one, and we have a suspicion that it was a model JN-4A, the same thing that we have here.

If you land at a place where they use these As, be careful as an old woman. These machines are a new model. The big dihedral angle prevents them from slipping. You can tilt them up to 90 degrees, but just about that time they are liable to stall and, if they do, nothing can keep you from dropping into a spinning nose dive, and you will need 2000 feet to get out of it. Instructor Norton says "on no account" pull a split-A turn under 2000 feet, and don't let their noses point down too much on turns or spirals. Otherwise they are good birds, speedy, climb fast, and answer the controls quickly, but are somewhat harder to land than the Bs. If you happen to fall into one of those spins, use reverse rudder. It's the only thing that will get you out; and so, when doing a spiral or short turn, always bear in mind that it's very easy to get into a spin, and be ready to poke the rudder in the opposite way from what you are turning in. Old Bart [Robert Bartholomew] was doing a tight spiral last Friday and fell into a spin. Being caught by surprise, he gave her right hand rudder, which was the direction he was turning in, and in consequence he dropped 1500 feet before he could pull out with his left rudder. He was only about 400 feet from the ground when he did straighten out.

Last Thursday [1 August] was an unlucky day for aviators. A Lieutenant Richardson fell 100 feet here in a spin while attempting to spiral. The Lord only knows what he was thinking about when he tried to pull a spiral that close to the ground. He will live. On the same day, Tiffany and Richards fell at the Mt. Clemens field in Michigan, also in a spin in an A. Luckily they landed in a lake. Richards, though in the front seat, was unhurt. Tiffany will probably lose an eye from a cut by glass. These "Baby" Standards are worse than the As. Don't fly one unless you have to. If you are so unfortunate as to get one, don't give them any bank. Our gang of "perpendicular bankers," Lindsley, Benson, and Bart [Bartholomew], won't bank more than 35 or 40 degrees, even when out of sight. It takes three times as much aileron to get you out as it does to go into same, and usually it takes several seconds for them to work.

They act like one of those old time muskets that you lit with a fuse and then waited a week or so to fire; but the rudder is very sensitive and it's damn easy to get yourself into a flat tailspin by excessive rudder on a flat turn, or even with a fair amount of bank. When doing a spiral with a conservative amount of bank, hold it and correct for slip or skid with rudder and elevator. They are the only things that will work quick enough.

Always come into the field with an A or "Baby" on a straight glide from an altitude of at least five hundred feet. That's a rule on this field. Of course, when taking off, you will have to turn under that altitude, but you can make a wide turn and take your time about getting altitude. These things can't be tilted about like those old Bs, but remember that the machine will take one hell of a bump before you are hurt, and if your motor quits and a house or a tree gets in your way, just run it down, aiming the old bird so that the engine will hit the ground first. We can't use glass goggles, so try and get yourself triplex or celluloid. And be damn careful.

George

GEORGE HUGHES TO LUCY HUGHES
Tuesday, 13 August 1917
Dear Mother:

We are having wonderful weather here at present; not so very hot during the day and at night a blanket feels mighty good. Gerard better make a strenuous effort to get here—by transfer or direct. From all accounts this is by far the best of the new fields. The others are at Mt. Clemens, Michigan, and Rantoul, Illinois, but neither one is as far along as this one. Besides we are well worked in and are being treated with the greatest of consideration.

To be sure, at first things went more or less crab fashion. The officers didn't know why we were here or what to do with us, and we were over-anxious to get things moving, all of which caused more or less of a row, but all is smoothed over now. We get all the flying it is possible to give us and all of us that make good will be taken on as instructors, sooner or later; and I believe those who do not will be given clerical positions.

Last Monday our mess was started up in the hall in back of us and believe me it surely is a dandy. Norton had charge of starting the mess and as luck would have it he ran onto a negro cook who was dissatisfied with his job in a fancy restaurant in Dayton and who was tickled to death to get out here at the field. He surely is a wonder at cooking. I have never been to a hotel yet where the cooking was any better. We also have dandy waiters and everything is kept spic and span, with not a fly in the place. It didn't take long for the news of that mess to spread around, and now all officers, including Major [Arthur] Christie* [first commanding officer of Wilbur Wright Field], eat with us. One end of the mess hall is reserved for officers and the other end for the cadets. They are the fledglings who have been sent here to get their flying education.

The purchasing sergeant who has charge of getting all the food is also a hotel man, and with the 75 cents daily allowance, which officers get, we are leading a pampered life, as far as food goes. We often have to go away leaving plums and oranges lying on the table. However, no matter how much I eat, it's not more than an hour before I feel ready for another meal, which shows that the grub must agree with me—or else I have a tape worm, which isn't likely. Most every night we go over to Fairfield and get a couple of watermelons and have a regular feast on the piazza. It only takes four of us to put away a big fifty-center. Taken all in all, we are leading a pretty gay life here.

By the end of this week we will be moved into the officers' quarters. Each one of these has three rooms, a bath, and a kitchenette, and every two suites share a screened-in porch. The only bad part of it is that we have to furnish them ourselves—but if we get taken in as instructors with prospects of staying here four or five months it won't be so bad. Bartholomew and I have our suite picked out and are waiting to see what we can really expect before settling down. Lindsley and Church have already moved in but the rest are going about it more cautiously. Church has lots of money and so he can do as he darned pleases and a few hundred won't make any difference.

Affectionately,

George

GEORGE HUGHES TO LUCY HUGHES
Friday, 17 August 1917
Dear Mother:

We moved into the officers' quarters yesterday and now we are making frantic efforts to fix them up decently. Most of the fellows have bunked up, two in a suite, but Bartholomew, Goldsborough and I decided it would be much better if three of us could join in and fix up a place together. So far we have merely moved in; we haven't had time to scrub up the floors as yet. We just swept them out and have contented ourselves with polishing up the enamel ware—such as the bath tub and the kitchen sink.

Things were in a terrible mess as the carpenters had just finished. However, we managed to clean them up fairly well. I started a good wood fire in the kitchen range and got the hot water tank well heated. It surely did seem fine to have warm water to wash in. Until now we have had nothing but cold water. We haven't bought any furniture; we intend to hang back and see what the rest of the crowd gets stung with, then profit by their experience. It's going on two months now since we received any pay, and most everyone is pretty low, but when we do get paid off we ought to have a fat roll.

Affectionately,
George

GEORGE HUGHES TO LUCY HUGHES
Tuesday, 28 August 1917
Dear Mother:

I imagine that Gerard has been sent to Rantoul. Two more men reported here Thursday from Mineola and they said that Gerard's orders were for Rantoul. It's a very good place. Much better than Mount Clemens according to all reports, but not quite as big as this field. As yet I have received no word from Gerard but suppose he'll be writing in a day or so.

I am now wearing my lieutenant's insignia and they already have me on as Officer of the Day for the night. There's no escaping it—but it isn't so bad since we no longer have to make an inspection after midnight. That's done by the sergeant for those of us who are instructors. I haven't taken the oath of office yet and will have to wait until hearing from Washington before doing so.

The reason we can't have any Curtiss machines is that the civilian instructors won't use any other and there aren't enough to go around—and more aren't to be had for love nor money. I suppose the reason the government continues to use Standards is that someone is interested in helping the company. However, the funny part of this business is that our machines are ordered by an aircraft board and most of its members evidently don't know a tail skid from a propeller and they dictate what the engine shall be like and all the rest of the details. As a result, witness the "Baby" Standard.

I asked the [Standard Aircraft] representative yesterday why the devil his firm continues putting a four-cylinder motor in an airplane, and he said that's what the aircraft board ordered and his company had nothing to do with it. The private concerns haven't the nerve to tell the government what's what in aviation and yet they are just getting a bad name for themselves by delivering machines specified by the board.

In England the manufacturers got sick of the fathead know-it-alls on the air boards and went to work and developed their own machines and engines. Then they told the government they could take or leave them but no changes would be permitted at all. As a result, they have engines that will average one hundred hours in the air without overhauling—which is far better than the best we can show. If an engine goes wrong it is sent to the factory and replaced by a new one. No repair work is allowed by a government official or employer.

Still these Standards are safe enough. We never go up when it's windy and take no chances whatsoever. All accidents here have been with Curtiss machines. About three Curtisses get smashed for every Standard. As Captain Peebles says, "when a man goes up in a Standard, he's so darned careful he always comes down safe again, while in a Curtiss, he feels so safe and cocksure that an accident often results."

I would like the following, if you can ship them out: my two army blankets, my heavy white sweater, sleeveless sweater, bath robe, bedroom slippers, and camera tripod. It's getting cold as blazes out here and I begin to fear that the winters must be tough if it can darn near produce frost in August. We almost freeze nights. We only have two blankets each, to be sure, but that should be aplenty for this season of the year. Last night I had to sleep in a woolen shirt. I intend to stick out on the piazza as long as possible. It's almost like being outdoors.

We have got our little suite pretty well fixed up now. You asked about the kitchen: no, we don't cook our own meals but we could if we wanted to as we have a regular range and kitchen equipment. The place is fixed up so that one could keep house if so inclined. We painted our bathroom floor steel gray and put up towel racks and all manner of little convenient fixtures. The part of the parlor floor not covered by the rug we stained a tobacco brown and it looks very fine indeed. The rug is a light blue shade which goes well with the brown border. We intend to paint the kitchen floor and will probably stain the bedroom floors the next rainy spell that comes along.

We have been up to our necks in mud the last four days. It started to rain Tuesday night and things got in such a mess that flying was called off until Saturday. You should have seen the trucks and automobiles that got stuck. Half the camp was detailed to dig them out. Some poor boob drove a horse and wagon out in front of G-2. The wagon went in over the hubs and the horse just settled the full length of his legs until his body finally buoyed him up. There's no lack of excitement around this place. I begin to see even now that I'll never be fit for ordinary civilian life again. This is certainly a grand and glorious existence we lead around here, with everything mapped out and nothing to worry about. Just living from day to day oblivious of the fact that there is such a thing as time. There's always something going on or to be done and the time flies.

Affectionately,

George

GEORGE HUGHES TO GERARD HUGHES
Thursday, 30 August 1917
Dear Gerard:

Your two letters just received. Rantoul must be one hell of a place for a flier to be confined to. We not only fly here all morning but also part of the afternoon, and then we fly our beds around the room at night. At least it felt that way when we first started. The motion of the bird got so ground into our bones that as soon as we would retire, the old bed would begin to bank up and sway around. We are immune now, the Lord be praised! I took to the air at six o'clock sharp this morning and flew until ten, then laid off until three o'clock, when I went up again and flew up to 4:20.

Old "Rusty" Bounds of the Standard Company treated me to a joy ride in my ship—the one with which I instruct. Damned if he didn't give me the ride of my life! I never dreamed these "Baby" Standards could be put through such gyrations. He came down to within 30 feet of the ground on the darnedest dive, then hauled her around on an eighty degree bank, then leveled off and coasted down the field about five feet off the ground, then opened up again and cut some powerful short turns just off the ground. The gang on the field were holding their breath for me—and no joke, either; but I didn't feel uneasy a single moment. That old boy sure can fly!

Talking about conservative flying: we get what they call "advanced flying" almost every afternoon. Captain Peebles is the guy who does it and he can only take up three of us a day. So far I have been up but once. We went up to about 4500 feet, then he began pulling off his stunts. He put her into a tailspin and let her flop around four or five times, then yanked her out with reverse rudder. Then he told me to get her out of the next one. Well, I stepped on the old rudder as viciously as I dared, but it wasn't enough, and he had to come to my rescue.

The secret of extricating yourself is to jam the rudder to the reverse as far as it will go and doing it damn quick. Otherwise you pick up terrific speed. As long as you are in the spin, you don't go very fast but the instant your tail and flippers are in neutral you begin to drop like a rock. The way to get into one is to start her skidding and at the same time pull her gradually into a stall, keeping horizontal stability with ailerons as long as possible. As soon as you stall, she'll flop over into a spin.

It isn't really bad stuff at all. You lose track of the ground, but you do not get very dizzy. While you are in the spin, keep your wheel well back against your chest and full rudder in the direction of spin and the two will hold up your speed; and as soon as you neutralize your wheel and reverse the rudder, out she comes—almost immediately. The Captain also pulled three loops, a bunch of stalls, and three or four side slips. We have been out of good ships for several days, but ten new Ds came in yesterday, and as soon as they are assembled, we'll start this advanced flying again.

The gang who are here are: Norton, Benson, Weatherley, King, Bartholomew, Lindsley, Lowe, Goldsborough, McCreery, McConnell, Church, Trowbridge, and myself. McConnell is married and lives just a door or two from me. Norton and King have been given command of squadrons of 150 men each. Goldsborough is commander of Cadet Unit No. 1. He took Norton's place. Things are booming along. Everyone is well satisfied. The officers are all a good bunch and are giving us every chance. I have been assigned to active duty but haven't received my commission and can't take the oath of office until it comes and I accept. It's a funny situation. I have to stand my turn as Officer of the Day. Must close now.

Ever,

George

JERRY'S COMMENTS

George's comments about how to get out of a spin reflect our deep concern about getting out of a spin. When we first learned how to fly, getting into a spin was one of our main concerns. Or, to be more exact, how to get out of one when we got into a spin. If we didn't know how to recover from a spin, we knew we would crash. A spin is basically an uncontrolled descending steep spiralling turn. It took us a while to realize that we could enter a spin—and get out of one—with a systematic set of cockpit procedures of the kind George describes. But in the meanwhile, several fliers lost their lives out of ignorance and fear, including poor Captain Taylor at Mineola.

GEORGE HUGHES TO LUCY HUGHES
Friday, 31 August 1917
Dear Mother:

Received two letters from Gerard at Rantoul. The gang there doesn't seem to be making out as well as we are here. But I guess if they will only sit tight, things will start their way in a short while. Everything seemed to be going against us when we first arrived here, but we couldn't be any better off now if we were to be given complete command and allowed to order things just as we desired.

Had another rain this morning and I only flew about ten minutes. I doubt very much if there is any flying at all this afternoon. Think I'll go in to Dayton after dinner and bum around for awhile. My class seems to be coming along very well now, and if the weather will only clear up so that I can give them a little extra time, they ought to get a good start toward becoming flyers. Three of them are very good indeed and the other three aren't so bad, but they are a little slower at catching on. Still, they are doing very well, and I expect that all of them will make good in time.

The weather here is now quite agreeable, very cool at night and just about right during the day. I doubt if it will hold this way very much longer. We are liable to have another hot spell before the summer is over. It doesn't seem possible that the summer is really almost over. Old Father Time uses a speedier machine than the "Baby" Standard by the way he goes by.

I don't know whether they figure on keeping us here all winter or not. I wish they would transfer us to San Antonio or San Diego for the winter, but I guess there is no chance of it. I congratulate myself every day that Gerard and I learned when we did; we had the best school and the best machines in the country. I would hate to be learning on a Standard with some green instructor, the way this bunch here and elsewhere have to do. Besides, all this flying here will make my chances of surviving all the greater—if I am ever shipped across. The "feel of the air," as they call it, can't be acquired except by long hours in the air, and that's what we are getting here. Must close now.

Affectionately,
George

GEORGE HUGHES TO LUCY HUGHES
Tuesday, 4 September 1917
Dear Mother:

We have started Sunday flying here, so now we get it every day in the week. But we do no instructing on Sunday, just joy-ride around and amuse ourselves. The Sunday work is primarily for the solo men who have been turned loose and need the time. My class is coming along very well and I expect that three or four of them will be ready to fly alone in a week or so, and the rest in a couple of weeks anyway. Tomorrow I believe all the Mineola gang—there are fourteen all told—will go on a cross-country flight, possibly to Springfield, though the destination is not definite. The object of the flight is to help out at some of the Labor Day celebrations, and stir up the public generally. Some of the enlisted men will be going along.

The morale of the enlisted men in this branch is far superior to any other military branch. The opportunities to rise are the greatest. Enlisted men are being given their commissions right along. About five got them while we were at Mineola. The work is no harder than in the infantry and far more interesting and agreeable—and has the advantage of including a darned good technical education. A man has the opportunity to learn all there is to know about airplane engines and aviation in general. They need men with a little intelligence in charge of these ships, and men sent over in these crews will never see the front but will stay back a safe distance where the hangars are, and the time spent in working on these machines is not wasted, the way drilling is.

Affectionately,

George

GEORGE HUGHES TO GERARD HUGHES
Friday, 7 September 1917
Dear Gerard:

When you go up to take pictures, better have someone with you. It's damn hard work trying alone, and almost impossible to get good results. Bart [Bartholomew] and I were up all yesterday afternoon chasing clouds across the skies in wild endeavors to get some good pictures of our own shadow. Damn near froze to death, as it was fairly cool on the ground and we went up 6500 feet and more. Cheer up. Perhaps when new orders come through, they'll be for this field and then you will be in luck, for sure. Bart is going to get married the first of October and Goldsborough and I will be alone. Lots of room! But don't say anything as I have heard no official announcement yet.

McCreery is just as wild as ever. He has a class now which he scares almost to death every morning. While he was still soloing he used to go above the clouds in a Baby Standard and proceed to loop it. He took a cadet up for a joy-ride and looped above the clouds. I don't know how many he has pulled by now. I guess he has lost track himself. I went up with him for a few turns around the field to practice landing from the front seat and liked to have died from nervous prostration. He pulled a turn banked to 80 degrees only about 75 feet off the ground. Too close for comfort when you are in a Standard! We have one stick control Standard which I flew this morning. She landed very nicely but the air was perfect. If those you are getting in are like this one, don't bank them past 45 degrees. It's one hell of a job to get them straight again. The stick control doesn't give enough leverage. My class is coming along pretty well now, about as good as anyone else's. I couldn't get any of them up this morning, as my old ship was on the fritz and choked up every time I tried to take off.

I have been assigned to the 47th Squadron as Supply Officer. I haven't found out just what my duties are, but I guess it isn't a very hard job. Goldsborough, King, and Norton have been made assistants to the officer in charge of flying. They have given up their classes and are in charge of the field during flying hours. They assign ships and check up on the work of the solo men. I saw a notice in today's paper that Bud Jacobs fell 300 feet at Mount Clemens and was not hurt. Damned lucky to say the least.

As ever,

George

GEORGE HUGHES TO GERARD HUGHES
Wednesday, 12 September 1917
Dear Gerard:

Just in case you didn't get the letter in which I explained about the tail spin, here it is again. The usual way of getting into one on purpose is to stall, with or without motor, and just as she flops over, give her full rudder in the direction in which you want to spin and keep elevator [control] well back against your chest. If you want to stall with motor on, be sure and cut it the instant you flop or you will get into one hell of a gyration. Captain Peebles said he got into one with the motor on full and damned near killed himself. Said he would never try it again.

The best way is to stall with the motor off. You go into a "fluttering leaf," as it's known here. You go into it easy and can come out in a fraction of a second. The usual way of getting into one unintentionally is to pull a very tight spiral, holding nose up until she stalls. To get out, neutralize the elevator and step on the rudder damned hard. If you have spun around only once or so, you'll come out quite easily. I wouldn't advise you to try it by yourself unless you have good altitude. McCreery gets above the clouds and pulls them all the time, but he doesn't seem to give a damn what he does anyway. His chief delight is looping a Baby Standard.

Concerning Standards: On making turns, 8s, or spirals, you have to give reverse aileron the moment you get into whatever bank you desire. They have a tendency to increase heeling up once you get them off an even keel. I did some [Figure] 8s with a 90 degree bank and had my ailerons 50 percent reversed when half way around, and it took all she had to straighten her up. That was with a dep [wheel] control. The old stick never would come up out of a 90 degree bank. Oh yes—in tail spins, the ailerons are in neutral all the time from start to finish. Can't you arrange to come here some Sunday? We fly from 8 AM until 3 PM. I'll take you up for a good ride.

I understand that Captain [Maxwell] Kirby,* at present our officer in charge of the training department, is to take charge of Rantoul. You'll get your belly full of flying if he does come out there. He's the damnedest man. Won't let us wear anything but leather helmets, but he comes down to the field in his auto bare-headed, without goggles or overcoat, hops right into a machine, and goes up without even getting rid of his cigar. Goes up as calm as if he was in his office chair and begins to loop at 1200 feet. We call him the "Cat's Whiskers." He wears his hat strap under his chin. You'll know him on sight.
George

GEORGE HUGHES TO LUCY HUGHES
Wednesday, 12 September 1917
Dear Mother:

Failed to write yesterday as I flew all the morning and then slept through the afternoon. I am beginning to feel as though I can really fly halfway decently at last. There is nothing like going up three or four hours a day to get you immune. Working the controls is getting to be almost a reflex action with me. Half the time, I am not conscious that I am working them.

I really enjoy myself more every time I go up. I am getting to where I can almost see the air. Flying takes you into a new and little-explored where you see the old earth at its best, as far as scenery is concerned. This morning the clouds were wonderful. I took my gang up above them and had a grand time just chasing around among them. It was quite bumpy and the clouds were all broken and floating around in big clumps, looking like huge puffs of fresh cotton.

It has been exceptionally cold here all day and I wouldn't be surprised if we were to have a frost tonight. This cool weather has put pep into us all and I feel ambitious as the devil; I think I will start running again. I am more than glad that I learned at Mineola. It's rough as all get-out out here. Just today one man, who has been flying alone several hours, reported to the Captain that he wants to give it up, as he feels he isn't fitted for the service. Most of the cadets, however, are doing very well indeed—though they surely do hate to go up in those Standards, and I don't blame them one bit. I would have been scared myself at the same stage of the game, but now I find it rather good fun to go up and wallow around.

Affectionately,

George

GEORGE HUGHES TO GERARD HUGHES
Sunday, 16 September 1917
Dear Gerard:

Don't be scared to use the rudder on the JNs. They stand a lot as long as you don't stall. For heaven's sake, try to get down here over some weekend. I'll guarantee you all kinds of flying. You'll go back feeling a new man. All us Standard drivers drew for one available Curtiss to be used for instruction. For once in my life I had a little luck and drew her. Church fell about fifty feet in a Standard with a pupil. Ship was demolished but no injuries. McCreery turned a man loose, and he, on seeing Church wreck, proceeded to follow suit. Side-swiped his landing gear and turned over. Another solo man ran into the top of one of the hangars; climbed out on to an open door and waited for the ladder. Murray McConnell leaves tonight for Fort Sill. The day before yesterday, my Standard caught fire and burned like hell for awhile. My Pyrene can was empty. It pays to inspect them. Am sending some photos. Excuse the jerkiness of this letter.

George

GEORGE HUGHES TO LUCY HUGHES
Sunday, 16 September 1917
Dear Mother:

Sorry to hear you have been worrying about me. Don't do it! I am still alive and kicking. The last seven days or so have been fine for flying and we have been going to it for all we are worth. It's rather hard work and I usually fall into bed by seven. It's quite dark by 6:30 now. The good old summer is just about past. The cool weather that we are getting seems to take the bumps out of the air and the cadets are getting along pretty well. I expect to turn several of mine loose next week. No, I am not doing any running just now—don't seem to be able to get up my nerve to start in, and there are so many darned sentinels around the place. Will write a decent letter Sunday.

Affectionately,

George

GEORGE HUGHES TO GERARD HUGHES

Monday, 17 September 1917

Dear Gerard:

I am forwarding your orders [assigning Gerard to flying duties] for "frequent and regular flights" in another envelope. I don't know how they happened to come to me. For hell's sake, go easy on those Standards. Don't try to pull stuff close to the ground. Goldsborough and I were just on the brow of the knoll where the mess hall is; it was 1:30 PM and we were on our way to the field. Well, one of those damn things was taking off and as it cleared the last hangar in the north unit its windward wing got cocked up. She started to drift like a bitch. I hollered at Paul to look and the next thing the pilot made a left—instead of a right—hand turn. This brought him tail to the wind, and all this time he kept her nose up and stepped on the rudder, skidded, stalled and flopped not more than seventy yards from where we were standing.

Flames burst out instantaneously; it was the most horrible sight I have ever seen. It seemed like an age before the two men were able to extricate themselves. All the time we were running like hell. The fellow in front was terribly burned. The man in back had his face pretty well cooked; his hands and arms too were bad. In about a minute and a half all the canvas was burned off, but the gas tank kept on blazing for a hell of a while. Both men will probably live, but their faces will show the marks everlasting.

Well, we congregated on the tower and had hardly finished talking when Sharp yells, "God! There goes another!" I wasn't fast enough to see it, but Sharp said it was a tail spin into the middle of Fairfield. We would never have found the damn thing if it hadn't been for Manning who was up at the time and landed alongside.

It turned out to be Sanford, who was joy-riding a sailor cousin. They went into a tailspin and couldn't get out, for some reason or other. Sharp said he was doing a right-hander and on coming out he evidently gave her too much rudder and skidded into a left spin and was too close to the ground to pull out of it. Sanford was pretty well dazed and had a couple of cuts about the face, but the poor devil in front was terribly smashed. Both legs were in tatters. The engine and [gas] tank had come back in on him. It's doubtful if he will live. It was damn tough luck.

The lad had a commission in the Navy. He had been transferred to the flying division and was just visiting here before going to a naval training station. He and Sanford were in a Curtiss. The passenger in the Standard [in the first accident] was a ground school cadet. He had stopped off on his way to Mineola to get a ride a little ahead of time. Such is life and luck!

Affectionately,
George

GEORGE HUGHES TO LUCY HUGHES
Saturday, 22 September 1917
Dear Mother:

My Curtiss seems to be holding out famously and continues to be one of the best on the field. It's no work at all to ride in it all morning and I am generally able to get the entire gang up every day, a thing which was impossible in a Standard. The best of them are continuously breaking down and you spend most of your time trying to get them to run.

If the weather holds good (it looks much like rain just now), I expect to turn one of my fledglings loose tomorrow morning. I have at last got this one ["Casey" Jones*] so he can make fairly decent landings. If I can only turn him out, it will make the rest of the class sit up and take notice. I now have seven men in the gang and the last addition is turning out to be a wonder. I have only had him for a week, yet he is better than some that have been flying for three weeks. I'd just like to turn him loose next week. I think it would make the rest open their eyes. It ought to have a good moral effect on the class generally.

Some time ago I took an infantry lieutenant up for a "joy ride." His people live in Dayton and last Saturday they asked me around for dinner. Their name is Matthews. The father and mother are getting well along in years and are much cut up about this war as they have four boys in one branch or other. They were very nice to me; showed me the best time possible; invited in a lively little Dayton girl, and we went to the country club. Luckily the girl was very popular and I had a good time of it. But the funny part of it was that the father, who is a lawyer, began talking about his grandfather Parrot and, among other things, the huge war orders of one kind or another that the Dayton manufacturers receive. Among the high moguls of the place is one family—the [John] Patter-sons.*

Affectionately,
George

GEORGE HUGHES TO LUCY HUGHES
Wednesday, 26 September 1917
Dear Mother:

Next time you are in Boston, I wish you would get me a couple more good blankets. There is going to be a great shortage of all kinds of clothing and bedding this winter. Even now it is impossible to obtain shoes or clothes from the Quartermaster, even though we are officers. I am still running around in the stuff that was issued to me at Mineola. Tried to get some things from the Quartermaster at Columbus—not a chance. The infantry camp at Chillicothe isn't half supplied. I believe a great number of the recruits have no equipment at all. They are a terrible rough crew—the scum of the earth from all reports; they don't dare give them guns for fear they will shoot up the place. I suppose they will murder half their officers the first time they get into battle. Damn glad I am not in that game.

Had my first spill yesterday. These blooming solo men are all the time coming around and asking me to help them on their landings. Yesterday, this bird came around and so I said, "Sure, take a lap around the field and land. Then I'll tell you what's wrong and make the next for you." Well, I was sitting in the front seat enjoying the scenery while this fledgling was coming in to land. He was drifting to beat the band, so just as we were about to touch down, I kicked the rudder. The next thing I knew I was hanging on the belt and the ship was standing on its nose, straight up as a young ash [tree].

We had landed in a piece of very rough ploughed ground and the wheels settled in, not being able to keep up with the speed of the fuselage, and we simply tipped up. The old gang sure had the laugh on me, for up until then I hadn't been charged with so much as a bent [wheel] spoke, and I was beginning to think that I was pretty good. But I can't boast any more, since I was directly responsible for what happened.

If I had been looking out on the left, instead of the right side, I would have seen the rough ground and would have taken hold of the machine and dodged it. It taught me a lesson. I'll look out on both sides before landing next time. It is the most ignominious feeling I know of to find yourself dangling on your belt and see the old ship standing on her nose right in front of everyone! The only things broken were the propeller and my watch crystal.

Affectionately,
George

GEORGE HUGHES TO GERARD HUGHES
Thursday, 27 September 1917
Dⅽⅿ Oⅽⅰⅿⅾ.

For Pete's sake, try to come down here over a Sunday. Ask Major Kirby for permission. Tell him you have a brother instructing here and you'd like to get a day off to visit the place. We start flying at 6 AM, Sundays included, and keep it up until 4 PM. So if you could manage to spend Saturday and Sunday here, you would be able to get several hours of flying.

McCreery just had one hell of a fall this morning. He was up instructing in spirals. Either he or the student tried to pull a spiral close to the ground and nose-dived about one hundred feet. Luckily they hit in very soft ground. The engine was completely buried. Both men were still conscious but fairly well banged up. It happened only an hour or so ago, and the hospital refused to tell us how they are, but we think they will both recover. Mac has been inviting just such an accident by pulling split-ass turns close to the ground. They put him on restriction to post for two weeks last week for going up and looping and tail spinning. He had the sun between him and the field but it so happened that Major Peebles was up some 6000 feet, just about in the same spot, and saw him go spinning by. Got his number and socked it to him. You are supposed to wait for advanced instruction in that stuff and as soon as Peebles passes on you, you can spin and loop all you want. Mac, however, couldn't wait and has been pulling loops ever since he got here.
George

GEORGE HUGHES TO LUCY HUGHES
Tuesday, 2 October 1917
Dear Mother:

I have turned two men loose so far and both are doing fine. Neither of them has broken anything yet and the first one out is now almost ready to take his final tests. I expect to turn out two or three more this next week. As soon as I turn one loose I get a new man, so I have seven of them all the time. The last two are pretty good and I guess I won't have any trouble with them.

I got my flight reports yesterday giving my total time in the air since arriving at this place and I was somewhat surprised to see that it totaled up to 101 hours and 40 minutes. I think I must lead the rest of the gang by several hours. Lieutenant Benson, one of our Mineolaites, only had 77 hours and a few odd minutes and he is no slouch. The rest haven't received their time records.

It will be interesting to see who really has the most time, but to tell you the truth I hardly think anyone has my record beaten since all the rest of the crew are flying Standards and that means half their mornings are spent on the ground waiting for repairs. There's no need to worry about me as I fly with a 90 percent safety margin. That turning over on my nose didn't amount to anything as regards danger. It just made me mad to have such a simple upset right out in front of everyone.

It breezed up so strong this morning that flying was called off and we are having a regular loafing session for once. I expect we will be bothered with the wind here this fall more than anything else. I think this section must be right in the storm path of all the lows that originate to the west and end in New England, thereby adding much to the fame of the weather in that last-mentioned place.

We are having the most wonderful meals at the officers' club that you ever heard of. Every change seems to be for the better around here. You could not live better at any hotel than we do at present. The party that is running it for us used to have an inn in Osborne—a small town close by—and it was famous for its chicken dinners. Quite a few of the officers used to eat there but when our club was opened one of the captains persuaded the inn-keeper to come in and run our mess. I guess it will cost us a pretty penny but we might as well spend our dough that way as not. Good food is half of life around here when you work and travel the way we do.

Affectionately,
George

GEORGE HUGHES TO LUCY HUGHES
Thursday, 4 October 1917
Dear Mother:

The express package containing the blankets arrived okay last night. Those things will come in mighty handy as it is now getting quite cold, and the prospects of our being able to obtain supplies from the government grow no better. In fact, there is some talk to the effect that the enlisted men will have to freeze or buy their own supplies from private dealers. It certainly is a crime. I am enclosing a photo of my class [Fig. 9]. The second man in from the left is the one I turned loose first [Charles S. "Casey" Jones] and the next to last man on the right is one I sometimes despair of being able to turn loose at all. All the others are doing okay. My time record still seems to hold good. The nearest approach so far is Bartholomew's—90 hours. He is one of my roommates, so it's all right.

Affectionately,
George

Fig. 9. George Hughes and Students, Wilbur Wright Field, Dayton, Ohio. From left to right: Orstrom, Charles "Casey" Jones, Henry, Morsback, George Hughes, Hahn, Suder, Franzheim. "Casey" Jones, later associated with Curtiss Field near Mineola, continued his association with the Hughes brothers after the war.

GEORGE HUGHES TO GERARD HUGHES
Friday, 5 October 1917
Dear Gerard:

It's too bad you can't break away long enough to get down here. If that damn QM would just come across with a little pay, I think I could manage to get up to Rantoul for some weekend. "Babe" Benson left for Fort Wood last Friday. He is going across [to France] in charge of School Unit No. 4. McCreery is up and around, just as wild as ever. He went up Sunday and looped and spun and did everything else on the calendar—even though he had but one arm and about half an eye. He won't be able to go back to instructing for a few days yet. He certainly was a lucky bird to escape with a whole hide.

A certain lieutenant by the name of Schroeder [Rudolph W. "Shorty" Schroeder*] blew in here yesterday from Rantoul driving a Standard. He claims his time in the air was just three hours—total mileage from Rantoul is over 300. It was some going for one of those birds, even if it was blowing a gale in our direction. Wishing to return the compliment that we sent you in the person of the old "Cat's Whiskers" [Major Kirby], he went up and looped that old crate twenty-eight times, one after the other; then he took two passengers in the front cockpit and flew down to the Wright Company field at Dayton. This afternoon he blew in again and started around the field banked up in a left hand turn some 75 feet off the ground. He kept going round and round right in the middle of the field. Everyone else was making right hand turns.

About this time I came along and saw this guy going wild up there and naturally thought it was a solo bird in distress. It wasn't long before he was cocked up to about 90 degrees and started hell-bent for the ground. I never suffered so before and was about to have a hemorrhage when he suddenly flattened out, connected with the ground, and zoomed up about thirty feet. If I had had a gun handy I would have taken a crack at the bastard for scaring me out of half a year's growth.

Well, he kept up this wild stuff for half an hour or so. King was in charge of the field and simply went wild, and when Schroeder came down he tried to put him under arrest. Believe me, some row ensued, and Walter simply bawled hell out of Schroeder. They damn near had a fight. I wasn't present at the discussion, but I guess King laid it on a little too thick, from all accounts.

George

JERRY'S COMMENTS

One of the more interesting individuals assigned at Chanute while I was there was Lieutenant Rudolph W "Shorty" Schroeder. He was one of the most un-handsome men you could ever meet and yet one of the most likable. He was a splendid pilot, a "natural." He was an excellent mechanic and had a perfect ear for the tune of a motor. I saw him once take a knife and whittle on a wooden propeller because he said it was out of balance and made the engine vibrate. Would you believe it? When he was finished, the motor smoothed right down and started to purr for Shorty.

When we learned to fly at Mineola, those old Jennies were equipped with wheels which you used to operate the flippers [elevators] and ailerons. All the aircraft at Rantoul (and from then on) had "sticks" instead of "wheels." Shorty very kindly took me up in a Standard and gave me my first lesson with a stick. Shorty rose in rank to Major, and in the 1920s he flew an experimental LePere plane and established a new world's record for altitude. Wonderful fellow—wonderful personality!

GEORGE HUGHES TO GERARD HUGHES
Thursday, 11 October 1917
HAVE BEEN ORDERED ON FOREIGN SERVICE LEAVE HERE NEXT WEEK CAN YOU GET DOWN GFH 527 PM

JERRY'S COMMENTS

George sent me this telegram as soon as he learned he had been selected to command the 12th Aero Squadron and take it across the Atlantic to France. One day he was a flying instructor and the next he was a squadron commander. Just like that. I received permission to visit him the following weekend, traveling by train from Rantoul to Dayton and back.

GEORGE HUGHES TO LUCY HUGHES
Sunday, 14 October 1917
Dear Mother:

No definite date has been set for leaving this post and I doubt if we will know until about a day before we really pull up stakes. We may be here a week longer but not more than two weeks at the most. So far I am the only officer attached to the squadron and unless we pick up more on the way I doubt very much if I will be able to break away long enough for a visit home.

There should be at least three officers to look after the squadron, and I believe the full complement of officers is nineteen, counting the flight officers, so we will undoubtedly have some more attached along the route. This is a school unit and as far as I can ascertain is booked for southern France which, if true, will be pretty soft. Sounds good to me! It's getting colder than blazes at this place. It's blowing about twenty miles per hour this morning and the field is so muddy that we can't use it.

I had the luck to get the best squadron in the place, but I am having a terrible time trying to hold on to it. The school here is trying to take away about half of the men and give me "scrubs" in place of expert mechanics. The men of the squadron are very much cut up about it, as the 12th [Aero Squadron] has always ranked first everywhere it has been. It was the first even in San Antonio, which is our biggest post. But now, if they take away the best men and replace them with second graders, the men feel that it will be a lame duck squadron. Naturally, they feel it keenly and they have been entreating me to to do my best to hold the squadron together.

This noon we are going to hold squadron drill. The other three squadrons which are going [the 13th, 18th, and 19th] have been drilling for several weeks but the 12th ought to be able to catch up with them since it ranked first at San Antonio. I stand a good chance of coming out of this Army a poor man. At present I am directly responsible for all supplies, mess expenditures and company funds, and any shortages will have to be made good. Usually there are officers [in charge] of these separate divisions. Luckily we have complete winter outfits so I won't have to worry about that. The 12th, I believe, is the only one with complete supplies.

I was with the 47th but got transferred over at the last minute. I wasn't expecting to go across for some time yet and was more than surprised when I got my orders. I got a wire from Gerard saying he will be down over Sunday for a visit. Well, the first snow storm of the season has arrived. Just started a few minutes ago. It's mostly flakes but is enough to show that it will be none too hot here this winter. I'll let you know when I leave and give you plenty of time to reach New York if I can't get home.
Affectionately,
George

GEORGE HUGHES TO LUCY HUGHES
Friday, 19 October 1917
Dear Mother:

Nothing definite has been issued as to when we leave here. The way things look now, it may be a couple of weeks; then again, we are liable to get orders any minute. There's no way of finding out, and we won't know until a day or so before we are to leave. I expect that we will stop in New York two or three weeks when we get there, so I may be able to get up to Oranlle.

Gerard was here Sunday. He arrived Friday night and returned Sunday evening. He is the picture of health and seems to be getting pretty well along now. Everything is evidently going much smoother up at Rantoul since one of our majors [Major Kirby] went there and cleaned the place up. We managed to get about three hours in the air together and I showed him what I know about driving one of the busses. He flies very well but naturally not as well as if he had been able to get in more time. Considering how little practice he has had since leaving Mineola, I think he is doing remarkably well—and it ought not to take him long to develop a good feel of the air, now that they are getting more flying.

If the weather is good tomorrow, all the ships available will go to Columbus to aid the Liberty Bond campaign. The total distance is 162 miles. Will write full account. It ought to be some affair.

Affectionately,

George

Apparently George never did write a "full account" of his Liberty Bond flight to Columbus. Undoubtedly his time was occupied with more pressing duties, overseeing the movement of approximately 150 men and their equipment first to New York, and then overseas to France.

3

Jerry Hughes, Flight Instructor, Chanute Field

After spending a month at the home of his mother in Ossippee (or Granite), New Hampshire, Jerry received notice of his new assignment, to Chanute Field, Rantoul, Illinois. Like Wilbur Wright Field in Dayton, Chanute Field was recently built, construction having been authorized on May 11, 1917, and construction begun May 31. Chanute Field was not finished until August, and when it was completed, it lacked adequate aircraft to fulfill its flying training assignment.

Jerry arrived at Rantoul around the first of September. Jerry was not particularly happy about being assigned there, especially when he learned that neither aircraft nor students had arrived. In fact, some of the flight instructors initially sent to Chanute Field were reassigned to fields in Texas soon after he arrived. The field at Rantoul was isolated, far from any large city, and much smaller than the Wright Field complex to which his brother was assigned. In addition, he was separated from his brother for the first time in many months. His initial letters to his mother clearly indicate his grumpiness about his situation—he wasn't happy about his remote location, about not flying, about having to be an officer.

Soon a new commanding officer arrived, Major Maxwell Kirby, who had come from Dayton; George had told Jerry that Kirby would make an impact, and that apparently was the case. About the first of October adequate aircraft had arrived so that Jerry could begin to fly again. He reports to his mother late in September that he has been able to obtain only 30 minutes of flying time—certainly much less than his brother was picking up in Dayton. But the flying pace eventually increased, for he tells his mother, in a letter written late in October, that they have rushed to complete flying tests for some of the students assigned there. The flight instruction program at Chanute was not without its price, however; Jerry reports on at least seven aircraft accidents at Chanute, most caused by spins. But no one was killed, and Jerry comments on their good luck in avoiding any deaths associated with training.

JERRY'S COMMENTS

Chanute Field at Rantoul, Illinois, was one-unit field, located on what had been a big corn field. It was as flat as a pancake and was a full mile square in size. When high winds blew across those dry corn fields at Rantoul, extraordinary dust storms would develop. Traveling through such a storm was like driving through a heavy blizzard in New Hampshire—you couldn't see the front end of your car.

Since all the new training centers had been built practically overnight, and starting from scratch, there were several problems associated with their operation. Each post had its big hangars with huge doors, barracks, dining rooms and kitchens, officers' quarters and headquarters buildings—then there were machine shops and all that. All of these buildings had to be furnished and equipped. The necessary personnel had to be recruited and trained.

By the end of 1917 most fields were lacking, not only in planes but in men. There was still a need for ordinary enlisted men, mechanics, cooks, stenographers—plus the need for commissioned officers from the ranks of second lieutenant to colonel. As for planes, Curtiss was going full blast trying to turn out enough Jennies, but it was a matter of some months before every training field had enough aircraft to offer a full course of flight instruction. Certainly there were not enough aircraft available in July of that first year of 1917, not at Chanute Field. In the meantime, hundreds of cadets were piling into the ground schools, and they would soon be coming to us for their first lessons.

Major Tom Hanley* was our first commanding officer. His most spectacular bit of flying at Chanute came about this way: he took up a spanking new LWF. As he came down to land on that broad expanse of the flying field he apparently didn't see a Standard sitting squarely in the middle of the field. A cadet was soloing and had landed to catch his breath. He was just sitting there before taking off again. Major Hanley came floating in in that beautiful new LWF and landed plunk! right on top of the Standard. Fortunately, the cadet had taken to his heels and run away—otherwise he would have been killed. Of course, the cadet should have given his Standard the gun and got clear that way, but he figured the safest way for him was to jump out and run for it. Hanley suffered a bad bruise on his nose.

Our second commanding officer was little Major Maxwell Kirby.* We called him "the cat's whiskers"; he got into the newspapers with one stunt he pulled shortly after he arrived. He took a Jennie up solo one day and, not liking the way the controls in the back seat worked, he crawled out and over into the front seat. The back seat had a wheel control and the front seat had a stick. He liked the front seat controls better and landed in the front seat after taking off in the back seat. It's a stunt I wouldn't recommend to anyone but the most rugged.

Rod Tower and Edward W. "Lem" Killgore, fellow students at Mineola, were with me at Chanute. At first, we were designated as Officers in Charge of Flying, with no particular duties until there were planes and cadets for us to be in charge of. We got in some flying, which was welcome, because we were hungry to get up in the air again. Mostly we sat around and waited. Mr. and Mrs. Morgan Brooks and their two daughters lived in Champaign, Illinois, about an hour's drive away. The Brooks family had been friends of our mother in Boston. Mr. Brooks was on the faculty of the University of Illinois and was very much interested in aviation. Their two daughters were attractive and fun to be with, and I occasionally broke up the boredom by traveling to Champaign.

GERARD HUGHES TO LUCY HUGHES
Sunday, 9 September 1917
Dear Mother:

Things are running smoothly here. I do absolutely nothing as yet—not even flying. Haven't got my quarters fixed up yet. Today is Sunday and sleepy as usual. There's no news. Went to the movies in Champaign. It is quite a large town. Chicago papers are terrible. No news except murders and silly talk. No real news. We read the *New York Times* but it is usually two days late. Don't like being an officer. Have to be on good behavior all the time, and whenever you approach an enlisted man he stiffens up and salutes you as though you were the Czar. It doesn't seem natural or right. You feel like an outcast from society. Haven't been to see the Brooks. Scared!
Affectionately,
Gerard

GERARD HUGHES TO LUCY HUGHES
Tuesday, 11 September 1917
Dear Mother:

I bought some furniture for my suite today; just a rough table and a couple of chairs. Don't know how long we will be here, so don't want to invest too heavily. Twenty-five fliers from here leave for San Antonio in the morning. They have not received their commissions yet. It may mean France for them. Nobody seems to know. Had my first flight in two months yesterday. Felt very natural. The officer's French class started last night. It consists of 24 lessons of one-half hour each. I guess I will get a little something out of it.
Affectionately,
Gerard

GERARD HUGHES TO LUCY HUGHES
Wednesday, 19 September 1917
Dear Mother:

I haven't got in any flying yet—except that I went up with Lem Killgore once to look around. Rantoul, from the air, is a very small cluster of houses and trees and all about, as far as the eye can see, are large fields of corn and oats, with a few trees lining the boundaries [Fig. 10]. The aviation field is one square mile. The place is horribly monotonous on account of the absence of hills; also there is no place to go. Champaign, a fair-sized town in which the University of Illinois is situated, attracts most of the soldiers over weekends.

Here they fly on Sundays—which makes it hard to keep track of the days. I am just hanging around here doing nothing and waiting to be assigned to duty as a lieutenant. I haven't been to call on the Brooks since they visited me. I will have to go down there soon. You pronounce Chanute "Shanute"—at least that is the way it is pronounced here. I am not teaching a class. In fact, I have been in the air only about thirty minutes since I arrived. I expect with our new commander we will be put to instructing. I hope so anyway.

Affectionately,
Gerard

GERARD HUGHES TO LUCY HUGHES
Thursday, 27 September 1917
Dear Mother:

Our new commanding officer is fine. He has made a general shake-up in the jobs around the camp; he has ordered all army insignia taken off automobiles, and has forbidden the wearing of flying equipment off the post. "Ground Flying" is what they call that stuff. Fellows would put signs saying U.S. ARMY AVIATION SECTION and the like on their cars, and would wear helmets, goggles and leather coats downtown. It's the cheapest sort of a display and is absolutely taboo in any well-regulated camp.

Our former C.O. [Major Hanley] allowed the officers to bring women into their quarters on the post. (Never mention that to anyone.) You can imagine that things were not in the best of shape here. The new C.O. has changed all that with a bang. The French officer who is detailed here was hardly treated with respect by the former C.O., a thing which is pretty terrible when you think of it. Well, Major Kirby is a different man and a few weeks from now this place will be a real camp.

Affectionately,
Gerard

Fig. 10. Rantoul, Illinois, and Chanute Field. Chanute Field (named after Chicago aviation pioneer Octave Chanute) is located to the southeast of the city of Rantoul. The new hangars and other support structures are clearly visible. The landing area is the grassy field to the right (south) of the hangars.

GERARD HUGHES TO CLAUDETTE DE BOUTILLIER [one of two sisters, Boston friends]
Thursday, 27 September 1917
Dear Claude:

Your letter was received and enjoyed with the keenest of pleasure. It is so seldom that one receives a truly delightful letter such as yours, one which is long enough and interesting enough to carry a person back completely to days gone by and surround him again with the faces of friends.

George is enjoying himself immensely down in Fairfield. He is instructing his first class in flying. He writes me that they are doing well. He has high hopes for three, especially. The other three (he has six) have not caught on as quickly as the others, but they are doing satisfactorily. He gets in about five hours of flying every day. He is also given advance instruction by another officer. The latter takes him up and shows him how to loop, sideslip, stall, and how to get in and out of tail spins, nose spins, and the like. These terms probably sound technical to you but they are merely various maneouvers of a machine. Tail spins and nose spins have caused many an aviator to fall. You often get into them unintentionally and unless you are high enough up (at least 2000 feet) you will hit the ground before you can get out.

Two men got into a tail spin here yesterday. They fell over 1000 feet and landed in a farmer's yard about a mile north of camp. The old farmer ran over to the machine, which was all smashed to pieces, and (according to his statement) "when I see the airplane I thought somethin' was wrong with it, so I runs in the house and telephones over to the field." One of the men was slightly injured but the other was smashed up quite badly.

The day before yesterday "Bud" Jacobs of our old Mineola class fell with a pupil at Mount Clemens. I don't know what the trouble was. They fell 300 feet but neither one was seriously injured. About three weeks ago two of our old class—Tiffany and Richards (the latter a Harvard 1915 man)—fell into a lake at Mount Clemens. Neither was badly hurt, although one of Tiffany's eyes was badly cut by the glass in his goggles. Captain Taylor, who was in charge of our training at Mineola, fell about a week after I left. He was instantly killed. They say he fainted in the air and fell on the controls. The man with him was unable to bring the machine down on that account. This fellow is a sergeant and only had his jaw fractured. I'm glad I'm not with George. We always worry about each other, the one on the ground being nervous about the one in the air. It gets to be a strain, I can tell you, when it comes every day.

I have very good quarters here. At present I have a suite to myself —two bedrooms, study, bath, and kitchenette. A first lieutenant is entitled to all this, but we are rather crowded and so I will have to share my abode with someone pretty soon, I expect. I don't know how long I shall be here. I think the War Department will send the different aero squadrons to France as soon as they are filled and equipped.

Each squadron has about twenty officers, including the major who commands, and they are the men who do the flying and the fighting. The enlisted personnel (150 men) consist of mechanics, cooks, and administrative types who do the work of the squadron. There are only about three officers in my squadron, and there are only a little over 200 officers in the country who can fly—if there are that many. The rest are being trained.

We will have to wait since the squadrons will have to be filled by men who have yet to be trained and commissioned, and it takes time to get trained and to receive one's commission, I can assure you. It's a tremendous business turning out 20,000 aviators, but when we get them ready, they will do the country proud.

Sincerely,

your friend, Gerard

GERARD HUGHES TO YVETTE DE BOUTILLIER [the second of two sisters], Thursday, 27 September 1917

Dear Yvette:

I was delighted to hear from you. As you know, a soldier's chief pleasure is letters from his friends; and they are especially a pleasure in a place like this where there is so little that is exciting or amusing.

Until a few days ago this aviation camp was in the last stages of despair. Our Commanding Officer was not the man for the position and he allowed the place to run down. Discipline slackened, work was inefficient, and so little flying was done that Chanute Field was more of a ground school than a flying field. The result was a new Commanding Officer. His name is Major Kirby and he was in charge of flying at Dayton, where George is, until he came here. George wrote me about him, saying that he was a "bearcat" and that if he ever came to this field he would make things hum.

He arrived, and he hadn't been on the ground many hours before he went out to the field, asked for a machine, and without coat, helmet, or goggles, climbed into the back seat of the Curtiss. Up he went, taking time only to throw away his cigar. He flew around for half an hour or so, diving and looping. Then down he came. When he taxied up to where the crowd had gathered, what was their astonishment to see the little fellow in the front seat. You know these machines have two seats—front and back. Well, while up in the air a couple of thousand feet, he calmly climbed out of one and into the other.

The crowd gaped with wonder. It was a stunt that they had never heard of before, on this field at least. For several days it was the chief topic of conversation. Some argued that Kirby must have stalled the machine and jumped in the front seat as it slid from under him. Others held that he put the bird into a nose dive and fell in. The *Chicago Tribune* came out with Kirby's picture and half of a column about the "new aerial thrill." The stunt showed what kind of a man our new Commanding Officer is. He established a reputation for himself and has been living up to it ever since. He has speeded up this camp several hundred percent and it won't be long before it is one of the best in the country.

Illinois must hold all the records for dusty roads. Several days ago Lieutenant Killgore (a fellow Mineola graduate) and I drove to Champaign, a town some twenty miles away. All the way down it was like driving in a heavy fog. The dust raised by passing cars was so thick you could hardly see. We choked and spluttered along until our eyes were so full we were just about blinded.

Pretty soon a car went tearing by raising an unusually heavy cloud. Killgore was driving our big Cadillac and being temporarily blinded by the dust, he swerved over into the middle of the road. Just then another machine approached us and before we could turn to avoid them BANG! there was a shriek of tortured metal. We had slashed them. After the dust had settled a little, we looked around for dead bodies. There were none, but we had ripped off the other man's mud guard and his front wheel was missing. One of our mud guards was badly crumpled, but otherwise we weren't scratched. Well, such is the life of a soldier exiled to the corn fields of Illinois.

Sincerely,
Gerard

GERARD HUGHES TO LUCY HUGHES
Monday, 8 October 1917
Dear Mother:

We are beginning to get more flying here and may be able to take our JMA tests before long. They rate you as a Junior Military Aviator. When we pass our JMA we will get $250 a month. And if by any chance we get to be captains, that will be materially increased. I called on the Brooks on Sunday. When I first got there, I helped Mrs. Brooks hang a couple of pictures; then Frances and the other sister, Frona (whom I'm now convinced isn't married) and I made candy. Then we went and investigated the new women's dormitory at the University of Illinois. It is enormous—with a full-sized mirror in the hall for the fair ones to look at themselves in. The building was to be turned over the next day to the aviators at the ground school. Then they had me to supper. Then I went home. Is my razor strop hanging in the attic anyplace?

Affectionately,

Gerard

JERRY'S COMMENTS

I was instructing at Chanute when I got a telegram from George, saying that he had received orders to go overseas, and could I come over and see him before he left? I immediately got permission and traveled by train to Dayton. When I arrived, I learned that he was on his way to France; he had been given command of the 12th Aero Squadron and had orders to lead it to Europe.

GERARD HUGHES TO LUCY HUGHES

Sunday, 21 October 1917

Dear Mother:

I went to Dayton. Took me eight hours. Took the train to Indianapolis and changed. Arrived in Dayton and went to the Miami Hotel where I met some of the old Mineola gang. It was wonderful seeing them again. They said George was on his way in. He arrived half an hour later in an old jitney. He looked very well and much pleased with life in general. We drove out to the field, after finally getting the Ford to run. Bartholomew was away, so I slept in his bed. The spirit at Dayton is very fine. It is the old Mineola spirit, no doubt injected by the fourteen men of our class who went to Fairfield. Everybody is happy, treated like heroes by the city. Feted, feasted, and made much of by the entire populace; dancing at the Country Club every night; boots and spurs and all the rest.

When I got up in the morning it was damp and terribly cold—a penetrating wind was blowing. Ate breakfast at their mess hall. It is fine. Table linen, good service and dishes, ferns and rubber plants as decorations. Food very good. A whole flock of machines were lined up ready to fly when we reached the field. A great roar of motors in the chill air. Then off they went, one, two, three, until there were fifteen or more machines in the air.

George still had his class and turned two loose that day (Saturday). I stood on the observation tower overlooking the field. The field is enormous; it stretches far to the left and right and over a mile across. Bare as a bone—no grass—dust flying up in clouds. Many men were being turned loose to fly for the first time and in the space of ten minutes three machines piled up, breaking landing gears, wings or what not. No one was hurt at all. I called on the C.O., as a matter of military courtesy. Met all of the gang. All were tickled to death with Dayton. Some like it so well they would just as soon stay there and not go to war at all.

George and I went up and flew for an hour in the afternoon. He certainly can handle a machine now. He can make a perfect landing every time, no matter what the weather conditions. All of which is natural enough considering he has had over 150 hours actually in the air. He has more flying time than any other of the Mineola men at Dayton. His class is coming along slowly. I think he expects too much of them. He is very exacting. Won't turn them loose until they land perfectly. Poor policy, I think.

Saturday night we went into Dayton, to the Country Club and around, then back to camp. Sunday we flew in the morning. Then again in the afternoon. Got an excellent view of the field. Went to a show in Dayton, and then I took a train for Chicago. Had a nice sleep, arriving in Chicago in time to catch a train to Rantoul—arrived safely.

George was in excellent spirits. He doesn't show much emotion over anything, but I think he was highly elated over being put in command of the 12th Squadron. It's the best at Dayton, if not in the country. The best equipped certainly. I don't know how long he will be in command. As far as I could learn, he will have command of it at the front. You have every right to be proud of your eldest son.
Affectionately,
Gerard

JERRY'S COMMENTS
I said good-bye to my brother and headed back to Rantoul. I didn't think at the time about what an extraordinary thing it was that the Army had taken a young first lieutenant, with no previous command experience or real Army training, and placed him in charge of a full squadron of men and directed him to lead them on an expedition across the Atlantic to France. I have given it considerable thought since!

GERARD HUGHES TO LUCY HUGHES
Monday, 22 October 1917
Dear Mother:
On Thursday we received word from Washington that all men passing their Reserve Military Aviator tests on or before October 20th would be commissioned second lieutenants. We have seventy men here who

should have had their RMAs if this place had been on the job. Dodge, Killgore, and I tried to determine what men out of the seventy should be given a chance to try for their RMAs. We were in a hole, for we know that whatever way we chose, there would be a howl.

We did the best we could and finally chose twenty-eight names. These men drew lots for preference. The next day we were up at four o'clock in the morning; a vicious wind was howling, cold and forbidding. Angry clouds obscured the sky. As soon as there was light enough to see, we started with a rush. Some men were sent out on cross-country flights; some were put through the test for landing for the mark; some the test of climbing out of the prescribed field. All day long we kept at it, until there was not enough light to see. We started with nine machines and had four in commission at the end. One was a total wreck. The pilot had his face rather badly smashed. The others had motor trouble or something else. Anyway, we got through sixteen RMAs. Which is a record, I guess. It was an awful day's work, believe me!

The other day Lem Killgore and I flew down to Champaign. We circled over the city and then came back. It took us quite a while to get down. We were up about 7000 feet. Went to see "It Pays to Advertise" with Frances Brooks and her sister Friday night. It was acted by a fraternity at the University. It was well acted and very funny. Took Frances to the Illinois-Wisconsin football game Saturday. It rained, which spoiled it. This is a hectic life. Two of the officers flew to Chicago Saturday. One smashed his machine getting out of the field at Fort Sheridan. He landed in a tree. The other one got there okay. Dayton was going to send twenty-five machines over to Columbus last Thursday. I haven't heard whether they did or not.

Rod Tower gave a great exhibition of flying today. He is the one who flew to Hackensack, New Jersey, instead of Smith's Point for our RMA test at Mineola—remember? Well, he took off over the hangars without sufficient speed. Landed gracefully in the electric wires and then in the company street. He wasn't even shaken up. It a new kind of machine, an LWF. He had never flown it before, so that accounts for it— to a certain extent.

Affectionately,

Gerard

GERARD HUGHES TO LUCY HUGHES
Sunday, 4 November 1917
Dear Mother:

Yesterday we put through some more RMAs. There was quite a wind blowing. Kilgore was in charge of the portion of the test for climbing out of the field. Two of his men got into tail spins less than 300 feet above the ground. The first man was going straight at the ground with motor full on. Luck was with him, however, and he pulled out of it about fifteen feet above the ground. The next man did the very same thing, but he didn't pull out. The machine was demolished. The pilot got a broken arm and some scratches. I don't think our men have had enough hours nor good enough instruction to be turned loose, let alone to try for their RMAs.

Affectionately,

Gerard

GERARD HUGHES TO LUCY HUGHES
Monday, 5 November 1917
Dear Mother:

I was glad to hear from you and learn that George was getting along okay. There is no doubt that this aviation has been the making of him. It was not that he lacked executive ability, but that he had no confidence in himself. He has always been that way—retiring and self-deprecating. When he got into this game and found himself, and saw that he was a good deal better than the average, his latent ability just naturally blossomed out. If he keeps it up he will get promoted.

There is more opportunity for ability to get its reward in aviation than in any other branch of the service. Also aviation will be more in the public eye than any other and it will mean something to be in it. You must have been pretty busy equipping that son of yours. What he should have bought in the way of a raincoat is a "trench coat," to be had at Brooks Brothers for $60. They are a raincoat and an overcoat all in one.

This war is sickening, what with the Russians and Italians giving in. Germany is at their last gasp, and if only the Italians had kept up their winning streak there wouldn't have been anything to it. There is no prospect of my going to France yet awhile. Thank George for the flight reports. Tell me what his address is.

Affectionately,

Gerard

GERARD HUGHES TO LUCY HUGHES
Tuesday, 6 November 1917
Dear Mother:

Went down to Urbana yesterday. Found myself in the University Co-op, and before I knew it had bought about $20 worth of books. It's a bad habit. Went to a movie, then I drifted over to the Brooks. Had supper without being asked, and left on the nine o'clock car. They are a wonderful family. Always busy doing something extraordinary. Frances is trying out for a part in a pageant. Dr. Brooks was so busy thinking of his propeller yesterday that he ran into somebody with his car and bent the axle. It didn't worry him in the slightest.

Tell George, if you see him, that I flew an LWF for the first time yesterday. I slipped it over on our gang the way I did in the Standard, being the first one to fly the LWF since Rod Tower smashed one of them. I got up to 1500 feet and pulled a tight spiral with the motor on. When I came down, the motor died out in the middle of the field. I walked in to the hangars and on the way I picked up a dead duck. I swore that I had caught it round the neck while I was in the spiral. They almost believed me, but I spoiled it all by laughing.

Affectionately,
Gerard

The LWF was one of the less common aircraft in the Air Service inventory. Gerry joked that LWF stood for "laminated wood fuselage," which it had, but the initials stood for Lowe, Willard and Fowler, the makers of the plane. This aircraft, which was reported to suffer from a lack of structural integrity, was little used in the flight training program. Gerry reported that it was great fun to fly, with a phenomenal gliding ratio.

JERRY'S COMMENTS

Gradually the instructors who I had been flying with were reassigned, as we had more instructors than flyable aircraft to instruct with. They were all good men and a pleasure to fly with [Fig. 11]. One in particular who helped me a lot was Rudolph "Shorty" Schroeder.* He showed me how to handle a Standard with skill and confidence. When he left Rantoul he went to Texas before ending up at Dayton as Chief Test Pilot at Wright Field. Another dynamic person was H. W. Flickinger.* He later became president of Republic Aircraft.

GERARD HUGHES TO LUCY HUGHES
Friday, 9 November 1917
Dear Mother:

I should like a new pair of socks very much. Another thing, I badly need a muffler of generous length and ample width. Frances Brooks made me a wonderful helmet and is now knitting one for George. Went over to hear a couple of old duffers from the University of Illinois—the President and the Dean—rave and rant, telling how nobly they [men

Fig. 11. Chanute Field Flying Instructors. From left to right: R. G. Page, John Foote, Charles D'Olive, H. W. Flickinger (and his dog, "Spike"), Henry Smith, Lem Killgore, Percy Dodge, Bryan McMullen, William Lewis, Rudolph "Shorty" Schroeder, and Gerard "Jerry" Hughes. John Foote was later killed in an aircraft accident, Charles D'Olive became an ace with the 93rd Aero Squadron, H. W. Flickinger became president of Republic Aircraft, Bryan McMullen became commander of the 258th Aero Squadron after the Armistice, and "Shorty" Schroeder became famous as a test pilot at Wilbur Wright Field, where he set three altitude records in open-cockpit biplanes. The group is standing in front of a Standard training aircraft, with its distinctive vertical radiator located behind and above the engine. Picture taken on a chilly day in October 1917.

from the University] were doing in the war. Said that 1700 graduates and undergraduates were in the service. Their enrollment is as large as Harvard's, and Harvard has 5000 men in the war! You would be surprised to see the multitude of able-bodied young loafers around the college. Their football team is not impaired by the war; nor are their other activities apparently. They are lukewarm I'm afraid.

And then the old President got up before the "Ground School Aviators"—who were at the meeting en masse, 350 strong, and says, "You noble young heroes who have chosen the most dangerous calling which the war affords, we oldsters salute you!" (or words to that effect). In my opinion the ground schools ruin the men more than they aid them. They scare them to death with reports of breaking wires and tail spins, and give them swelled heads over the idea that they are heroes. When the men reach a flying field, their heads are full of the wrong dope—and it takes some time to straighten them out.

Got a postal card from George today, saying he left Dayton the 31st. I guess he is glad to get started. I wish to goodness I could get out of here.

Affectionately

Gerard

GERARD HUGHES TO LUCY HUGHES
Friday, 23 November 1917
Dear Mother:

It's snowing here today. Think I'll go to Chicago this afternoon. This place stops as flying school on the 15th of December, but stays open as a school for mechanics. Squadrons will come here for bit of training before being sent abroad. Whether we remain, I don't know. Either we will stay awhile and go with one of the squadrons from here or else we will go south to one of the southern flying schools. I have not flown much. Only once in awhile, mostly in LWFs.

Affectionately,

Gerard

GERARD HUGHES TO LUCY HUGHES
Saturday, 24 November 1917
Dear Mother

I'm in Chicago on a spending bee. Putting up at the best hotel. Expensive meals. Operas. Plays. Movies. Goodbye money! Blooey! Well, Chicago is not so bad. Michigan Avenue is a great place to walk up and down. You see all sorts of things. I'm going to see Galli-Curci tonight. Tomorrow afternoon, Galli-Curci in Rigoletto. Last night saw William Gillette in "A Successful Calamity." It was fine. Liked it very much. Would like to see George Arliss in "Hamilton," but must wend my weary way back to Rantoul tomorrow night. Do you know whether George has sailed or not? I have had a couple of letters from him, but he said nothing about when he would leave. He wouldn't know anyway, for that matter. Well, I must be off to the opera.

Affectionately,

Gerard

GERARD HUGHES TO LUCY HUGHES
3 December 1917
Dear Mother:

I spent Thanksgiving with the Brooks. First of all, we had dinner at the University Club. Quite a few people were there—professors and their families grouped around various tables. The afternoon was spent at the house. Frances and Frona were to be Red Cross nurses in the pageant which was to be presented in the evening. They made their costumes. Needless to say, they looked very well in their white capes and all, especially Frona. Who is quite tall and, as I perhaps have told you, very good-looking.

The pageant was very good. The masque was a symbolic representation of America's attitude during the course of the war. The action centered on a Mother-figure, representing America. Various shadows flit about her as she sits beneath a spreading oak musing on war. She carries an American shield on one arm and holds an American flag in the other. She is disgusted with the war, but offers aid to all sides through the Red Cross. Then Britain—tall and stately—appears. She carries the Union Jack and is dressed in a long flowing red dress. She asks America why she doesn't enter the conflict on the side of humanity.

Next comes France—petite and moving swiftly. She also implores America to come into the war. Then there is a sudden hush. From the back of the stage appears a woman, tall and gaunt, her face as pale as death. She moves slowly but proudly to the front, her black dress contrasting strangely with the brilliant flag whose broken staff she carries in her hand. It is the orange flag of Belgium. She kneels before Mother America, burying her face in her lap. Then she rises, and with figure set and tense, she speaks a few words. The other nations dip their flags in salute.

Another silence and then shadows appear bearing something in their hands. One has a Red Cross flag torn and mutilated by a shell. The second bears a life preserver on which is written *S.S. Lusitania*. Other shadows shrink back at the sight. America stands horrified; then suddenly, in a vehement outburst, she calls for a naked sword and girds it to her side, while the other nations salute. Belgium approaches her, kneels, kisses the Stars and Stripes and simply says, "America!"

The whole thing lasted an hour and there was no clapping to spoil the effect. Belgium was acted by a Mrs. Scott. She did it very well indeed. The part which she took is the most impressive thing I have ever seen. The simplicity of it was what made it doubly effective. The other parts were acted very well, too. In short, the pageant was quite a success, to my way of thinking.

A couple of students ran into each other on Friday. They were up probably 300 feet. People who saw the accident say that there was a terrible crash when they met. Both men are in the hospital, but will recover, I think. This field has been the luckiest one in the country in regard to deaths. We have had some of the darnedest wrecks and yet nobody has been killed, whereas at other fields men have been killed in accidents where machines were hardly damaged.

This post was a wild place on Thanksgiving. You talk about those "terrible women" in "How to Live at the Front." I guess they haven't anything on some of the married women of Chicago. Certain officers whom I know very well pulled what they themselves called "the most brazen party ever held on Chanute Field." There have been some pretty brazen ones. But I guess they were right in their assertion. I will leave the description to your imagination because the extreme of your imagination will not surpass the actual fact. Even at that you can't blame the men much. We have been in this place three months or more and they are getting reckless. Those damn women were the most to blame. Flying stops on the 15th of the month and then we move.

Judge Landis of Chicago—of national reputation, especially Standard Oil—spent the day with us on Sunday. He has a son in the aviation service who is already in France. The judge is keenly interested in everything connected with flying. He said this after Lieutenant Schroeder had taken him up for a ride. He also said that he had never had the loss of his youth brought home so forcibly as when he thought that he was barred from entering the service.

He is over sixty but full of fire and fight. White hair, with a face like a hatchet and eyes like a couple of knives. When introduced to him, he wanted to know where you were from and all about you. When I said I was from Massachusetts, he said "I congratulate you." I don't know why. In the evening he gave a stirring talk on the war and the pacifists in Chicago, whom he is fighting tooth and nail.

Affectionately,
Gerard

GERARD HUGHES TO LUCY HUGHES
Friday, 7 December 1917
Dear Mother:

Called on the Brooks yesterday. There is snow on the ground now and it is very cold. Three days ago I went the highest I have ever been. Took an LWF and went up to 8600 feet. It got cold up there and the engine began to lose power, so I had to come down. I was bent on hitting 12,000 feet, but it was no use. The next day I went up to 7300 feet and the motor got cold again. Wonderful sight, far above the clouds. They look like a barren waste of snow.

Affectionately,
Gerard

GERARD HUGHES TO LUCY HUGHES
Monday, 10 December 1917
Dear Mother:

I won't know until my assignment orders come where I shall be. I may go to Fort Sill, Oklahoma. Duncan Fuller (Harvard 1915), of our old Mineola gang, leaves for that place tonight. John Baker was sent there from Mount Clemens. It's a big artillery post and a school for aerial observation. I should prefer to stay here, I think. At least for a while. All of the old Mineola bunch who are capable enough will be majors before the war is over. Two are commanding squadrons at Fairfield now, and a squadron commander is made a major. I hope that George will have the stuff to land such a title. Those of us from Mineola certainly caught the tide at its flood. As usual, when I go from home cooking to army grub my stomach suffers. I have been feeling low for a week—but it's gradually wearing off.
Affectionately,
Gerard

JERRY'S COMMENTS

Finally, as winter approached, orders came through for a contingent of men, including me, to leave Rantoul and proceed to Rich Field, at Waco Texas. It was then that I parted company with Rod Tower and Lem Killgore.

GERARD HUGHES TO LUCY HUGHES
Friday, 14 December 1917
Dear Mother:

We are all ready to pull out if we get the transportation. It has been delayed a day so far. We should have left this afternoon, but won't go until tomorrow. We have been pretty busy getting packed up and straightening out affairs. I will be going to Waco with the 39th Aero Squadron. "Mac" McMullen is in command. He has been assistant adjutant at this post for quite awhile. He is a very good soldier and a nice fellow. He was in the Texas Militia [National Guard] and comes from around Dallas. Lieutenant Smith, former C.O. of the 39th, recommended me as C.O., and it was fixed for me to take it to Waco, but McMullen wanted to get back to Texas, so it was given to him. He was going to take it alone, but he and I fixed it up with the Colonel, so I'm going along as Supply Officer. Hope to hell we get out of here tomorrow. It's still cold as blazes!
Affectionately,
Gerard

Jerry continued to fly until flying activities were curtailed by the winter weather. But even with three types of aircraft to fly, Jerry did not spend much time in the air, for his flight record shows that he totaled less than 15 hours of flying time during the four months he spent at Chanute, less time than he had accumulated at Mineola, when he was only a student.

4

George Hughes en Route to France
with the 12th Aero Squadron

As Jerry said, one day George Hughes was an instructor at Wilbur Wright Field, and the next day he was a squadron commander, responsible for overseeing the welfare of 150 restless, anxious enlisted men and a few officers who had received orders to travel to France to take part in the war effort. George was probably selected for the position because of his maturity and aggressiveness as an instructor. Whatever the cause, George's life changed abruptly on October 11.

As commander of the 12th Aero Squadron, George was responsible for ensuring that the ten officers and 150 enlisted men who made up the squadron arrived in France intact. He was also supposed to ensure that the unit arrived with the necessary supplies and equipment. This was a formidable task, as the units often were underequipped when they left the United States, and few supplies were yet available in France. The Air Service practice in World War I was to form the nucleus of an Air Service squadron in the United States and then send it to France as an entire unit. The men assigned to the squadron consisted primarily of staff officers and administrative, support, and maintenance men. The flying officers joined the unit later, after it had arrived in France.

The reason for the two-phase plan was simple: staff officers and maintenance men could be trained relatively quickly, but flight training for pilots and observers required much longer periods of time, especially early in the war, when American training fields were just in the process of being constructed (as they were at Wright and Chanute Fields, for example), and experienced instructors were not available. To obtain flight training as quickly as possible at a time when America had few training resources, American flight students were often sent to training programs run by the French, British, or Italians. Occasionally those new aircrew members became part of the British or French or Italian air forces because American combat units were not fully operational. A fully functional American combat preparation structure did not become established until the late summer of 1918. In the meantime, a piecemeal approach to unit combat readiness was adopted.

The men in a newly formed unit had no idea of the kind of aircraft that might eventually be assigned to the unit; it could be pursuit (or "chasse"), bombing, or reconnaissance aircraft. The specific combat assignment was determined eventually on the basis of aircraft availability and perceived need for a particular flying mission. The Americans had to rely on the aircraft production capability and generosity of the British and French, and they did not know in advance which aircraft would be made available to them. Usually the officer who was sent over with the squadron as its commander was replaced by a more senior officer after the unit arrived in France.

JERRY'S COMMENTS

When George left Wright Field with the 12th Aero Squadron, he had to deal with a different set of problems than he was faced with before. The 12th Aero Squadron traveled to New York City by troop train and arrived at Camp Mills, in Garden City, after night had fallen. It was November, a cold wave had hit the area, and the temperature had fallen below zero. The men had to remain on the train overnight. They had no blankets with them and wouldn't receive them until the next day. The steam engine was just about to uncouple from the rest of the train and remove the one source of heat available to the men. But George persuaded the engineer to stay hooked on to the cars and keep steam up all night. George's first letter to me was written after he had been visited by our mother and sister at Mineola.

GEORGE HUGHES TO GERARD HUGHES
Thursday, 15 November 1917
Dear Gerard:

Mother and Jeanie returned to Granite last night after a very pleasant stop here in New York. Jeanie worked like a trooper and put my company accounts into shape. The old duffer who had the squadron before me hadn't paid any bills since June and there was a stack of them big enough to scare an expert accountant. But I have them all figured out now. Accounts balance to within 6 cents and we have cash on hand of $1400, so things aren't as bad as they might be.

But to begin at the beginning: We left Dayton the afternoon of the 31st and after an uncomfortable 24 hours spent on day coaches, we arrived at Weehawkin, a place on the New Jersey side just opposite 42nd street. Here they informed us we were to lay over under quarantine. The 13th (another Dayton Squadron) had been suspected of having diptheria and were to be held in Dayton, but were turned loose at the last minute and managed to clean up, pack, and get on board in three hours. Well, we protested loudly and they sent to Governor's Island for a doctor who arrived about 7 PM. He took our word for it that there were no cases among us. By "us" I mean the 12th and 13th, as the 19th and 20th went over by a different route. So we were given permission to unload and were taken up the river on a ferry to Long Island City where there was no train to take us to Mineola. After much telephoning and cussing, a train was made up for us, and along about 10:30 we got under way. The cars were ice cold when we got into them but by the time we reached Mineola, or rather Garden City, they were well heated up and we made arrangements to stay in them all night, so we felt we weren't so bad off after all.

When we reached the concentration camp—that is, the old LWF field [Mitchel Field]—the trains ran right out to it over that old electric line that formerly was never used. We were met by a young lieutenant who said that a telegram had come from Washington to unload us immediately and quarantine us in barracks just completed but which had no heat, light, water, and, of course, no cots. The men were supposed to sleep on the floor under their three little blankets. Naturally, Trowbridge (First Lieutenant and C.O. of the 13th Squadron) and I were supposed to stay with our squadrons. Well, believe me, I didn't go to bed on the floor of that dump of an ice chest. There was a chill in there that went right through you, due to the fact that the place had never been warmed up and the atmosphere was somewhat damp.

As soon as the men were settled, I went out front to a sentinel post where there was a fire and waited for the sun to come up. It was then about 12:30. I managed to get a couple of cat naps and was much better off next morning than if I had slept indoors. About 5:30 the baggage car with our cook stoves, grub, and cooks came along and I got them backed onto a siding just off the end of our barracks. When breakfast was ready I roused the squadron from their pleasant dreams and a more down-and-out gang you never saw.

During the day I managed to get cots for every man but could get no heat stoves from the Quartermaster. This field [Mitchel Field] is now known as Field Two, and the old field is now known as Field One [later known as Hazelhurst Field No. 1, and still later as Curtiss Field] [See Fig. 3]. We were still "under quarantine," and I spent the damnedest night trying to sleep on a cot with no mattress. About froze. The canvas just wouldn't heat up. Well, that brought us to Saturday, November 2.

The first sergeant suggested that straw would help out a lot, so I got a truck and went to Field One to Captain Ricker, who gave me an order for 3000 pounds of straw off a dealer in Mineola. Poking around in the warehouse, I found that Ricker had a bunch of stoves. I persuaded him to part with eight of them on a memo receipt. They were big train station agent models and I couldn't haul but four, but when I got them to the barracks, I found that they would be aplenty, so let the others go and went on to Mineola for the straw. That night was more comfortable: got the place heated up, and everyone had a good straw mattress.

Sunday they lifted the quarantine and I beat it into town and damn me if it wasn't a real relief to get a good bath and sleep in a civilized bed. However, the news of the straw and the stoves soon spread around camp and the rest of the gang [from the other Dayton squadrons] came around like a bunch of wolves. They raised such a rumpus that they managed to get away with two of our stoves, although there were plenty over at the other field. A damn dirty trick, in my estimation, but I couldn't do anything but state my sentiments. We were in a barracks that was getting heat, while the 13th wasn't. Besides, we had other things to worry about. The men all needed baths but there was no water except a little cold water that came in now and then. I went over to Hempstead to see if I could find a public bath house. On inquiring, I found that the Garden City Hotel had offered its showers and pool to all soldiers. I got a truck and sent the men over in bunches of 24 at a time and got them cleaned up. Since then, things have been peaceful, though we have been kept busy as the deuce getting the paperwork straightened out.

The day before yesterday headquarters came down on us like a ton of bricks and now all officers have to drill their squadrons from 8 to 10:50 AM, at 11 we go to an officers' meeting; 1:30 to 3:30 we drill again; 4:35 we hold retreat at our individual barracks; and during the night at least one commissioned officer must be present in the barracks at all times. I have a lieutenant attached, Quinlan by name. He's a live wire. Best one I have seen around here. Also got a medic—unknown quantity as yet. The gang who are here with me are: McCreery, C.O. [commanding officer] of the 19th; Henry Lindsley, C.O. of the 20th Trowbridge, C.O. of the 13th; Richards, Supply Officer of the 9th; Trainer, Supply Officer of the 8th; and Tillinghast, Supply Officer.

The men are beginning to get restless now; they have nothing to do and are being mighty well fed. Last night eight men were absent without leave, two cooks went on strike, and my mess sergeant and assistant mess sergeant have beat it off to the Lord knows where. And all this out of a clear sky; we were getting along famously until this morning. I proceeded to break my mess sergeants and cooks and put the eight absentees on hard labor duty and am going to put the gang on slum detail for a while. This managing a squadron isn't what it's cracked up to be. You have to stick around the whole damn time, and the better you treat the bastards the worse they behave.

I went over to Field One today and tried to get a ride in one of the machines. But you can't get in without a pass, and once in all you can do is turn around and go out again. They won't hardly let you look at a ship. As for getting into one, they act as though they want to put you into the guardhouse just for merely asking for a ride. You need a guide to show you the way around. About the only buildings I recognized were the old Wright hangars and the big green ones that were completed before we left. The new buildings stretch in an unbroken row from the old main entrance to the auto parkway. In fact there are about three or four rows running all the way.

The majority of ships are the Curtiss As and Ds, with only five or six of the old Bs left—the same old tubs that were here in our day [four months earlier] and have survived until now. No Standards whatsoever, and only about three LWFs. Speaking of LWF, the old LWF field is packed with all kinds of buildings. They start on the edge of the old polo grounds and run right down to the tree nursery where the ground begins to fall and where one of the figure eight pylons used to be. From there on to Clinton Road, is a solid mass of tents, known as Camp Mills. The doughboys put up there. It's a hell of a disappointment coming back. Nobody left that we know! Can't get a ride! So I wish to the devil that they would ship us on.

As ever,

George

GEORGE HUGHES TO LUCY HUGHES
Monday, 19 November 1917
Dear Mother:

We are still here at Garden City and there seem to be no prospects of getting away for a week or so at least. I suppose there are no boats to take us across in. Awful bore sticking around here doing nothing! Too much good food and the lack of hard work is beginning to tell on the men. Can't hardly hold them down. They beat it into town whenever they damn please and don't return until all their money is gone! Last week my mess sergeant and his assistant took French leave and two cooks went on strike at the same time, and the consequence was that breakfast was held an hour late and I got the deuce for appearing late with my squadron at Battalion Drill.

I busted the whole gang of absentees to the ranks and put in new men. Since then things have been going pretty well in the kitchen. That old gang had the idea that we couldn't get along without them, and I guess it was quite a jolt to them when they discovered otherwise. The rest of the squadron has been cutting around so that I confined them all to the barracks Saturday night and Sunday I started them on a hike bright and early. We took along lunches and marched to a place called Bar Beach, up on Hempstead Harbor. It was after 5:00 PM when we finally got back. I guess the round trip must have been fully eighteen miles. It had the desired effect, all right, all right! Every one of the devils stayed home last night and I wasn't plagued by a lot of nuts asking for passes. About twenty fell into bed as soon as we reached the camp and the rest didn't burn much electricity after supper.

Affectionately,

George

GEORGE HUGHES TO LUCY HUGHES
Sunday, 25 November 1917
Dear Mother:

A regular cold wave struck this place last night and found us all still here—worse luck. The Lord knows when we will be able to pull out, but not before the end of next week at the soonest. I am letting the cooks prepare for a banging big feast on Thanksgiving as it isn't likely we'll be gone by then. At present I am hugging the steam pipes in the orderly room in a vain endeavor to keep warm. I guess it will be powerful cold tonight.

I had a new officer attached to the squadron yesterday. He is going to take over the supply end, which will be a big help. He's damn capable, one of the self-made type; his schooling ended in the ninth grade, but he managed to get into the officers' reserve corps and pulled down a first lieutenant non-flying commission. I made some changes in the squadron itself that are going to help out. My former first sergeant was a good fellow. So much so that he couldn't enforce discipline. The men were too damn slow at doing what he ordered them to do, so I got him to resign and have installed an old boy, hard as nails, serving his second enlistment, and he's pounding the stuffings out of this gang. I made the change on Friday night and turned him loose on the gang Saturday morning, which gave him a good chance to make himself felt by having a regular spring housecleaning. He had the men move everything out of the barracks, scrub all the floors and windows, and rake all the grounds round about. To use plain English, he just raised hell with the gang and I believe the start he got will keep him going through the rest of the war.

I also appointed him an assistant, another hard-shelled second enlistment man; and between the two I guess things are going to hum around this place. There's one other thing; when the old wind gets blowing around the corner of the building, all I have to do is look out the window at the flapping tents of the doughboys across the way and then I don't need to be told how well off we really are.

Affectionately,

George

GEORGE HUGHES TO GERARD HUGHES

Monday, 3 December 1917 (9 PM)

Dear Gerard:

Things are beginning to move at last. All our junk is on board a baggage car and tonight, about midnight, three hours from now, we will start for the port of embarkation. Major Fitzgerald* is in charge of our wing of nine squadrons. I have no idea how many men will be on one boat or what kind of a boat it will be. There are all kinds of rumors which indicate that it could be anything from a Mississippi River raft up to the *Das Vaterland* [a large German luxury passenger ship seized by the Americans after war was declared and later renamed the *Leviathan*].

I expect we will be loaded on board whatever it is before daylight tomorrow, but probably won't leave port for twenty-four hours or so after that. At any rate, I will be able to write you all about it from the other side. Best of luck to you down south in Waco. Oh yes—give my regards to Miss [Frona] Brooks and thank her for that helmet; use all that soft stuff you are so good at. Affectionately, George

P.S. Unless you have use for a bedding roll before you cross, don't buy one until you get here. The local canteen deals out all that kind of junk at 5% above wholesale. Damn sight cheaper than you can get it in town.

G.

GEORGE'S COMMENTS [WRITTEN IN HIS PHOTO ALBUM]

December 3, 1917

We left Mineola at midnight, presumably to fool the enemy, and arrived next morning at Philadelphia, where we embarked without delay on the *Northland*. From there we went to Halifax, arriving the day after the big explosion which laid waste a large portion of the city. Major Fitzgerald* was in command of all troops on board and after much persuasion he consented to a few of us going ashore on urgent business, mainly because he wanted to go himself. We lay in Halifax a week waiting for our convoy to form.

GEORGE HUGHES TO GERARD HUGHES
December 1917, On board [the *Northland*] and at sea
Dear Gerard:

Take my advice: when you get ready to embark, bring along an old hat with a chain attached thereto. Also a pair of low-cut arctics. About the only way you can keep from getting seasick is to stay on deck and keep moving around. In doing so you get your feet soaked and run a damn good chance of losing your hat. Even if you do manage to hang on to it, the soaking of brine it gets will ruin it.

If you have anything to so with a squadron, be sure and pack up a field desk with stationery and blank forms, especially charge sheets, not to mention morning and sick reports. In fact, you need everything for the daily routine business of a running a squadron on shore. We were foolish enough to believe some damn fool who said we wouldn't need them on board; but you do—I'll tell the world—and we have had one devil of a time getting ours up out of the hold. It's kicking up just enough sea outside to make it interesting but not enough to cause us any inconvenience. About 50% of the men or better are down and out. The main reason is that they stay down in the close and crowded steerage. Even staying inside of an outside cabin gets me to wobbling a little and I soon make tracks for the outside. This staying under cover ain't what it's cracked up to be. I prefer to stay outside, even if I do get soaked.

Of the gang on board, the only ones you know are Lieutenant Tilbrook and Captain Heinz (quite seasick). Of the old Mineola bunch, McCreery and Trowbridge. Henry Lindsley* had to drop out. His squadron was put under quarantine just a day or so before we left. I feel that it is time for me to go on deck again—just for a little while—don't you know.

*   *   *

I didn't reach the open air any too soon.

*   *   *

Don't tell me you have never been seasick, because you don't know a damn thing about it, and you never will until you get aboard one of these ships in a heavy sea. As "Wild Bill" McCreery says, you want to eat a lot so you won't be shooting blanks when your time comes.

You know well enough when you're about to be shipped out because they confine you to camp for about twenty-four hours prior to leaving. But don't believe any damn rumors about the port you are going out from, because we woke up a long ways from where we expected to embark. Oh yes: some more hot advice if you happen to have a squadron. About two hours or so before you are to finally leave, line up the whole bunch according as their names appear on the passenger list. The first man on the list being the right flank man front rank, next man right flank rear rank—then back to the front rank and so on. In this way you can shoot them on board in a column of twos with no trouble at all; and as they go on board and are assigned bunks by one of the ship's representatives, check off their names on a duplicate copy of the passenger list. This is a stunt that will save you a lot of time rounding them all up again, and you are required to make a personal check before the ship pulls out. Anyone AWOL should be reported and his service record [personnel file] sent back.

More advice: never let go of a service record without getting a receipt, and whenever you send in a ration return (one is due every ten days on shore) always get a receipt for it. In fact, get a receipt for every damn thing you do if you want to be on the safe side. Trust to no man's honesty. When things go wrong and documents turn up missing, it's every man for himself and the devil catch the hindermost, which means *you* if you haven't got something down in black and white that will relieve you of all responsibility. Also: while you have the men lined up prior to leaving, search the privates for booze, and impress on them that every man pulled in for some infraction on board ship will be made a living example. No smoking below deck at all, and on deck only between sunrise and sunset. Anyone showing a light on deck after dark will catch everlasting hell.

Oh yes: I might add that the Sam Browne belt is worn aboard ship, though you have to wait for your Wing Commander to authorize it. Major Fitzgerald* is in command of our nine squadrons; there are no other troops on board. When you get this little billet-doux you will know I am safe on t'other side, as it will be held until then and then mailed. You may then inform the rest of the family.
George

GEORGE'S COMMENTS

There were about eight ships in our convoy; the *Northland* occupied a central position with the others grouped about us in the form of a flying wedge, which gave us a feeling of great security. But we didn't have as much as a single submarine scare all the way across although the weather was excellent throughout. We arrived in Liverpool Christmas Eve and were taken off in lighters as the *Leviathan* was taking up the entire dock. From Liverpool we went to Le Havre, France, via Southampton. At Le Havre we lay over for a couple of days at one of those misnamed "rest camps," where we slept on board floors inside small round tents.

GEORGE HUGHES TO GERARD HUGHES
Saturday, 29 December 1917, France
Dear Gerard:

We arrived on the sunny shores of France a day or so ago and have been freezing ever since. We are located at a so-called rest camp, waiting for orders to proceed inland. In the meantime we are tearing around in an effort to stay warm. All the men, and all the officers also, are quartered in conical tents, ten to a tent. Of course, no cots! We keep warm by huddling up close.

It snowed about half an inch the day we arrived, but most of it soon melted. Last night we had a little snow—just enough to whiten the ground—but damn me if it wasn't cold. Got up at 6:30 and romped around until after reveille; gave the men a short run at double time, then made tracks down to the officers' hut, hoping to find a warm room and hot water in which to clean up. The front door was still locked when I arrived and there were no signs of life. I prowled around and managed to get in through the kitchen and made my way to the bathroom. All the damn hot and cold water pipes were frozen tight as a drum. I was about to give up I disgust when I stumbled onto a bucket of water—or rather ice—on the floor. Busted a hole in the top and proceeded to shave with spartan fortitude. Froze a couple of fingers on my right hand.

It's a great life if you don't weaken. But hell! I'm no worse off than the rest, and when I see the others shivering around me, it helps to warm me up. Taken all in all, it's not so worse! I expect we will move out almost any time now. Major Fitzgerald is no longer in command. It was only a provisional wing anyway. He has gone on to Headquarters—wherever that may be—and the rest of us will be scattered around the country. There's a rumor to the effect that all of us officers will be detailed and sent to school.

There doesn't seem to be any great scarcity of supplies here. If you have the dough you can get almost anything. Clothes and shoes are somewhat more expensive than back home. Whip-cord suits cost $61 and shoes cost about 25% more. Leather goods are much cheaper in England; you can get Sam Browne belts for $7.50 that sell for $15.00 in New York. Boots are also reasonable, but food is scarce as hell there. They are on what they call "war rations" and damn me if you can get any more than just so much, no matter how much dough you have.

When you come across, get yourself assigned to a life raft. Let the aristocrats take the over-loaded rowboats. Keep an old fatigue uniform handy. Whenever a sub downs a transport, it tries to shoot every man in uniform. The rest of the convoy never stops if one of the bunch gets hit, but puts on full steam ahead and does its damnedest to get away, which of course is the only thing to do. When you come across the Channel, you'll find the accommodations poor, so as soon as you embark, get hold of one of the ship's crew and tell him that you want to buy a stateroom from one of the ship's officers. My Supply Officer was a traveling sales-man. The bastard can get anything he sets out after. Says he just goes after them as though he wanted to sell a bill-of-goods and didn't have a cent left in the world. Darned if he didn't get the Second Officer's cabin for the trip across the Channel. Three of us put up in it, and we were better off than the Major himself. He nearly fell over when he found out where we put up! The rest of the officers slept on wooden benches and the men sat up. It's a case of dog-eat-dog and you just have to go after things tooth and nail.

Tobacco is scarce here—and no mere talk, either. Good cigars run as high as 70 cents in American money. So, if you have anything to do with a squadron, I would advise that you take $100 from other funds, if the accounts will stand it, and buy up a bunch of cigarettes and tobacco and ship it with the squadron baggage. I bought up a big bunch of Camels in Halifax but they cost a damn sight more even there than back in the States. Chocolate is also pretty scarce here. There's a law here which prohibits the purchase of sweets to be eaten on the spot. You have to take them away and eat them in secret. I suppose if you attempted it on the open street you'd get knocked out and robbed. A good thing to carry along with you in case of emergency is a small bottle of Horlick's Malted Milk Tablets—provided you can stomach them.

Oh yes! Old Henry Lindsley's* father, Major Lindsley, came over in the same convoy we did. I believe he is in command of the 163rd Infantry, though I am not sure. The biggest boat in the world [the *Vater-land/Leviathan*] hove into port the day before we did. She occupied the whole blooming dock, so we had to come ashore in lighters. I believe she had close to 8,000 troops on board. Also a bunch of nurses and others. Report has it that all supplies are shipped to the front for the troops there and the shortage here is due to that. As soon as we move along—which I hope will be damn soon—I'll let you know just what is what. At present we are still on the sea coast.

As ever,

George

P.S. Get your money changed into English coinage before you leave or bring it in American Exchange, such as express notes. You will get better exchange rates that way. Tradesmen are the same the world over—

nothing but a bunch of robbers. They'll try to trim you every time on your change. U. S. silver is no good here.

G.

GEORGE'S COMMENTS

We were most uncomfortable at Le Havre and were glad when orders came to go by train to St. Maixent. On first sight, the light French rolling stock looked like mere toys to an American. The freight cars had but four wheels and generally had a brakeman's cabin at one end. We rode in these from Le Havre to St. Maixent [Fig. 12]. At St. Maixent we—the 12th, 16th, 19th, and 10th squadrons—were quartered in an old monastery, which was supposed to date back to Caesar's time and to have been the headquarters of Napoleon. Be that as it may, it had a very ancient appearance that would give credence to any story regarding its antiquity. At St. Maixent we had a worse time even than at Le Havre; food was in extremely short supply and wood to cook with was even scarcer. The enlisted men had a tough time but the officers used to get one or two meals a day at the Cheval Blanc, a very good little inn.

The Air Service camp at St. Maixent was located in the west central section of France; newly arrived men were tested and equipped as necessary for the duties to which their unit was assigned (Mauer I, 73). When a squadron was sent overseas, the men in the unit didn't know what type of aircraft would be assigned to their unit, or if their unit would be involved in training or combat. At St. Maixent that decision was made. In the case of the 12th Aero Squadron, the decision was to send them to the front. It was not yet decided whether the unit would be a bombing or an observation squadron. Both kinds of missions required two-place aircraft, with a pilot and an observer flying as a team.

GEORGE'S COMMENTS

On the the 14th of January the 12th Aero Squadron again received orders to move, this time to Chaumont. We were two days enroute and as usual, when we arrived no one knew the why or wherefore of our coming. We were stationed at the headquarters field on Hill 402, run for the exclusive benefit of certain staff officers. Lieutenant John Mitchell,* brother to Chief of the Air Service General William "Billy" Mitchell,* was in command of "the Hill," and we got along fine together. He was receiving flying instruction from Adjutant Fumat, a well-known French pilot. Adjutant Fumat gave us several hops in an old Nieuport 18-meter training aircraft, but unfortunately we had to move on before we were able to solo.

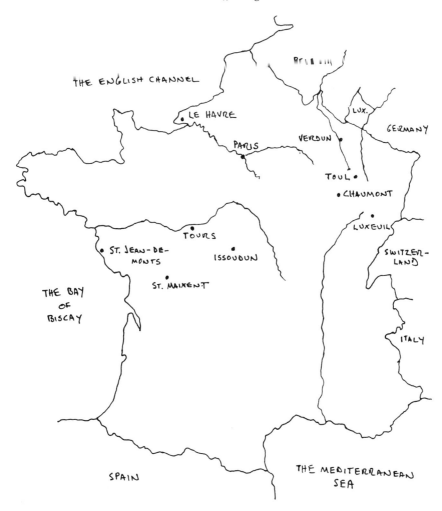

THE ENGLISH CHANNEL

BELGIUM

LE HAVRE

LUX.

PARIS

VERDUN

GERMANY

TOUL

CHAUMONT

LUXEUIL

TOURS

ST. JEAN-DE-MONTS

ISSOUDUN

SWITZER-LAND

ST. MAIXENT

THE BAY OF BISCAY

ITALY

SPAIN

THE MEDITERRANEAN SEA

Fig. 12. Map of France. Cities shown are those visited by George Hughes and the men of the 12th Aero Squadron on the way to the front lines. Also shows sites where Jerry Hughes trained in October and November of 1918.

We had a very interesting time at the Hill, getting acquainted with the latest types of French chasse [pursuit] planes which General Mitchell had for his own use. The field came by degrees to be a way station for French pilots ferrying planes to their advance fields from the Paris factories. We gave them such a glad welcome that they began dropping in on us a little too frequently. Every visiting French pilot would ask for a couple of pieces of white bread to show to his mess-mates at the front.

Chaumont was located in eastern France, not far from the portion of the front lines to which American forces had been assigned. Chau-

mont served as the headquarters for General "Billy" Mitchell, who planned the buildup of Air Service squadrons and assigned them their combat tasks. Apparently General Mitchell and his staff decided that the 12th Aero Squadron would become an observation squadron; it was sent to a training field at Amanty, where training aircraft were provided. Another American squadron was already assigned to Amanty, the 1st Aero Squadron. In addition, a British bombing squadron flying Handley-Page aircraft was also assigned there.

GEORGE'S COMMENTS

The 12th remained at the Hill until February 1st, when Major Harry Brown* took command and moved us to Amanty [Figs. 13 and 14], where we began our training in preparation for flying over the front. At the time of our arrival, Amanty was occupied by the 1st Aero Squadron, under the command of Major Ralph Royce,* who was conducting an advance school for observers. Later on it became the base for the 1st Day Bombardment Group. For several weeks we pilots hauled embryo observers around the countryside in our ARs [Avion Renault aircraft], clumsy old French tubs [Fig. 15]. Domremy, the birthplace of Joan of Arc, was a few miles south of our airdrome at Amanty and was a favorite joyride location for us, especially as the church and a nearby chateau aroused our photographic desires and gave us an excuse for low flying.

GEORGE HUGHES TO GERARD HUGHES
Friday, March 15, 1918
Dear Gerard:

Get all the practice you can driving the old bus from the front seat. Over here things are just the reverse from back home. The pilot's seat is always up front here. The rear seat is reserved for your observer, who has a machine gun rack mounted on the edge of the cockpit, which gives him a considerable arc of fire. The seat of a Nieuport or SPAD is set so close up to the wings that you might as well be in the front seat of a Curtiss, but I believe the scout machine is more or less going out of business. It hardly has any chance against a bunch of two-seaters in formation, and that's the way most of the raids are carried out.

I am going to try to get in on the bombing game. I believe it's going to be a big factor in the war before very long, and it's by far more interesting than the other branches, especially now that the scouting end is beginning to take a back place. In the bombing business you get a lot of cross-country flying; also a considerable amount of fighting, as the Boche generally send up a bunch of machines to give you battle, and as soon as you unload your bombs you are free to raise hell as you please.

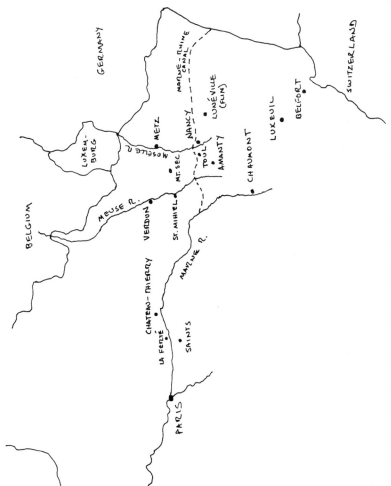

Fig. 13. Map of Eastern France. Shows training locations and battle sites in which the 12th and 258th Aero Squadrons were involved.

Fig. 14. Staff Officers of the 12th Aero Squadron. Picture taken at Amanty (near Toul), France, about the first of March 1918. From left to right: Charles Wade, Dan Bell, Tom Quinlan, Frank Luhr, George Hughes (wings on uniform), Robert Ideson (medical officer), Wilbur Kennedy. Many serious faces, and they're not in the war yet.

Fig. 15. An Avion Renault AR-1. The men of the 12th Aero Squadron trained for their combat missions in this aircraft and flew it over the front lines in May and June. The pilot sat in the front, and the observer sat in the rear. It was a stable aircraft, but slow. This aircraft displays the insignia of the 1st Aero Squadron. Individual standing in front not identified.

In reconnaissance and photography, however, you have to fly around a small sector while the archies [German anti-aircraft fire] take pot shots at you, and this business of doing the hootchy-kootchy over the front lines doesn't appeal to me very much—though there are those who prefer it to bombing.

The British are the boys who are raising hell in the air. The French aren't a bit backward in admitting that the English are the real aerial bulldogs. The other day a bunch of Bristol fighters went on a little trip into Hunland and after dropping a ton or so of bombs on some Boche town, they closed in on a bunch of Fokkers that came up after them and shot down fourteen. Not satisfied with that, they flew back home at an altitude of about 100 feet in the air expending their machine gun ammunition on everything in sight and just raised hell generally. That's the stuff to be in; gives you a chance to give the boche a real kick in the backside.

At present I am flying a large two-seater reconnaissance machine [the AR] that handles just like the Curtiss. Most of the work is taking observers on practice flights. I got in a couple of good three and a half hour photographic trips, then a bunch of new pilots came in and I was given the pleasant little task of converting them to these birds. All of the pilots were fresh from the Nieuport training school [the 3rd Aviation Instruction Center at Issoudun] and thought they knew the whole business. There were about thirty of them and I sure had a merry time.

We have but one dual control machine [flight controls located in both front and rear seats] and you are set back just far enough [in the rear seat, where the instructor would sit] that you get the full force of the propeller blast. God! Talk about wind. It almost blows you out of the seat when you are sitting in the rear, while up front you hardly feel the wind at all. It sure is some job trying to navigate from the rear cockpit and I was damn glad when it was over with.

Even with the instruction I gave the boneheads, they managed to bust up six perfectly good birds trying to set them on the ground, while one supreme bonehead ran one bus with an empty radiator until the damn pistons melted and forced him to come down. He ought to have been court-martialed.

George

GEORGE HUGHES TO GERARD HUGHES
Friday, 22 March 1918
Dear Gerard:

I had about given you up for dead or lost. Had not heard a damn word from you since I left Garden City, at least not until today, when your letter of 22 December arrived, much tattered and torn but intact. It certainly must have done some traveling.

Henry Lindsley* was detached from his squadron in England and sent to Issoudun, the big training field here in France. Carroll Weatherley is also down there, but according to the dope, is doing no flying. He is merely in charge of a squadron. Issoudun is a Nieuport training station with every grade of ship down to the smallest speed scout. Old Tilbrook I believe is also down there with the bunch that he brought from Chanute. As yet I haven't heard what has become of McCreery and Captain Hinds* and Trowbridge.

Major Harry Brown* is now in command of the 12th and we are out in the woods [at Amanty] one hell of a ways from nowhere. However, we have a well-stocked Quartermaster close at hand where you can get anything in the line of clothing—socks, shoes, underwear, britches and blouses. The britches are of English make, exceptionally good material but damn poor design. In order to get a pair that would accommodate my calves I had to go four sizes too big in the waist and seat of the pants. The tops of them just about touched my arm pits. But I'd rather have them too large at the waist than too small. They do fine for rough work and are built to last a lifetime.

On coming across, the best thing to do is to bring a couple of good suits and buy things from the QM for rough wear. These britches only cost six dollars a pair, which is cheaper than you can get them anywhere else. But there is one thing you certainly want to bring with you and that is a good pair of rubber boots. I have a pair of hip boots—Goodyear—glove fit, I believe they are, and I wouldn't sell them for anything and I am the only one who has a pair.

When it gets muddy it sure gets sloppy. We are right in the midst of a spell right now. The day before yesterday it took to snowing and now we are up to our ankles in mud. Regular New England—Boston —thawing weather. Believe me these boots are just the thing, especially for motorcycle riding. I have taken to riding one. Down in the sections where there are more streets, officers aren't allowed to run motor vehicles. But up here in the woods no one cares. But some of these damn fool officers break up more good transportation than they are worth.

I suppose it won't be long before some nut smashes up a machine; then they will put the cork on us too. But in the meantime, whenever I need to go anywhere, I just hop on an old Harley and go. When I first started in on them I wasn't satisfied unless I was making fifty miles an hour. Got spilled twice and didn't break anything, and now twenty-five per is plenty good enough for yours truly, especially on these roads.

A couple of weeks ago two officers in the squadron got a motorcycle and started gaily off. They hadn't gone over two miles when they struck a bad stretch of road, lots of deep ruts and along the way numerous heaps of gravel for repairs. They struck the ruts, shot across the road into a heap of gravel, and landed on the other side in a puddle with the machine on top of them. They surely were a sight when they got back. Their clothes were practically ruined, but luckily the motorcycle wasn't damaged and the accident had the good effect of curing them of their desire to ride out alone.

Besides the boots, be sure and supply yourself with a good canteen, preferable an issue one—and a mess kit. I got a good one from Abercrombie and Fitch in New York, quite compact and easy to identify. Also bring a cot. You will be out of luck if you don't. Besides, you can make a sleeper out of these damn French coaches by setting up your cot in the aisle. It's a whole lot better than sitting up all night when you are traveling. It's also a good thing to have some kind of a bag to sling over your shoulder so that you can keep your indispensable articles in it and your travel orders.

That reminds me: never make a move unless you have an order authorizing you to do the same and keep hold of all your orders. Have them handy where you can produce them. Especially have a copy of your orders authorizing you to proceed on foreign service. If you don't have it, you are apt to have trouble getting your pay, unless you can go personally to the paying QM. Your voucher would never be honored through the mail. So much for that.

Did you ever get that letter I wrote from Halifax telling you what to bring in the way of blank forms and the like? Bring a field desk stocked with every damn thing you would need on land to run a squadron for two months. Also a typewriter. Don't listen to what anyone else may tell you. Have muster rolls, pay rolls, property transfer sheets, summary court-martial sheets, and anything else you can think of.

Also be prepared to give calisthenics a couple of times a day and to lecture on the duties of a soldier and a non-com [noncommissioned officer]. Be prepared to interpret Army regulations, especially those that are to be read every so often. Be able to explain the workings of the automatic pistol. Then you will be able to get by okay; otherwise you will have a bum trip. The Manual of Physical Training—U.S.Army, 1914— has lots of good dope in it.

When you get ready to embark, try and work it so that your squadron won't be the first to go on board, either bow or stern. The first go to the bottom of the ship or steerage. The next ones in get the upper decks. The last bunch usually gets the best pickings, so if your place in line will put you first, either in the front or rear of the ship, give some fool order that will get your men so jumbled up that the next squadron will have to go ahead. March the men down to the other end of the pier and forgot to give a command to halt if necessary.

As soon as you get aboard, hunt up the ship's steward and reserve the unoccupied 3rd Class cabins for your sergeants. They will be damn glad to pay the damages, which won't amount to much. Of course, if it's a regular U.S. Army transport, there won't be any left-over cabins; but it's ten to one you'll come on a steamer of some private company, so go after them hot-foot. Anything you can do to put your men in a comfortable place will be repaid by them in more ways than one. If there is any money in your squadron fund, buy up a stock of barber supplies, a fair amount of cigarettes and tobacco, safety matches, coffee, and anything else essential to daily life.

All of these can be had from a good QM but you are apt to travel around for three or four weeks before you finally get to one. At least that was our case. However, by the time you get here, things ought to be running slick as greased lightning. Still, anything you may bring will always come in handy and you won't have any difficulty getting rid of it. If you can get around it, don't turn in any clothing or equipment at Garden City. Hang on to every damn thing you can because you'll be able to use it, and if you can get through Mineola with it you can lug it the rest of the way. The best way is to equip yourself so that you could spend three weeks in the woods away from civilization, not including food, and you'll come out okay. By that time you'll come to a QM where you can buy anything from a pair of pants to a bottle of Listerine.

If you don't like Resistal [flying] goggles, supply yourself with a couple of good pair of the kind you do like. Also a leather helmet that will accommodate a woolen one underneath. The rest of the flying equipment they issue here is fine—Teddy Bear union suits fur-lined throughout and big overshoes lined with goatskin, wool inside. They will slip over your shoes but I find it warmer to wear them over a couple of pair of heavy socks. If you buy gloves, don't buy them fur-lined. They are the coldest things you can put on. Fur outside with wool cloth lining are okay, but not fur inside. Personally I like leather ones with detachable linings.

Speaking of boots: the only way to keep them fit for wear is to stuff a towel into each foot as far as possible every time you take them off. That will absorb the moisture and keep them in good shape. Rubber boots are conducive to trench foot, so it's well not to wear them for any continued length of time without removing them and drying them out, especially if the temperature is just a little above freezing, the way it is a good part of the time over here in winter.

In the meantime, study your French. Work up an everyday vocabulary of common words and verbs. Learn all you can about motors, airplane construction, and design, and get as much time in the air as possible. And don't be in too big a sweat to get across. When you do come, bring a bunch of those Liberty motors and airplanes that we hear so much about. The papers here claim that the motor is so powerful that you have to throttle it down to maneuver the plane, the straight-away speed being too terrific to permit of any abrupt turning. If you have any dope on what it can really do, let us hear about it.

The fastest thing over here is the single place SPAD which has a 220 hp motor and makes [censored] miles an hour under 12000 feet. Don't believe any bull you may hear to the contrary, because it's going to take some designing and motor building to drag a pair of wings and a fuselage through the air any faster.

Hell! This letter just got interrupted. A couple of guys came and said they saw a wild boar down the road a mile or so. I grabbed my old .45 revolver and took off. We picked up the old boy's opening tracks in the snow and pursued him for a devil of a ways. You can tell from this that we are out in the woods all right, when wild pigs come almost up to our back door.

Among others here at [Amanty] are Lieutenants [Arthur] Coyle,* [John] Reynolds,* and [Daniel] Morse.* These officers were at Mineola when we were there. Coyle went on a bombing trip the other day with a French squadron. His pilot was a green one and on the way back they fell out of formation and were promptly attacked by three Boches, though Coyle only saw two of them at first. These two were up above him and kept playing around, taking long distance shots at him. All of a sudden he became aware of a stream of tracer bullets whizzing by his tail, coming from below. Every third bullet is usually a tracer and it looks like a streak of fire. You can follow its course from start to finish; saves the trouble of sighting when you want to fire fast.

Well, by some streak of luck, they managed to get into a bank of clouds and by dodging around they shook the Boche—but got well lost, and just managed to get back across the lines. It was a close call, and Coyle was sure glad to get back. When a man falls out of formation, he might as well make up his mind to it—he is sure to have to fight his way back. These damn Boche are always laying for a chance like that.

I hope to hell this letter doesn't get sunk. I'd hate to have to try and reproduce it.
George

5

Jerry Hughes, Flight Instructor, Rich Field

While George Hughes was traveling to France, Jerry Hughes was traveling too, from Chanute Field to Rich Field, near Waco, Texas. Rich Field had been officially declared open on December 1, 1917, a little more than two weeks before Jerry Hughes arrived shortly after December 15. As had been the case at Chanute Field, the facilities were not complete, and there was clear evidence of recent construction efforts in the amounts of loose dirt that rose into the air when the wind blew, as it apparently did with great strength during the months of January and February. Jerry's early letters from Rich Field show him in an unhappy mood, complaining about the cold, the lack of appropriate culture in the local community, and his sense of isolation. He suggested that his mother and sister come down to Texas to keep him company for a while. After some hesitation, they eventually joined him on March 4. Jerry's mood improved perceptibly after his mother and sister arrived. They remained with Jerry at Rich Field until the hot weather arrived, returning to New Hampshire some time after June 1. While they were in Texas with Jerry, he wrote no letters home, and there is a three-month break in his correspondence. It is likely that he wrote to his brother George in France, but those letters have not survived. Fortunately, he filled in many of the details of his Waco days in his later narrative.

By the middle of January he was flying again, checking out in a Standard, an aircraft he grew fond of during his days in Texas. Jerry was initially in charge of solo students, sixty-five of them, to be exact, and supervising them made him as "nervous as a cat." He instructed sometimes as much as three to four hours a day, and was proud that the students rated him as one of the best instructors in the program. He developed great proficiency in the Standard training aircraft, at one point spinning down continuously from altitudes of 9000 and 11000 feet.

Probably as a result of his mother's stay, Jerry grew curious to see his old family homestead in Boerne, Texas, and early in July, after his mother and sister had returned to New Hampshire, he drove down to the San Antonio area to revisit the ranch. Although nothing in the letter that he wrote describing that trip seems unusual, he said later that the visit had a major emotional impact on him. Perhaps out of frustration and loneliness, Jerry developed a romantic interest in a girl who lived in the Dallas-Fort Worth area. But once again, events associated with the war intervened, and on August 25, after seven months of flight instruction duties, he received orders sending him to France. His time in Texas had served him well, however; while he was there he had accumulated over three hundred hours of flying time, had soloed over 25 students, and had demonstrated his expertise in surviving difficult situations in flight while others around him had been less fortunate.

JERRY'S COMMENTS

After leaving Rantoul, we traveled south in a troop train and finally arrived at Waco, Texas, just before Christmas. Rich Field, newly-built like most of the other posts, was located on what had been a cotton field. It was not level, like Chanute, but laid out on a pretty good slope. There were little ditches and gullies and various other depressions, none of which provided aid or comfort to pilots taking off or landing. The local political boys must have had considerable clout to have persuaded the Army to build a flying field at that location.

The high winds howled across that old cotton field as though the devil himself was blowing in. The force of the wind was so great that it took the black soil off the open fields and deposited it in the drainage ditches which surrounded the buildings. I kept the windows in my quarters shut, but the dirt came into every room and covered everything. The bathtub had at least a quarter of an inch of black dirt in it. But at least I had a bathtub. I had a nice little apartment all for myself and took my meals in the Officers' Mess. It was a choice living situation, especially after the austere conditions at Rantoul.

GERARD HUGHES TO LUCY HUGHES
Wednesday, 2 January 1918
Dear Mother:

The weather has been good, except for the strong wind which prevails. I haven't seen a newspaper for a week. It's just like being on a desert island, being in this part of the country. The people don't know what's going on in the world and they don't care to know. They are glad that we are at war because it brings a lot of soldiers to town with a lot of easy money. They live on a lower plane down here than in the north. There is no doubt about it.
Affectionately,
Gerard

GERARD HUGHES TO LUCY HUGHES
Friday, 4 January 1918
Dear Mother:

George's first letter has come and am sending it on to you. His letter is exceptionally well-written and very interesting. Don't mind the cuss words. We always cuss when we write to each other. Saturday was a wonderful day. Balmy and warm. I went up in a Standard with only my knitted sweater on. Sunday was not so warm but comfortable. Monday morning it was cold as Iceland with ground covered with hail. Wind blowing like fury. And so the weather goes. Jumping from zero to ninety degrees, up and down, up and down. It's more trying than northeast weather. This is a baneful existence. No chance of going any further than Waco, and there is nothing attractive in that burg. Nothing but routine work on the post; no parties allowed or anything. The only recreation is gambling, because reading requires too much effort when one is tired.
Affectionately,
Gerard

JERRY'S COMMENTS

After arriving at Rich Field, I wrote to Mrs. Brooks, in Illinois, thanking her for her hospitality and describing our train trip down and arrival in Waco.

GERARD HUGHES TO MRS. MORGAN BROOKS, URBANA, ILLINOIS
7 January 1918
Dear Mrs. Brooks:

Much to our surprise the palatial Pullman cars in which we rode from Rantoul held together all the way to Texas. They were of the vintage of 1860—being lighted by candles (most of which were missing). Luckily we were hauled most of the way by freight engines which were unable to attain great speed. Otherwise something would have undoubtedly given way. The men in the squadron had a dining car in which meals were cooked and served. On its previous trip this car had flown its true colors and carried a load of horses. When we reached Rich Field it was on fire. Our field range had been badly set up and the result was a burnt horse-car.

The three officers with the squadron (Mac McMullen, Doc—the doctor, and myself) did not eat in the dining car—but jumped off at every large station and scampered to the lunch room. It was quite convenient being able to stop and start our train when we felt like it! At Little Rock we ordered lamb. Doc said it wasn't lamb. He said he knew lamb when he saw it—and that what was served to us was mountain goat. Mac claimed it was wild Arkansas horse. Whatever it was, it was so bad we couldn't eat it. We allowed the squadron to get off the train at Little Rock and as a result we left the city with six men missing. They reached Rich Field about a day late.

We received rather a cool welcome at the post here. Apparently the C.O. thought McMullen was too young or inexperienced to be in command of a squadron. I was taken out of the organization right away, and was made as assistant to Major [Clinton W.] Russell* (in charge of flying). A few days later Dr. Fowler was relieved from duty with the 39th, and then McMullen was relieved of command. By this time, however, they had learned that Mac knew as much as they—and so he was made Assistant Adjutant. Major Hanley,* who was in charge of flying at Rantoul, is now here. He too is an assistant to Major Russell.

The cold here is very penetrating—and a person feels it more than in the north. The wind blows incessantly and two thirds of the time we cannot fly. We have no equipment for the repair and over-hauling of engines and planes—nor have we any spare parts. As far as I can learn the same condition exists at all the southern schools. It was the same at Rantoul—but Washington cannot profit by experience. They blindly send us a wire to average four hours a day per plane, and turn out 100 Reserve Military Aviators a month! It would be a joke if the matter were not so serious. Washington's reply, when we ask for equipment, is "Fly what planes and motors you have until they fall to pieces." There is criminal negligence somewhere—or else someone owns a lot of aeroplane stock.

I don't like this part of the country. A person can't get anything to eat—neither here at camp nor in Waco. And the newspapers are terrible. One can get the *New York Times* or the *Chicago Tribune* but they are a week old. The people do not seem very much interested in the war—except in that it has brought a lot of soldiers for them to rob. Camp McArthur is here at Waco with 25,000 men—comprising the National Guard from Michigan and Wisconsin. Grippe and measles are pretty common at the camp and in the city. As soon as I arrived I managed to get a severe cold which laid me up for a week. I managed to avoid going in the hospital—and thus save myself from sure death. At Camp Bowie not long ago they were killing them off at the rate of sixteen per day. Lack of preparedness is already taking its toll.

I certainly miss all of you and your kind hospitality. It is hard for one to express appreciation which is deeply felt—so please know that it comes from the bottom of my heart when I say—I thank you.

Sincerely,

Gerard H. Hughes

GERARD HUGHES TO LUCY HUGHES
Friday, 11 January 1918
Dear Mother:

When I awoke at five this morning I stuck out my hand and lo! I knew what was on my bed, for I had felt it before. It was snow! I dug my way out, galloped around and built a fire, and shook and shivered as with the ague. In my parlor—even with windows closed and blinds drawn—there was a huge pile of snow on the table. I swept it all up, and couldn't fit it all into a large pail. Water pipes frozen solid. Wind howling and whining like fury. Cold as blazes—a sort of unnatural cold—penetrating, biting, irritating.

I sat all morning close to my red hot stove and froze. The wind was so strong that it came right into the room. I'm on the north side of the building and so receive the brunt of the blast. The south side was comfortable all day. The wind has died down now. In the morning the wind will be from the south and then it will be hot again. I pity the poor men over at Camp MacArthur in tents—and only three blankets.

Affectionately,
Gerard

GERARD HUGHES TO LUCY HUGHES
Thursday, 17 January 1918
Dear Mother:

More snow and rain succeeded in making the field a sea of mud. We flew today and as a result broke twenty propellers. The wheels throw up the mud and when the wooden prop strikes even a small piece of dirt, it is very liable to split. I'm in charge of the soloists. I have five instructors who help me keep track of them. There are fifty-six solo men now and it is quite a mob to keep track of. I think I told you about how they ask questions. I'm getting nervous as a cat. Too much coffee for one thing; that, and watching those solo birds try their best to break their necks. They take off close over the hangars, skid around turns, and raise the deuce generally.

Affectionately,
Gerard

JERRY'S COMMENTS

We had four or five civilian instructors at Rich Field, but the others were lieutenants like me. My best friends included William Kuhn (from the University of Pennsylvania), Russell Klyver (from Franklin College, Indiana) [Fig. 16], Maurice Sharpe (from DePauw University), Bryan "Mac" McMullen (of the Texas National Guard), and Dick Chamberlain.

Fig. 16. Jerry Hughes and Russell Klyver, Rich Field. Klyver was one of Jerry's two best friends at Rich Field. The other was William Kuhn, who died when he flew his training aircraft into another aircraft flown by Jerry and Klyver. Klyver accompanied Jerry to France and died in December 1918 flying another pilot's aircraft as Jerry watched from the ground.

Kuhn and Klyver had received their flight training at Gerstner Field, Lake Charles, Louisiana.

They told me of a strange accident which happened at Gerstner Field before they left. An officer named John Purroy Mitchel.* who had resigned his position as mayor of New York City in order to enter the Army, was going through flight training. Mitchel went up in a Thomas-Morse Scout to do some aerobatics. In doing a wing-over or a loop, he pulled the plane into an inverted position, and fell out. He struck the ground and died. The big question was how could a man of his obvious intelligence forget one of the cardinal rules of flying: "Buckle Your Seat Belt"? Part of the training field at Mineola was subsequently named in his honor. Klyver and Kuhn said that there was a lot of speculation at Gerstner. Was he really that careless? Had he committed suicide? Both Kuhn and Klyver had flown the Thomas-Morse Scout and condemned it as tricky and nasty to fly. But fall out of it? Not likely!

GERARD HUGHES TO LUCY HUGHES
Monday, 28 January 1918
Dear Mother:

I've got a scheme. Don't know whether it will work or how you would like it. How about coming down here to Waco? We could take one of the married quarters—no rent or anything. I have just as much right to have my mother and sister here as some of these 2nd Lieutenants have in having their wives. I'm the second-ranking 2nd Lieutenant at that. Come on down. Stay here until you get tired of it then leave. I'm feeling exceedingly well. Am out on the field before sunrise and stay there until the sun sets, except for lunch. We had another norther and a second snow storm. It is warm and balmy now.
Affectionately,
Gerard

JERRY'S COMMENTS

I tried hard to persuade my mother and sister to come to Texas and keep house for me for a short while in the spring of 1918. I told them that the warm weather and the experience of seeing a military operation would do them good. But I think I was lonely. Possibly the pressures of instructing and worry about George had something to do with my request.

GERARD HUGHES TO LUCY HUGHES
Wednesday, 6 February 1918
Dear Mother:

Have had no word from you in several days. Things are going all right around here. Had a big wind the other day which nearly filled the place with dirt. An anemometer on one of the hangars read 45 miles an hour, which means that there was some gale aloft. Five machines which were sitting on the ground were turned right over on their backs by the wind. I see by this morning's paper that the German subs sank another transport. It will be a good thing for the nation. Wake them up a bit. Those strikes in Germany gave people a sort of idea that the war was over. I have heard nothing from George.

Affectionately,
Gerard

GERARD HUGHES TO LUCY HUGHES
Tuesday, 19 February 1918
Dear Mother:

We can get all the kitchen things we need right here, so don't worry about bringing them when you come. The only other things I can think of is some sheets and blankets and pillow-slips. If you don't want to bring them, we can buy them. This is going to be a sort of newly-wed proposition. I want to experiment with my mother so that I will know how years hence. I think I will start making notes on it. Perhaps later, write a book on "How to Live on Love and Gumbo" or "Family Life in an Aviation Camp."

Affectionately,
Gerard

JERRY'S COMMENTS

One day in February, seven of us were given the job of ferrying some Curtiss planes down to San Antonio. This trip was largely uneventful, except for our landing at Austin. We landed at what had been a polo field, located close to the city. This spot was really too small for flying purposes, but its proximity to Austin made it attractive for us to use, so we just swooped in and landed there. After having a bite to eat in town, we walked back to our ships and began figuring how we could take off and climb out of there. A very strong wind was blowing, which proved to be a blessing. We knew that the steady strong wind would be the one factor that would enable us to extricate ourselves from a tight situation. Those who had brought passengers told them it would be wiser to take the train back to Waco. All went except Smith, my passenger.

One by one the boys took off and made it, except for Leo Post. He turned from his takeoff heading too soon and caught his wing on a chimney, causing him to crash-land. Fortunately he was uninjured. I was the last to go. I had brought Sergeant Smith along as a passenger. He and I had helped all the others get away. I turned to Smith and said, "Sergeant, how about it? Do you want to stick with me and risk the takeoff?"

Without hesitation, Smith said, "Lieutenant, I will go with you." Simple as that. Strange, how men will lay their lives so gently in the hands of fate.

We placed the tail of our Jennie right back against the fence. The motor was running well. We settled ourselves in our seats, he in the front, I in the rear. Everything seemed okay. We gave her the gun, full throttle, and headed straight into that gale of wind. We lifted off the ground and I aimed directly at the trees and houses that sat on the hill in front of us. I kept pulling back gently on the stick, just enough to keep the plane climbing without sacrificing any flying speed or control over the aircraft. We cleared the hill nicely and after gaining a little more altitude, we swung to the right and headed for the Colorado River. From then on it was easy sailing; we reached Kelly Field without incident and turned our Jennies over to the proper authorities.

GERARD HUGHES TO LUCY HUGHES
Friday, 22 February 1918
Dear Mother:

Hope you are well and that you will let me know when you are coming. I wired you last night asking if you could come before the 4th of March. You see, I have moved into my married quarters and I don't like to hang onto them for two or three weeks by myself; and the sooner you come the more time we will have together. You probably will not be able to stand it for very long, but it ought to be a unique experience for you. You will be right next to military preparation and will be able to feel the pulse of a nation at war. For me it is common and everyday, but to you it would be extremely interesting or unusual. So if you can stand it for just a couple of weeks it will be worth your while—just for the experience. I received a letter from George. His tide seems to be carrying him on towards an ambitious goal. His opportunity is unexcelled.
Affectionately,
Gerard

JERRY'S COMMENTS

My appeals to my mother to visit me in Texas were successful, and she and my sister Jeanie arrived on March 4th. To accommodate our travels around Waco I bought a brand new Dodge touring car. We had a lot of fun with that car. After my mother and sister left, we used it for activities on the field. One stunt we pulled was to close the big hangar doors so that there was just enough room (six inches on each side) for the Dodge to pass through. We would then get in the machine at the other end of the building and drive through the opening at full speed. Fortunately we never hit the doors. If we had, it might have ended our flying careers. We figured that this stunt sharpened our eyes and our nerves for the day when we might be in mortal combat, fighting for our lives over the front.

On April 9th, Margaret Wilson, President Wilson's daughter, visited the army bases at Waco. She had been making a nation-wide tour to inspect the new Army camps. When she left on the train for Austin, a bunch of us from Rich Field gave her the opportunity to see what a Standard Aircraft looked like close up as it flew alongside her car window. These days it would be called buzzing, but in those days no one complained.

The planes we flew at Rich Field included Curtiss Jennies and Standards, built by the Standard Aircraft Company. The Standard had a four-cylinder Hall-Scott motor, with considerably less power than the eight-cylinder OX-5s with which Curtiss equipped his Jennies. Of the two ships, I liked the Standard best, and I used one of these exclusively when I gave flight instruction. The Standard did have some drawbacks. The little four-cylinder engine vibrated like the devil, and when you came in after a few hours of flying, your body would tingle all over. It really gave you a massage! And it threw oil all over. I invariably finished the day with my face and goggles smeared with oil. However, I became extremely fond of this little aircraft and loved to fly it. My favorite was #1690.

On April 11th I decided to give that ship a workout. I wanted to see how high she would climb, and to see how far down I could spin her from that height and then pull out. I finally got her up a little over 9000 feet and then I put her in a spin. Both the Curtiss and the Standard would turn nice and easy in a spin—not too fast, just comfortably. To count your turns you had to concentrate upon some large object on the ground—a lake or a town or the flying field itself, for instance. Each time you turned past that landmark you counted a turn. I counted up to thirty-nine and decided that was enough. I still had some altitude above the ground and wasn't too dizzy, but I thought that was enough of a workout.

The next day, however, I began thinking, "Old 1690 can do better than that." So up we went for another try. This time we reached 11000 feet. She wouldn't climb a foot higher and started to wallow around. I put her into a spin and this time counted to forty-five before I pulled out. When I pulled out, I was fairly close to the ground and was extremely dizzy. I decided that was enough, and didn't spin again, at least at Rich Field.

The man who taught me to put a plane in and out of a spin was George "Buck" Weaver,* a civilian instructor at Waco. He was a happy-go-lucky fellow who took me up in a Standard one day and showed me the tricks of the maneuver. After the war, Buck started manufacturing airplanes himself. He started the Weaver Aircraft Company and called his aircraft the "WACO." He built them out of a little town north of Dayton [Troy, Ohio]. Later I ran into his wife, Mattie, in New York City. She told me over and over how she was robbed of her interest in the Weaver Aircraft Company. She told me that she was the first woman to pass the necessary tests to become a glider pilot. She said she was "robbed" of license number 1 by some character who finagled his wife in after Mattie, but that woman got license Number 1 and Mattie got license Number 2. [Charles Lindbergh's wife, Anne Morrow Lindbergh, was awarded license Number 1.]

On May 25th an order came through calling for two planes to fly up to a small town north of Waco to aid the good folks up there in a Liberty Bond drive. Kuhn and Klyver got the assignment. I wasn't busy that day, so I told Klyver I would ride along with him for the fun of it. Bill Kuhn asked me if he could use my airplane, old faithful 1690. I said, "Yes, of course." She was an unusually fine ship, and I wouldn't let just anybody fly her. But Bill was different; he was a wonderful fellow and an excellent pilot. He took one of the mechanics, William Snyder, with him in case we had any problems with our planes.

We headed across the Brazos River and were flying along smoothly at 1500 feet when Kuhn decided to get a little playful and slipped over and then under us. I was looking down at him, wondering what he had in mind, and why he was so close, when suddenly his plane came up and smashed into us.

Perhaps his ship was caught by a sudden updraft of hot air from the cotton fields below; but whatever the cause, he was unable to correct in time, and the two ships collided. As a result of the impact, the two ships were locked together, and started falling, spinning around together, until finally we started to separate. For a brief moment, after we broke apart, we remained linked by some strands of wire, but the centrifugal force finally caused us to disengage. Kuhn's plane went spinning down out of control and struck the earth. He and Snyder were killed. Our controls were still functional, and Klyver was able to bring the ship under control, and we landed close by the wreckage of the other plane. What had started out as a happy day, an escape from the routine of training, ended suddenly in tragedy.

Eventually the hot weather increased, and it grew too warm for comfortable living. This was in the days before air conditioning. Early in June I accompanied my mother and my sister on the train back to their home in New Hampshire. I returned to Waco shortly after.

GERARD HUGHES TO LUCY HUGHES
Monday, 17 June 1918
Dear Mother:

I write this as we are approaching St. Louis enroute to Texas. Saw no one I knew in Boston. Spent a few hours in New York and then hit the road again. Found a most affable companion in my compartment on the train, a first lieutenant just back from the front with a gold chevron on his left arm for six months' service in the front line trenches and a gold chevron on his right arm for a wound. He was with the first American forces that were sent over and was assigned to British and French troops for instruction. Later his division took over a sector on the front and were properly shelled, gassed, and attacked. He gave some pretty good descriptions of the Germans. Described their latest gas—called mustard gas, because of its color. It attacks any part of the body that is at all moist and eats away the flesh. It will eat right through your clothing. It's very deadly. It is already very hot and dusty and dirty. It's an outrage to have to go back down here to Waco where it is hottern'ell.
Affectionately,
Gerard

GERARD HUGHES TO LUCY HUGHES
Monday, 24 June 1918
Dear Mother:

I've been on the go all the time since I got here. On arriving, I found a couple of letters from George, which I am forwarding. Things are about the same here—very hot. Orders came to stop flying and pack up all the Standards. They are to be replaced with Curtiss machines. I found a letter from Frona Brooks waiting for me here, and I didn't go near Rantoul!
Affectionately,
Gerard

JERRY'S COMMENTS

We spent the summer of 1918 instructing students, always in the hope that one day orders would come through sending us to France. My log book shows that I put in as much as six to eight hours a day instructing students. Late in June several of us flew down to Houston, landing at Ellington Field. We then took a train down to Galveston and spent the night there. The hotel put us up in some sort of attic. It had wonderful ventilation and a marvelous breeze came from the Gulf and gave us chills. It was a welcome change from the excessive heat during the days.

GERARD HUGHES TO LUCY HUGHES
Sunday 30 June 1918
Dear Mother:

I think I'll be making a trip to San Antonio soon. I am getting curious to see the old homestead. Have you received any letters from George lately? He is always making resolutions about writing and then you don't hear from him for about two months. I suppose things are pretty active along the front now. One thing before I forget it: if I ever crack up in a machine, for goodness' sake bury me up where it is cool, and not down here!
Affectionately,
Gerard

JERRY'S COMMENTS

During one of the hottest days of summer, when it was too hot to fly, I began thinking, "There is one thing I would like to do before I leave Texas. I would like to visit the old ranch where I was born." I got permission to leave the post for a few days and started driving south in the Dodge toward the town of Boerne. It meant driving early in the morning and in the evening. It was too hot in the middle of the day. I slept under the trees at night.

GERARD HUGHES TO LUCY HUGHES
Wednesday, 3 July 1918
Dear Mother:

I got the Dodge out and started for San Antonio about 9 pm. It did not take me long to get out of Waco. After driving about 80 miles I stopped in a wheat field and after spreading my cot (I brought one along), I lay down and had a comfortable sleep until daybreak, when I started on again. At Austin I got something to eat and changed a tire. I picked up a bum. He was an auto-trader. Just like the old horse-traders. He buys or steals a car and sells it for double its worth. He was company, any way, and he drove the car over the worst part of the journey. He could drive, too!

In San Antonio I ate and washed up and found a place for the night. The next day I drove up to Boerne. The road out to the ranch was familiar, except smaller than I remember. Everything had shrunk. The sand was the same. Jeanie's playroom in the cowbarn still had the wallpaper which she put on it. McFarland was there and I went into the house for a minute. The living room was hardly recognizable. I found father's grave without difficulty. The fence around it needs painting. I shall see that it is done.

Land around there has gone up tremendously. The old goat land is now $10 an acre, where it used to be $1 an acre. The price for other land has also gone up. After leaving the ranch I drove around Boerne for a bit and then went back to San Antonio. It was very hot in San Antonio and all the time I was there I kept wondering how you ever stood it—living in that God-forsaken country. It is terrible. In Boerne they have had no crops for three years and the earth is simply blowing away. Tomorrow is the 4th of July and everybody is taking off, most of them going to Dallas.

Affectionately,
Gerard

JERRY'S COMMENTS

When I read this letter years later I was astonished. I had absolutely no recollection of the details which I described. It had been sixteen years since my mother and brother and sister and I had left our farm there after my father's sudden death in a railroad accident. I remembered driving down to San Antonio and then up to the town of Boerne. I drove through Boerne and then out to the ranch. The house and barns were still there. I parked the car and started to walk toward the building where I was born and which we had left with so much sorrow in our hearts. It was then that I was hit by an overwhelming spasm of grief. I felt as though a heavy blow had struck me in the solar plexus. When I came upon the old familiar ground and saw the old familiar scene unfold before me, I was so overcome by emotion that I hurriedly got back into the car and drove as hard as I could back to Waco. I don't remember meeting McFarland or going into the house or visiting my father's grave. I don't remember visiting friends or relatives in San Antonio or Boerne. As I looked back on the day when we children were forced to leave the ranch, I felt as Adam must have felt when he was driven from the Garden of Eden.

GERARD HUGHES TO LUCY HUGHES
Wednesday, 10 July 1918
Dear Mother:

Just finished a long letter to Frona Brooks. Also one to Virginia Jackson up in Fort Worth. I have flown up there twice to see her and will fly up there again this weekend for the same purpose. May marry the girl for aught I know. No news here. Our swimming pool was formally opened today. We gave a little aerial exhibition and the divers did tricks in the water. Will let you know more about Virginia later. Very nice little girl—plays the piano, swims, laughs, talks just like any ordinary person, but. . . .
Affectionately,
Gerard

JERRY'S COMMENTS

We spent the entire summer hoping we would be allowed to go to France. We were sick and tired of teaching flying cadets. Then we began to get the news that some of the youngsters whom we had instructed had begun to reach the front. Some of them were getting into action, possibly becoming "aces." It was too much to bear! To amuse ourselves, we had some picnics and invited some of the local girls. As a matter of fact, Dick Chamberlain met and married a local Waco girl. The only thing I remember about her was that she used too much rouge. Silly, the things that we remember!

GERARD HUGHES TO JEANIE HUGHES
Wednesday, 17 July 1918
Dear Jeanie:

I haven't been in a writing mood for an awfully long time. George hasn't written me since May 31st, when he told me about having his machine riddled with bullets. Young Klyver has a girl back in Indiana who is going to Wellesley this year. I told him my girl was going to Smith College (taking the liberty of addressing Frona in such familiar terms). Then Klyver gets carried away and bets that he has the best girl, whereupon I asked him how I could prove it, and lo! he wants you to be the judge! He wants you to look up his girl if you ever get a chance while in Boston. Old Chamberlain has gone crazy over a Waco girl and it serves as an endless source of delight for Sharpe and Klyver. But it doesn't seem to bother him much.

The weather is getting cooler around here now, especially the nights. The hostess house is open now, and is run by a very nice flock of old and young ladies. We eat lunch and supper over there and get excellent food. I must go and play some tennis. After that I will drill the flying officers for a half hour. This afternoon more tennis and a nap or downtown to a movie. This evening perhaps fly or perhaps not—then off for a swim—then back to bed.

Affectionately,

Gerard

GERARD HUGHES TO LUCY HUGHES

Saturday, 27 July 1918

Dear Mother:

Klyver and I flew to Grainger, Texas, the other day and gave an exhibition. The town was having a Red Cross picnic. The main feature of the picnic was a cake weighing over 400 pounds and standing six feet high. They raffled off the cake and got $1000 for it. They auctioned it off piece by piece and got a lot more. Everything was free for us and we enjoyed ourselves. We ignored the girls absolutely. Klyver played with some little ones, about eight or nine years old. During the afternoon we walked away from the crowd, lay down on the ground, and went fast asleep. Just as indifferent as could be.

At five o'clock we flew—and believe me, we nearly scared that crowd to death. Klyver was on the controls and dove down near the crowd and did some pretty work. When we landed the people went crazy—wanted to shake our hands. Little kids would feel our trousers to see if we were real. There were over 2000 people there. They clamored for us to stay and all the rest but we hopped in and flew away.

Affectionately,

Gerard

JERRY'S COMMENTS

As the summer began to wane, my instructor friends and I began to become more aggressive in our flying. We had accumulated considerable time in the air, and our skill and confidence had increased immeasurably. We were not taking unnecessary risks, but we were doing things that would not have been done by green pilots. For instance, one day I came in quite low over the hangars, and not wanting to glide too far out into the landing field, I side-slipped close down over the roof of one of the hangars. I knew exactly what I was doing, and there was really nothing wrong with the maneuver. The trouble was, however, that old Captain Frank Coffyn* was standing right there at the time and he acted as though I had scared the be-Jesus out of him. He was the Officer-in-Charge of Flying at the time, and proceeded to ground me for two days.

Coffyn was quite a guy. He had been taught to fly by the Wright brothers some years before. He got quite a reputation in those days by flying one of old "pushers" [an aircraft with an engine mounted in the rear] under the Brooklyn and Manhattan Bridges. He told me once that he was the first man to land a plane on a ship. He may have made such a landing, but he was not the first. The records show that Eugene Ely was the first. When the war started, Coffyn, as an old-timer pilot, was given a captain's commission right away and sent to Waco. Somewhere along the line he might have had a nervous breakdown, because although he was not a very old man, his hair was white, and he refused to fly a plane himself.

We pilots were given an extra 10% in pay because of the hazardous nature of our work. To merit this bonus, we were required to put in four hours of actual flying time each month. Since Coffyn wouldn't take a ship up himself, he usually got Dick Chamberlain, whom he considered safe and sane, to take him up and fly him around for the necessary time. He never asked me to take him up.

I guess Major Clinton W. Russell,* our commanding officer (and later a general), decided he could spare Klyver and me. After all, new men were arriving on the post daily and there were plenty of qualified pilots to fill in the ranks. At any rate, orders came through in late August directing Klyver and me to proceed immediately to New York for embarkation at Hoboken and thence to France. My days as a flying instructor had ended.

6

George Hughes with the 12th Aero Squadron
over the Front

At Amanty, France, the 1st and 12th Aero Squadrons began an extended period of training in preparation for becoming combat ready. The squadrons initially received obsolescent two-place Avion Renault (AR) aircraft, designed for observation tasks. The French-built AR was a reliable aircraft, but it was old and slow and was a good target for German gunners. The men in the unit joked that the initials AR stood not for Avion Renault but for "Antique Rattletrap." The French had been using them as training aircraft for pilots and observers who then flew more maneuverable aircraft like the Breguet and Salmson, aircraft not yet available to the Americans.

The pilots and observers began to learn their flying duties and to develop techniques for working as teams. The pilot's main task was to follow the pre-assigned route of flight over and near the front lines, while the observer operated the camera equipment and fired the Lewis gun. The cold weather and snow-covered fields hampered training. Flying slow observation aircraft over the front lines was not as glamorous a way of life as flying single-seat pursuit aircraft, but it was just as hazardous, if not more so. Flying at altitudes ranging from 1500 to 5000 feet, the squadron aircraft were engaged in spotting enemy activity behind the trenches, taking photographs, or assisting Army units in adjusting their artillery fire. These tasks required continued exposure to enemy fire. Photographic work was especially demanding, for it called for the pilot to maintain the aircraft on a steady, straight track while the observer operated the camera. Flying a steady course gave the German gunners their best opportunity to shoot the aircraft down. This kind of flying could test the nerve of any flier.

The 12th Aero Squadron was commanded by Major Harry Brown* for all of February and most of March. On March 29 Major Brown was transferred to bombing operations, and Major Lewis Brereton* was assigned as squadron commander (Fig. 17).

Fig. 17. Major Lewis Brereton and General "Billy" Mitchell (Credit: U.S. Air Force). This picture was taken after Brereton left his position as commanding officer of the 12th Aero Squadron. Brereton (left) was a no-nonsense, strong-minded officer. Billy Mitchell (right) was a colorful, opinionated leader who argued unsuccessfully after the war for a separate air service. His outspokenness earned him a court-martial in 1925.

GEORGE HUGHES TO LUCY HUGHES
Saturday, 30 March 1918
Dear Mother:

What do you know! Your Christmas box, containing the fruit cake, some socks, and several magazines, came in yesterday. The cake certainly reminded me of home, and everyone who tasted a bit of it was loud in his praise thereof.

According to reports, the Germans are making a tremendous drive on the British front [along the Somme River, begun 21 March], but everyone here feels sure the British will be able to drive them back before it's over. I imagine the Germans will do their best to break through somewhere before the summer is over, for they surely must know that their time is about up, in spite of their apparent victories over Russia, for when the U. S. finally comes into its own and gets on a real war basis, then we will make Hunland a devilish hot place for the Germans to be. I only wish that we were doing it right now, but one can't expect to do the impossible overnight.

It's getting to be very springlike here. The bushes are taking on a decidedly green tinge and numerous song birds keep up a lively chorus around our shack, and I expect it will be summer before we know it. I suppose the weather around Waco must be at its best about now. How is Gerard getting along? I certainly don't envy him if he is instructing on the baby Standards. I certainly had my fill of them in Dayton. They are the worst craft that ever cruised the skies—notwithstanding the fact that "Shorty" Schroeder* looped one of them thirty-eight times.

Affectionately,
George

GEORGE HUGHES TO GERARD HUGHES
Saturday, 6 April 1918
Dear Gerard:

The other day, as I was coming out of our commissary sales room loaded with canned goods, guess who I should see coming across the road from the railroad station to meet me? None other than old "Pop" Hinds.* He said he was just in from Paris where he left McCreery, who is a ferry pilot bringing Handley Pages across from England. Well, old "Pop" is now assigned to the 12th. He is going to take my place as engineering officer, but that doesn't worry me very much as I expect to go to a bombing school before very long. Pop sure is a comical old duck. We have lots of fun kidding him. But confound his soul, he reamed me at Poker last night. The engineering officer with the 1st [Aero Squadron] is Guy Gilpatric,* an old-time exhibition flyer, wise enough to quit with a whole carcass.

I came awfully close to getting a trip over the lines with a French night bombing squadron. The commander of the outfit had never flown a tractor machine [aircraft with an engine in the front] and I took him up for several lessons. He promised me a ride, but this last German drive put the lid on my little scheme. I certainly would have liked to have gone on a trip with them. Every little bit of experience helps in this business and I want to get in on all I can.

There isn't much doing here in the way of promotion and as far as I can see there's no particular need for it just now. The thing that is worrying us mostly is that bill to take away the flying bonus and the fact that they are refusing to announce the flyers over here as being on such duty until the bill is definitely settled. Of course that doesn't affect me as I have my old orders [placing him on flying status] with me, but it is rather hard on the recent RMAs [reserve military aviators] who were sent across without them. Every once in a while we see a notice to the effect that so-and-so back home has been announced on flying duty and a general tornado of oaths ensues. Be sure and let me know if any of those bums get promoted back home and what the prospects of the JMA [junior military aviator] are.

As ever,

George

JERRY'S COMMENTS

When we passed our flying tests at Mineola and were qualified to receive our commissions, we were designated as Reserve Military Aviators (RMAs). The next step above that was Junior Military Aviator (JMA). Practically every regular Army pilot was rated as a JMA. This was especially true of the West Pointers [graduates of West Point, the U. S. Military Academy]. There were a few full-blown MAs—Military Aviators—men like General Foulois* and a handful of others. After the war these ratings seemed to disappear and I never heard of them again.

GEORGE HUGHES TO GERARD HUGHES

Saturday, 13 April 1918

Dear Gerard:

For Pete's sake, train those cadets to fly from the front seat. All [two-place] fighting machines are piloted from the bow and anyone who feels out of place up front will have a bum time of it. One man came in yesterday and pancaked from about 15 feet in the air: busted his landing gear and turned turtle. Luckily no one was hurt, but it was a damn close call. Drayton says McCreery went through Issoudun in a gale of wind. The first time he got into a "Baby" Nieuport he went up and pulled every imaginable stunt. At present he is a ferry pilot bringing machines across the Channel. "Babe" Benson is at some field in England. I expect that Drayton will be attached to the 12th as we are still short of pilots.

I don't see why they don't let us go after our own ships instead of using those damn ferry pilots. They down here as fast as they can, jump out, and beat it back to Paris on the next train. Then we spend the following week or two trying to get the machines they brought into commission. One machine had the engine practically ruined. It had been overheated to such an extent that the fool pilot ought to have been kicked all the way back to Paris or discharged for the good of the service.
As ever,
George

GEORGE HUGHES TO LUCY HUGHES
Saturday, 13 April 1918
Dear Mother:

The first ten days of April were terribly unfavorable for flying— nothing but rain and fog without a letup. Today it is also very cloudy, but as yet no rain, though it looks like it might any moment. Spring seems to be about the same over here as it is back home; we have to go through a certain amount of mud and rain before winter is finally done. The surprising thing about it here, however, is the length of time the underbrush has been green without any signs of life in the trees above. I suppose it's this way the world over, only I notice it more now that we are living in the middle of the woods where I can't possibly overlook it.

I finished a story by Mrs. Humphry Ward entitled "Missing." It's a war story about a young officer who gets married while on leave and then returns to the front, shortly reported to be "wounded and missing." And of course his young and beautiful wife has to worry herself sick. Why do the fair ones carry on in such a foolish fashion anyway? That's what war is for, and one might as well accept the inevitable with the best grace possible. In other words, don't make the Hun guns any more effective than they are now. It's bad enough when they get a man at the front without having someone at home die as a direct result also, just as though the bullet had kept going and got the second victim before stopping.

It looks as though my application for bombing stands a very good chance of going through, but I expect it will be a week or two before I hear definitely. I only hope it does as I think it will be the business I will like. It's a young branch of the service and offers lots of possibilities. Something I am looking for.
 Affectionately,
George

GEORGE'S COMMENTS

On April 13th, [Frederick] Luhr* and [Wilbur] Kennedy* being down with a broken propeller, I set out in aircraft no. 8 carrying Sergeants Fay and Bamber, a new propeller, and a bunch of tools in the rear. I located the place where Luhr and Kennedy had landed, but on landing hooked on to a willow stump which I failed to see, and busted the ship beyond repair. Fortunately, no one was hurt.

GEORGE HUGHES TO GERARD HUGHES
Sunday, April 28, 1918
Dear Gerard:

While it's fresh on my mind: you can buy all kinds of heavy underwear and socks from the QM but it's damn near impossible to get summer wear that's of any account. I brought plenty along so I am fixed okay. I don't believe they plan on getting in any of the summer stuff such as we have back home because it doesn't get hot enough. Films and filmpacks are something else that it is almost impossible to buy over here—and I suppose prices are soaring back home.

McCreery came in here yesterday driving a Salmson, a very fast two-seater with a radial motor of over two hundred horsepower. I guess it's one of the best two-seaters we have at present. Mac is now stationed at Paris, at Orly Field, in the capacity of tester and ferry pilot. He stopped for supper, then went back to Paris on the night train. He is having a devil of a good time. Flies ships down from the factories to all the various schools and thereby sees a considerable amount of the countryside. However, he likes his tester job best of all. He gets a chance to fly and try out all the various types. I should judge that he raises cain generally. His chief delight is, as he says, the Nieuport Scouts and "beating the hell out of them."

You remember Major [James] Dunsworth* of Rantoul? I believe you wrote me about him in the most affectionate terms. Well, he's here at our field and, being the ranking officer, he is in command. Tilbrook is with his squadron at Issoudun. It's officially known as Aviation Instruction Center No. 3. The bombing school is Aviation Instruction Center No. 7.

Speaking of motors: one of the best things you can do is keep a "trouble book," putting down exactly what ailed the thing and what you did to put it back in working order. The more you know about them the better off you'll be if you ever get over here, because the pilots who can diagnose a motor and its troubles are scarce articles. It's darned near impossible, however, to get anywhere unless you draw up some sort of an easy schedule to do your studying. An hour or so a day that you can always find time for. That's what I am doing, for I'd hate to go back to the States not knowing any more about motors than I did on coming across. That trouble chart in the back of the Curtiss book is pretty good. It has the whole thing boiled down about the way you like it. Better try and get ahold of one of them.

As ever,

George

Shortly after May 1, the 12th was assigned to patrol the front lines near the Seicheprey sector, flying out of an airfield at Ourches, near Toul (Fig. 13). In this part of the front, the 1st and the 12th Aero Squadrons began to engage in typical observation unit work, which included artillery fire adjustment, photographic reconnaissance, close-range reconnaissance (over the trenches), long-range reconnaissance (behind the front lines), and contact patrols. In artillery fire adjustment missions, the aircraft provided information about the accuracy of artillery fire to artillery units. Long- and short-range reconnaissance missions required observation of enemy troop or supply movements along or behind the front lines, while photographic reconnaissance missions required the pilot to fly in a straight line as the observer operated a camera which took photographs of the ground beneath, usually territory along or near the front. Contact patrols required the aircraft to fly overhead in support of the movements of specific infantry units as they moved across the front. Fortunately, the area of the front to which the 12th and the other two squadrons were initially assigned was relatively quiet. According to official reports, enemy aircraft activity was almost non-existent. On the other hand, anti-aircraft fire was "exceedingly dense, active, and accurate" (Mauer I, 183).

According to the official history of the 639th Aero Squadron, one of the support units at Ourches, the moment that the 1st and 12th Aero Squadrons began to fly combat missions defined the onset of the war:

"Daily the ships of the 1st and 12th would fly over the lines to take photographs of the enemy's positions and activities, or to act in liaison with the Infantry or assist the big guns in regulating the direction of their fire. When they came back from a trip, those of us who could would gather close to the pilot or observer and listen to the story of the day's experiences. When planes returned riddled with bullets it brought the actuality of it all home to us very vividly. The 1st Aero Squadron was equipped with biplace Spads, while the 12th had to get along temporarily with old A.R.'s. None of us will forget the days when ships never returned from a trip, or the days when aviators were killed accidentally on our own field; how quiet and sad the camp was on such days!" (Norton et al. 30).

Finally, after months of travel and training, George and the other members of the 12th Aero Squadron flew their first combat mission early in May. George and his observer, Captain Saunders, flew in one aircraft, while the squadron commander, Major Brereton, flew one of the other squadron aircraft.

GEORGE HUGHES TO GERARD HUGHES
Saturday, 4 May 1918
Dear Gerard:

So you want to know about the prospects of my getting into action? Well, I was up over the lines yesterday afternoon [for the first time] for about an hour. I didn't see any other planes, but the Hun batteries saw me. They took many a shot at me; they had my range down pretty good. I could hear the [anti-aircraft] shells when they broke, and believe me, I did some dodging around. Their method of fire is to shoot under you and make the shells break between you and home. The bastards hope to draw you in towards them and then throw a barrage around you and bracket you so your chances [of escaping] are damn slim. I got fired on four different times while monkeying around, then I finally saw another ship up in the clouds above me, so I beat it for home as I wasn't on any definite mission.

The Boche shot a few shells at that other ship but that didn't prove anything, as they generally shoot a few bursts around their own machines in a case like that to make you believe it is a ship of your own color, until they get within attacking distance. The bursts from the Hun anti-aircraft guns are black, while the Allies' are white, so you see it's quite a clever trick and often works. The Huns have also taken to flying an insignia similar to the Allies' except that the center is black instead of blue or red, as in the case of the French or British, so you see you have to watch your step pretty carefully.

If you ever get to the front be sure and always calibrate the ammunition for your machine gun. That is, see that every shell fits into the [firing] chamber freely. Lots of English pilots even go so far as to weigh every bullet. I keep my gun in my room and do all my cleaning myself. The [maintenance] men have so many guns to tend to that they can't give the time to each one that you can do to your own, and naturally they don't have the same interest in them as the guy who has to shoot them.

Old "Wild Bill" McCreery was up this way in a Nieuport 28 the other day. That devil certainly can fly. When he took off, he went up almost as straight as an elevator and when about 500 feet up, pulled a right, then a left roll, wing over wing, fell into a tailspin, and came out about 150 feet off the ground. At present he is a tester and a ferry pilot at Paris. He expects to get into a chasse squadron eventually.

I guess I am the first of the Mineola bunch to get to the front. Harry Drayton was down at our other field for a week or so, but was sent up the line and we ourselves have moved to a different station [Ourches]. I expect that we'll be here for some time to come.

As ever,

George

GEORGE HUGHES TO GERARD HUGHES
Thursday, 9 May 1918
Dear Gerard:

Here follows some good advice on flying at the front: First, don't fly in any one direction for more than fifteen seconds at a time. The first trip I took up along the lines I flew parallel to the lines for about five minutes on a straightaway course, turning neither to the right nor the left and at the same altitude, just as unconcerned as a man could be, when all of a sudden the bastards opened up and simply plastered the hell out of me. I like to tore the old bus to pieces getting away from there.

Your game is to keep them guessing. Change your course as often as possible, using every means. Skidding [using rudder exclusively to turn] is a very good way because you can change your course considerably before they notice it, whereas if you bank they can tell at once that you are turning. When things get too damn hot, heist her up on one side, pull the bottom out from under her, and sideslip a couple hundred feet or so [using top rudder to hold the nose up, descend rapidly in a bank]. Changes in altitude throw them off more than anything else and by the time they get it figured out, you can generally climb back to where you were in the first pace.

The bark of those high explosive shells going off around you puts action into your arms and legs but doesn't scare you especially. At least not half as bad as having them burst around you on the ground. I can swear to that because you know the Huns can drop to within a foot of where they want to on good old terra firma—but up in the air you can keep them guessing.

From what I have seen of things, I think two-seated chasse is about the best; then comes bombing. So if you ever get a choice, hop into one or the other, avoiding night bombing especially. The Huns have a hell of a clever device for catching night bombers. They let up balloons at hundred yard intervals to the height of about fifteen thousand feet. The wire cables holding them down make nasty snags for a bird to connect with.

As ever,

George

At the time that George flew with the 12th on the front, it was com-manded by Major Lewis Brereton,* a feisty, no-nonsense individual. The squadron's most experienced observer was Captain William Saunders, the squadron's operations officer, who flew many of his missions with George. The acting squadron operations officer after Saunders returned to the United States was Captain Elmer Haslett,* an observer with little combat experience but lots of personal nerve (Haslett 39). It seems evi-dent that the same personal bond that existed between George Hughes and Captain Saunders did not develop between George and Captain Haslett. George and Captain Haslett apparently flew at least one mis-sion together, according to documents found in George's photo album, but except for this one instance George does not mention Haslett. Nor does Haslett mention George in his postwar account of his activities in the squadron, Luck on the Wing.

JERRY'S COMMENTS

The work of the observation planes flying in active sectors of the front was extremely dangerous. When an observation plane was pho-tographing or mapping a certain area of the front, the pilot had to fly in a straight line at a set altitude. At those times there could be no twisting or turning no going up or down. No maneuvering to avoid enemy anti-air-craft fire. The pilot and the observer just had to sit there and take it.

For enemy gunners on the ground, a plane traveling in a straight line and at a constant altitude, especially a relatively low altitude under 3000 feet, made a perfect target. It is easy to imagine how the pilots and observers of the 12th felt as they flew through a more or less constant barrage of bursting anti-aircraft shells. Many of these men were among the unsung heroes of the war in the air. They were carrying on their haz-ardous work which was as dangerous, if not more so, than the work of the men in the pursuit or bombing squadrons. But, as George mentioned in his next letter to me, you didn't have to be flying in combat to be in danger of losing your life.

GEORGE HUGHES TO GERARD HUGHES
Friday, 17 May 1918
Dear Gerard:

You may have heard by now that poor old "Wild Bill" McCreery has been killed. [McCreery had been a fellow instructor with George at Wilbur Wright Field.] He and a friend were ferrying two Nieuport 28s from the factory to some airdrome and had stopped for gas. On taking off they evidently attempted to show the people what those little busses could do. Anyway, Mac dove down under the tail of his friend's machine and attempted to come up in front of him; but something went wrong, and the other bus chopped his tail off. His friend side-slipped down and escaped with minor injuries. That's the story I heard; I can't vouch for its accuracy.

About a week previously, Mac stopped at our field and on taking off went up in the darnedest zoom you ever saw, and scarcely had he leveled off when he pulled a right and then a left barrel roll and ended with a spin about 100 feet off the ground. He certainly could put those little busses through their paces. It was a shame he had to fall as he did, for he certainly could have made a name for himself if he had ever reached the front.

We lost two of our men over the lines the other day—a pilot and an observer [probably Cyril Angel* and W. K. Emerson,* killed on 14 May]. It was their first trip up there. We were unable to ascertain the exact cause of their fall, but we presume they were hit by anti-aircraft fire.

If you don't keep zig-zagging they can come awful close to you—as I can testify—but if you keep changing your direction slightly and at the same time vary your altitude with *great irregularity* you can keep them guessing. It's a good thing to change your course with the rudder about every thirty seconds, as they can't see your change as well as they can when you bank and turn. But the main thing, in my estimation, is change of altitude. If you give yourself a leeway of 1200 feet to play up and down in you are pretty safe.

Above all, beware of clouds. You make an extra good target when silhouetted against them; besides, they know the height of the clouds and can judge the bursts very easily. Moreover, by flying in a cloud you expose yourself to attack from above, unless the clouds are good and thick.

A word of caution about spins: those long tail spins may be good fun once in awhile, but they are a poor thing to indulge in to excess. Better cut them down to five or six turns and practice coming out of them so as to be headed in a specific direction. Endeavor to keep your flying as smooth as possible, doing stunts in such a way as to not depend on your motor to get out of, and without putting extra strain on your ship. I hear "Shorty" Schroeder is a captain. "Pop" Hinds sends his love and best wishes.

George

GEORGE HUGHES TO LUCY HUGHES [TEMPORARILY LIVING IN TEXAS WITH GERARD]
Sunday, 19 May 1918
Dear Mother:

I am glad you all bought a car and are having an interesting and enjoyable time at Waco. These are times when one should get all the pleasure one can out of life, for you never can tell what will happen next.

That you and Jeanie should follow Gerard around is the best thing possible, even if it does cost a little money. I only wish you would not address me in such endearing terms. It's a very bad thing to think of me in superlatives. One should take a sane view of life and this blooming war, for no matter what happens, the daily routine of affairs must go on regardless.

Tell Gerard to cut out all excessive wild flying and above all not to get the craze for this close-to-the-ground stunting. I used to think that I would like to take up aviation as a profession after the war, but now I am darned near convinced that it's a game that will get any man if he stays in it long enough, and if I ever get back to the States I am going to buy me a horse and a plough and the rest of the paraphernalia that goes with it. After one gets what they call "the feel of the air" he begins to forget the dangers of flying, grows careless and disrespectful of the laws of gravity, with the result that he gets caught napping some fine day.

We lost one of our aces [Raoul Lufbery*] this morning, a man who has been flying over here in this war on combat duty for over two years. In his haste to go up and chase some Hun planes he leaped into a little Nieuport speed scout, neglected to put on his safety straps, and was thrown out after reaching considerable altitude. If a man could only be as cautious every time he goes up as he was on his first solo he would probably never get caught; but he ain't, so there you are.

I have the honorary title of Senior Pilot and Flight Commander. Each squadron has three flights of six planes. Two flights are on duty each day, thus giving each flight every third day off. As far as possible we try to have the same pilots and observers work together at all times in order to get as much team play as possible.

The regular routine business consists of an alert crew, that is two pilots and their observers, who relieve each other in shifts so that there is always one ship ready for instant call for any work from daylight to dark. Then we send out a certain number of reconnaissance patrols each day. These patrols go out in formations of varying numbers, generally about three ships each. They fly up and down our sector just back of the lines. The rest of our work consists of photography and adjustment of battery fire [Army artillery fire] as necessary.

It's all quite interesting, but I still want to get into day bombardment work if possible, and intend to agitate the question again in the near future. Of course, the more experience I can get here, the better off I'll be. The more I know about the ways of the Hun the better will be my chances of bearding the lion in his den, so to speak.

Affectionately,

George

JERRY'S COMMENTS

Once again George was a little too hard on Mother's sensibilities, and the letter confirms his growing fatalism. George may have resented the fact that we were living the "soft life" in Waco while he was flying in combat regularly. Several photos in George's photo album indicate his combat activity. On May 3, the date of his first mission, he and his observer took photos near the front in the East Martincourt and North Richecourt sectors. On the May 18 he and his observer took photos of the front in the Apremont sector. On May 29 he and his observer, Lieutenant Lumsden, mapped an area between Mt. Sec and Seicheprey. But his most hazardous mission occurred on the morning of May 31.

GEORGE HUGHES TO GERARD HUGHES
Friday, 31 May 1918
Dear Gerard:

Had quite a bit of excitement today. Word came that the [American] infantry wanted some planes to work with them this morning. Those of us elected to go arose at the early hour of 2:30 AM. Had breakfast. I was the first to leave for the front. Got underway at 4:00 AM. Climbed to some 7000 feet.

This is the darnedest country for haze I ever saw. At 7000 feet we were just on the upper edge of it. Everything below was as completely hidden as though a black curtain had been drawn across to hide all from our view. Above was the clear blue and on our level the sky was rosy from the rays of the sun about to show itself.

The only blemish on the scenery were the bursts of the Hun Archies. They were simply plastering the sky three or four hundred feet above us in a vain endeavor to drive away three of our chasse machines. We dropped down to 5000 feet. Finally ended up less than 600 feet above the German trenches. We stayed around that darned place two hours or more, going back of the Hun lines at an altitude of less than a thousand feet.

How those devils did shoot at us—rifles, machine guns and every now and then the Archies would open up and plaster the skies. But I was always lucky enough to be elsewhere when they broke. One shell did break just under me so close that I expected to find myself minus a landing chassis. My observer amused himself by firing three or four drums of ammunition into the trenches, but I couldn't see a living soul even when we got down to where our wheels were dragging on the ground.

Finally I did see five Dutchmen standing on a hill. They, of course, command all the heights, and our men are down in the swamps. I came along just on their level. They looked at me like a firing squad getting ready to let drive at me. I turned around and beat it out of there "hell-bent for election."

Well, they simply perforated that ship of mine, but only one shot came close to me. It entered my lower left wing at a slight angle and came into the fuselage under my arm, passing somewhere along about the tip of my nose and piercing the center section of the wing some three inches back of the leading edge, just above my head. I'll bet those German officers sure cussed their gunners out, because they'll never get a chance like that gain. At least not at me for some time to come.
George

GEORGE'S COMMENTS

The latter part of May the Allied troops on the Beaumont sector decided to retaliate on the Huns at Seicheprey. The morning of the attack we were ordered to do a little low flying. Captain Saunders,* my observer, and I took off before daylight. Towards the end we flew at about 150 feet, just on a level with the top of Mt. Sec. We collected a goodly bunch of bullet holes; one bullet passed between my left arm and body. Luhr* and Haslett* relieved us and flew even lower. Haslett, our operations officer, was out to make a record for himself. He persuaded himself he lived a charmed life and would take any chance to distinguish himself.

After the Armistice Captain Saunders and I received the following citation for our efforts:

For gallantry in action, the commanding general cites the following officers:
Captain W. H. Saunders, Observer, 12th Aero Squadron
First Lieutenant G. F. Hughes

These officers flew in an A.R. airplane for more than two hours in the vicinity of LeBois de Gargantua [on 31 May 1918], performing adjustments of artillery fire despite an exceptionally heavy concentration of Hun anti-aircraft artillery fire. After completing reglages [adjustments] for two batteries and while conducting fire for amelioration for a third, they were brought down by shell fragments stopping their motor. In attempting to land on the rough terrain inside the American lines, the plane was smashed.

By command of Brigadier General William Mitchell,*
L. H. Brereton*
Lieutenant Colonel, Air Service, Chief of Staff

JERRY'S COMMENTS

George's participation in the events of late May must have affected his frame of mind, for he wrote only two letters home during the next four months. This was not like George, because until that time he always had something to say about his work or his experiences.

During May and June, the men of the 1st and 12th learned the routines of their various flying missions and developed a sense of confidence in their abilities to do their jobs, both pilots and observers alike. If there was one problem with operations in this area, it was that there was little coordination between the men in the infantry units on the ground and the pilots and observers in the aircraft overhead, for there was no effective radio communication system available to them and they had to learn one another's operational requirements and visual signals. Initially this was accomplished by a system of flags and panels placed on the ground and visual signals and messages tossed over the side by the men in the aircraft. But without preliminary training, and in bad weather and the pressures of combat, such a system did not work well.

GEORGE'S COMMENTS

The latter part of May we received notice that we were to move south to the Baccarat sector. Major Brereton* took me along to inspect the available airdromes; on the way we picked up some officers from the French Headquarters in Luneville. The field at Flin was finally selected as being the only one with enough room for the Salmson aircraft. The field was about 14 kilometers from the lines. We moved to Flin June 1st.

The flying activity in the Baccarat sector in the month of June was designed primarily to provide additional training for the pilots and observers in the 1st and 12th Aero Squadrons (Mauer I, 191). In addition, the squadrons were provided with larger, more capable aircraft, the Salmson, and additional training was necessary to become familiar with the operation of their new aircraft.

GEORGE'S COMMENTS

By the first of June the supply of Salmsons had increased so that the 12th and the 1st could be equipped with them. The 91st Aero Squadron was the only American squadron to be flying them before that time. To help convert our pilots from the old A.R. "wheel" control to the Salmson's "stick" control, we were given an old Sopwith two-seater [Sopwith A2] to train in. "Pop" Hinds later crashed while flying it and was killed.

Luhr, in attempting to take off across the narrow portion of the field at Flin, wrecked himself in a ditch. I was impressed with the fact that his observer, Lieutenant [Alvin] Goodale,* who was in the plane with Luhr, didn't lose his nerve. He contacted another pilot, Sig Thayer,* and the two of them successfully took off to complete a photo mission. This was Goodale's third attempt to complete this mission. I decided that Goodale was the observer for me, now that Captain Saunders had left for the States, and we flew together until I left the 12th. Goodale fell [on September 14] with Lieutenant [Edward] Orr* over the Argonne when they collided with a balloon cable and lost a wing. The first of July we moved to the Chateau-Thierry sector, operating first from Saints and then from La Ferte. Here we ran into a real war.

In July the 1st and 12th Aero Squadrons relocated to a new field about 40 km east of Paris, and became involved in some of the most intense combat activity they had seen, as they flew in support of the Allied resistance against the German attack along the Marne which came on July 15, and the Allied counteroffensive, which came on July 18.

George Hughes to Lucy Hughes
Monday, 15 July 1918
Dear Mother:

Just received four letters from you today. It's the first news I've had from home in five weeks. That was certainly a close call that Gerard had [a reference to Jerry's accident with Kuhn and Klyver in May] and I trust that he will refrain from close-order flying until he comes across to France. Then he'll have lots of opportunity for that sort of thing. It must be a great relief to be back at Granite after weathering the Texas heat.

The climate here in France has proven to be exceptionally mild so far. The nights are always cool enough for blankets and as a rule it seldom gets hot during the day. There is always a heavy dew at night which seems to help the crops. It's amazing how the grain grows here on the old farm lands that have been tilled since civilization commenced. The natives say this is a very bountiful year. Certainly the virgin soils of our western states couldn't do much better than the farms in this vicinity.

At present we are in a much more active sector than any we have been in before. I am scheduled for an early morning reconnaissance tomorrow and hope to be able to leave the ground by half past three. The sun doesn't rise until about five, but if the sky is clear I think I can make it okay. If not I will have to wait until it gets lighter. I always like to get away as early as possible, as the morning light makes it deceptive for the Huns manning the Archies.

Flying over the front is quite good fun when the gunners are missing you by a good safe margin, but it takes on quite a different aspect when they begin rocking your old boat. A reconnaissance is generally pretty easy to fly in such a way as to fool those devils on the ground, since you can change direction and elevation at your discretion. But a photo mission has to be flown at a constant altitude and in a straight line, which makes it perfect for the Dutchmen to shoot at you.

Of course, when they get too hot, you have to dive away and then return to your course later, trusting that their aim will deteriorate in the meantime. When you consider the factors that enter into estimating the range, it's miraculous how close they can come to you; quite as marvelous as flying itself.

Affectionately,

George

GEORGE HUGHES TO LUCY HUGHES
Thursday, 18 July 1918
Dear Mother:

Well, I got away okay with my daybreak reconnaissance the other morning. Those things are an awful lot of work. We arose at 2:30 AM, got a little something to eat, and were on the field ready to leave at 3:30. That ship that was to accompany me as protection had a little trouble getting started, so it was not until about 3:50 that I took to the air. I circled the field for about ten minutes trying to find the other ship and finally located it upside down in a grain field. The motor had failed and they had piled up. The pilot had the hard luck to break a leg.

Seeing they were down, we headed for the front alone. It was quite a wonderful sight. It was still about an hour before sunrise and the flashes of the artillery showed up most brilliantly in the semi-darkness. We were able to locate the positions of several new Hun batteries and got some other valuable information.

For the first half hour the Archies left us quite alone and as far as I could ascertain we were the only ship in the sky; but as it grew lighter I spotted four others. Three were in formation together and proved to be friendly chasse planes. They straightaway chased the fourth one back to Hunland where he belonged. They were unable to bring him down, though they gave him a good run for his money. We stayed up there some two hours and a half, then beat it for home to give the anti-aircraft guns a chance to cool off.

This dodging of Archie is great stuff, but the average pilot would rather have a fight with a Hun ship almost any time rather than be under fire from the ground. You stand a fair chance of bringing old Fritz down, but you are quite powerless against a battery on the ground, and the best you can do is escape with a whole hide. Statistics tell you that it's only one in about forty thousand shells that brings a ship down, but when a pilot begins to hear those old high explosives breaking around him, and the old ship begins to rock, he has the feeling that the forty thousandth shell may be about to arrive with his full name and address written on its side.

The night before my reconnaissance the cussed old Hun bombers came over and bombed a nearby town. Gosh, what a din and commotion! Searchlights swept the skies from all angles and our 75s [American anti-aircraft guns] kept up such a roar that you couldn't hear the bombs break. One landed on one of our fields, I believe, but the material damage wasn't great. Several fell short of one of our big hospitals crowded with wounded from the front but luckily none took effect. Those Huns are devils if there ever were such things.

Affectionately,

George

GEORGE'S COMMENTS

At first protected by a swarm of British and French pursuit pilots, we had things all our own way. At the drive on Hill 204 [near the town of Vaux] there must have been fully 150 Allied planes in the air at one time. It was like running a taxi on 5th avenue; it was all you could do to keep from colliding. But finally the Britishers went north and things got hot as the Huns began increasing their air forces [after the counter-offensive of July 18]. The day after I left the squadron for Orly Field we lost three ships in the 12th alone.

On July 23 I received orders transferring me to Orly Field in Paris where I was to assume command of the 183rd Flight Detachment. Before leaving I was directed to visit General Billy Mitchell's headquarters. After almost nine months I was leaving the 12th Aero Squadron.

The combat activity involved with the battles along the Marne (also known as the battle of Chateau-Thierry to American troops) was the most intense yet experienced by Americans, either on the ground or in the air. According to official reports, the loss of flying personnel and resources was significant:

On account of the large number of enemy pursuit squadrons operating in this sector there were numerous losses in carrying out the work of corps observation. . . . As a result it became increasingly difficult to carry out the work at hand and it was not infrequent that a flying personnel of from six to eight pilots and observers in each squadron exe-

cuted the missions scheduled for the day. This necessitated the execution of two or three mission per team per day (Mauer I, 217).

JERRY'S COMMENTS

George never talked much about his experiences with the 12th, except to say that he was shot down twice but never wounded or injured. He had machine bullets go through his flying suit but none ever touched him. He also said that he placed an iron stove lid beneath his seat cushion for protection. Each time he was shot down, his motor was knocked out by enemy fire. Each time he was able to crash-land his aircraft behind the American lines.

According to one of the men in the 12th, Lieutenant John C. "Jack" Kennedy,* George spent more time flying over the lines than any other two pilots—either in the 12th or 1st Aero Squadrons. When one of the men in the squadron wanted to go down to Paris for a rest or felt that his number might be up and he shouldn't fly that day, George took the flight for him. All of this effort didn't escape Major Brereton's attention, however, and just about the time of the big battle at St. Mihiel in July, Brereton recommended George for command of a newly forming unit, the 183rd Flight Detachment.

The period from May 1 to July 23, 1918, when George Hughes flew in combat with the 12th Aero Squadron, was the most hazardous of his flying experiences in France. However, George provided less information about this period in his letters home than he did at any other period during his time in the Air Service, and he never once mentioned either of his two forced landings. George wrote only six letters home during this twelve-week period. This fact in itself says something about the challenges and stresses George must have felt as a result of flying over the front.

7

George Hughes in the 258th Aero Squadron

On July 24, George Hughes received orders assigning him to the 183rd Flight Detachment. The mission of the 183rd Flight Detachment is not clear. According to George's statement, the unit was intended to be an observation unit attached to the British Army (Sloan 234). However, a set of orders in George's photo album describes the operation of an aerial "courier service" that was designed to operate between the towns of Fruges and Marquay with intermediate stops at Valheureux, Montonvillers, and Houtkerque. It is possible that such a courier service was set up to assist in transmitting messages for the newly formed American First Army, commanded by General John Pershing* (Maurer III, 14). But it is not clear that such a service was put into operation. Certainly it would have taken several weeks to establish it, especially if there were aircraft and equipment to be obtained. The operations order indicates that the unit was to have flown Sopwith aircraft (probably the two-place Sopwith A2), and George and others obtained some of these aircraft; a memo dated August 4, 1918, details George and six other men to ferry Sopwith A2 aircraft.

The memo establishing an "aeroplane courier service" is dated August 14. However, another set of orders, dated September 10, effectively canceled the courier service, and directed the men of the 183rd to proceed to Luxeuil, France, near the Swiss border, to form the core of a new squadron, the 258th Aero Squadron. An organizational chart dated September 12, 1918, shows both the 183rd (attached to British forces) and the 258th Aero Squadron in existence simultaneously (Thayer 178); this chart suggests that the decision to combine the two units into one was made during the first week of September. The orders dated September 10 identify George Hughes as the commanding officer of the 258th Aero Squadron. The 258th remained at Luxeuil from the middle of September until the first of November, gaining aircraft and personnel and developing operational proficiency.

George apparently wrote no letters home from the time he left the 12th Aero Squadron, in the middle of July, until October 2, a period of over two months. Possibly this interruption in correspondence home was due to travel and operational business associated with developing a new squadron. But there is something puzzling about the timing of his departure from the 12th (at the height of the battle of St. Mihiel) and his lack of communication with his family. Whatever the reason, once he moved to Luxeuil, George returned to his practice of letter-writing enthusiastically. As if to make up for his lack of communication, George wrote to his mother every day from October 2 through 18. This unbroken string of seventeen letters speaks for George's newly recovered sense of optimism. George appears to have found his old confidence again, and his old "take-charge" attitude is clearly evident in his October letters.

JERRY'S COMMENT

About the time of the big battle at St. Mihiel, George was ordered to leave the 12th and take command of the 183rd Flight Detachment. When George left the 12th, however, he did something that he wasn't supposed to do. He asked the squadron's chief maintenance man to leave the 12th and come with him. This sergeant had kept the planes in tip-top shape, and George did not want to part with him. The sergeant had a high regard for George and readily agreed to go with him. Unfortunately, his name was not on the roster of men who were to be part of the 183rd.

Just as they were about to depart for a location in Belgium, Major Brereton was informed of the situation and called George on the carpet. Brereton surveyed George with fire in his eyes and barked, "Lieutenant, do you know that I could have you court-martialed for this!!!" But Brereton eventually cooled down and even approved orders transferring the sergeant to the 183rd.

On September 10 the 183rd eventually became the core of a new squadron, the 258th, to which George was assigned as commander. The squadron received the more powerful Salmson two-place aircraft. The squadron took for its insignia the Lion of Belfort, in honor of a prominent landmark in Belfort, a large town near the field at Luxeuil. George was promoted to the rank of captain, a rare rank among operational flying officers in those days. His name appeared on the same set of orders, dated October 5, 1918, that listed Eddie Rickenbacker* for promotion to captain. In his first letter home he explained to our mother the location of his new unit in a code he had worked up in an effort to get around the censors.

GEORGE HUGHES TO LUCY HUGHES
Wednesday, 2 October 1918
Dear Mother:

Well, here I am back in camp again, where I found a lot of mail waiting for me, most of it written back around the first of August. I have just about got all my equipment together now and expect to stay home for a while. I certainly have done some running around. Often I would wake up in the morning unable to remember just where I was. The place I left this morning [Toul] is about as far from here [Luxeuil] as "Utopia" [Ossipee, New Hampshire] is from the "Hub" [Boston—a distance of about 100 miles] [See Fig. 13]. But the old Cadillac eats up the road in great style. The English rebuilt the motor and made it almost as good as new.

Affectionately,

George

GEORGE HUGHES TO LUCY HUGHES
Thursday, 3 October 1918
Dear Mother:

It has been a peach of a day. Hardly a cloud in the sky, but even at that it has been none too warm. We had the first frost of the season a night or so ago. I expect the leaves will be dropping before long now. The summer certainly has gone by like a shot! I hope they leave me here [at Luxeuil] for the winter. The country is beautiful and there is usually a heavy snowfall every year, so it ought to be like being back in New Hampshire.

Let's see—what did I do today? Spent the morning rearranging the guard posts and drawing up special orders for the guard and officer of the day. This afternoon I went up to see the Chief of the Air Service for this section and chewed the fat for an hour or so, thereby killing the afternoon in a grand way. I expect to stay around here for a few days to get the interior organization and work of the squadron in as good a shape as possible.

This business of one lieutenant running a gang of two hundred or so men and forty or fifty other lieutenants is quite a job. You have to keep on the tear to hold them in hand. But this bunch I have is really exceptional, and I don't expect to have any trouble with them.

Affectionately,

George

GEORGE HUGHES TO LUCY HUGHES
Friday, 4 October 1918
Dear Mother:

This morning I rose bright and early, had breakfast at 7:30; got to the office at 8:00; puttered around a while; made a few promotions, and stirred things up in a general way. Then I went up for a little flight—looped the loop a couple of times, spun, and stalled, just to show the gang that I haven't forgotten how to fly. These birds [Salmson aircraft] we have are pretty darned good for bi-place aircraft [Fig. 18]. They will do almost all the stunts, and I know of only one case of a wing being pulled off in the process. And that was done by a nut who didn't have any horse sense. These Salmsons aren't quite as fast on the climb or in level flight as the American DH-4, but they suit me just as well and have features that make them better for the kind of work that we are doing.

After dinner I took out the Cadillac, beat it up to Corps Headquarters, got my pay, put through some other business, and here I am back waiting to get supper. It's a great life. Especially when you are your own boss to a certain extent. The Chief of the Air Service is quite a ways away, and there's no one on the post that outranks me, so I can give them hell and do as I please.

Affectionately,
George

GEORGE HUGHES TO LUCY HUGHES
Saturday, 5 October 1918
Dear Mother:

This morning I went down the line to a French park [supply camp] to arrange for some aerial gunnery practice, draw spare parts, and the like. Got everything fixed up amicably and stopped in a fair-sized town for dinner. It was a very pretty place and almost large enough to be called a city. The country here is fine: nothing but mountains and woods, which remind me of New Hampshire more than any other section I have seen so far. The mountains are about the same size and look blue and quite inviting. I think I'll have to clean up an old rifle and go hunting.

There's one good thing about this country. If you go in a straight line for four or five miles you are bound to run into a hamlet no matter which way you go, so you ought not to stay lost for more than a day or so in these woods. I expect the wild pig ought to be quite plentiful with so much brush for them to hide in. The quail were most abundant up on the English sector, and on the low lands to the south—but you don't see so many around here, as the "pome de terre" [potato] seems to be more popular than wheat with the local farmers.

Fig. 18. Salmson Aircraft, 258th Aero Squadron. This aircraft was much more powerful and versatile than the AR-1 used by the pilots of the 12th Aero Squadron. As in the AR-1, the pilot sat in the front and the observer sat behind. By the end of the war, most observation squadrons were equipped with this aircraft or the American-made DH-4. The squadron's insignia, the Lion of Belfort, can be seen painted on the side of the aircraft.

Most of the work here is done with oxen. This afternoon I passed three teams of milk cows pulling wagons. Looked kind of funny—but as long as the women work like men in the fields, I suppose it's okay to hitch up the cows, too.

Affectionately,

George

GEORGE HUGHES TO LUCY HUGHES
Sunday, 6 October 1918
Dear Mother:

Am about five hours via Cadillac from camp [at Toul]. Came up to see about getting some spare airplanes; also a supply of flying clothes, goggles, and parts for ships. Supplies are now coming through from the States in great shape; we can get almost any amount of airplanes and equipment. I expect airplanes will be a drug on the market in a month or so.

Things are beginning to look pretty good for the Allies now. The American soldiers and equipment are coming over in such quantities that Germany is bound to be snowed under by next summer, if the war lasts that long. The American artillery coming to the front is about the best on the market. The bombardment they [the Americans] put down on the Huns at St. Mihiel made the ground rock for miles around, and they say the one [bombardment] up at Verdun made the ones down along the southern sector of the front look tame. We've got rapidity of fire and density that the French and English could never concentrate for any one drive. The war ought to be over in another year at the most.

Affectionately,

George

GEORGE HUGHES TO LUCY HUGHES
Monday, 7 October 1918
Dear Mother:

Have had quite a busy day. Ordered myself a new uniform, then came on down to one of our depots and put in a good half day's work collecting some supplies. That really is the part of the Supply Officer, but because I am much better known at this particular place than he will ever be, I preferred to go myself. It's a terrible thing, this collecting of supplies. I always start out loaded down with cigarettes, candy, and chewing gum, and then proceed to bribe the gang. First I go around to the storehouse and make a personal investigation to see just what they have in stock and how much. Then I go around to the officer in charge and camp in his office until I get what I want.

To illustrate: I wanted some "Teddy Bears"—fur-lined suits for fliers. On first inquiring, the stock clerk swore they didn't have a one.

But he had a bunch of suspicious-looking crates, so I proceeded to camp there, gave him some Lowney's chocolates, a little gum, and pretty soon he made the astounding discovery that those packing crates were all packed to the brim with "Teddy Bears"! Whereupon I beat it over to the office, where they swore that the last flying suit had been given out ten days before. But I finally convinced them otherwise, and came away with thirty and a truck load of other miscellaneous junk.

Also got an order allowing me to keep on hand six spare airplanes, and so now I am pretty well heeled; I have almost everything that it is possible for one to get, including three Dodges to go along with the Cadillac. I took a ride in a Dodge [the car Jerry, his mother, and sister drove in Waco] the other day. Gosh! But they feel funny after cruising around so long in the big bus [the Cadillac]; I felt as though I were riding in a kid's express cart. As for motorcycles, I have nine of those. The only thing that worries me is that some envious devil will come along and want a division of my spoils. They all want to know how it's done, but I only grin. It's no use telling anyone, because they'd soon have you backed off the map.

Affectionately,

George

GEORGE HUGHES TO LUCY HUGHES
Tuesday, 8 October 1918
Dear Mother:

The weather prohibited flying today; it drizzled all afternoon and this afternoon the gates opened up and the water came down in a perfect flood. About 4:00 it cleared up, and I went out for an hour's walk.

This field of ours is one of the biggest I have been on in France, and any one of the hangars will accommodate as many planes as three ordinary hangars. I should judge that the field is fully a mile long and at least a half mile across, and just as level as a billiards table. The men's barracks and the officers' quarters are excellent, and we have running water all over the camp. If we stay here very long it will spoil us for some of the fields I know of. At one place we were at during July [Saints], we slept under our planes and ate outdoors.

This place here is a palace in comparison. What's more, the nearest town [Luxeuil] is only a fifteen-minute walk away. It's quite a nice town —was a famous watering place before the war. People used to come from all around to take the baths and drink the water. So, all in all, we are fairly well fixed and I won't object to being left here all winter.

Affectionately,

George

GEORGE HUGHES TO LUCY HUGHES
Wednesday, 9 October 1918
Dear Mother:

I went up this morning and pulled a few stunts in one of our airplanes. After dinner I flew a little combat practice. These ships are pretty good for that, being fairly speedy and quite maneuverable. So it is easy for us to get together and simulate fighting.

It's especially good for the observers, as it gives them lots of practice swinging the tourelle around. The tourelle is the fixture to which the Lewis gun is attached. It is comprised of an iron U-shaped hoop attached to a revolving ring. This ring revolves around the observer, allowing him to point the gun in any direction on the horizon. The guns are attached directly to the U, the ends of which are hinged onto the revolving ring, thus allowing the guns to be elevated or lowered to a certain extant. One lever controls both [circular and up-and-down movement]. By pressing it halfway, you release the ring so that you can turn it. By pressing the lever all the way, both the U and the ring can be operated. It is quite a simple rig to tell about, but one needs to practice at it quite a bit to be expert.

It seems that I and my squadron are elected for contact patrol work for the duration of the war. We are running a school here to train the infantry of this section, along with other duties. A batch of infantry are coming in tonight to stay a week or so with us. The chief purpose of the work is to teach the doughboys how to work intelligently with the airplanes so as to make the most out of that form of communicating their whereabouts to headquarters.

In addition, we want to work up a feeling of friendship between the two branches of the service, and get both sides to appreciate the other fellow's point of view. The officers are to east at our mess so that we can get to know as many as possible, which ought to have the good result of closer cooperation in the actual work over the lines. Knowing the aviators in the plane above them ought to increase their confidence and interest in the work.

It ought to be fairly interesting and quite good fun for a while. I am willing to try almost anything once, but I don't like to have the squadron chalked up as an infantry liaison or contact patrol [mission] especially. Still, I don't intend to interfere with the natural course of events. I tried that once when I applied to get into bombing—and, lucky for me, they put my application in the waste basket. I'd be eating acorn soup [as a prisoner of war] or pushing up daisies now if I'd gotten into bombing then. So, let come what will; "ce ne fait rien" [it makes no difference].
Affectionately,
George

It seems clear that George Hughes's 258th Aero Squadron was heavily involved in liaison training with the American infantry to overcome the communications problems of the kind that had been experienced by the 1st and 12th Aero Squadrons along the front lines in May and June. George's letters provide evidence of the thorough familiarity that men of the infantry were expected to have with the operational procedures of the observation squadrons.

GEORGE HUGHES TO LUCY HUGHES
Thursday, 10 October 1918
Dear Mother:

The visiting doughboys all came in okay last night. The Chief of Air Service for this area is stopping with us to get things running. I expect he will depart after a week or so. This morning we took all the infantry officers up for a ride; also got a couple of the [enlisted] men up for a short tour. We let them all have a good look at the planes and explained the workings—the whys and wherefores of flying.

This afternoon we explained the various [communication] panels and how to use them. Then we walked over the terrain on which the maneuvers are to take place. About that time a plane came overhead and fired off the full list of fireworks and rockets so that the men could see them and have their meaning explained. Everything went along quite well, especially for the first day. Tomorrow we hope to run off the first of a series of problems.

Affectionately,
George

GEORGE HUGHES TO LUCY HUGHES
Friday, 11 October 1918
Dear Mother:

We had quite a day of it—or at least the gang did. I have things running in such a fashion that I feel like the most useless person in the world. While everyone else is working their heads off, I just bum around or sit tight in my office. As long as you have a big gang around, you might as well work them, in my opinion. One of the pilots had the nerve to tell me it was the best-run squadron he'd been in so far. If things keep going on as good, I'll be satisfied.

We ran off a couple of problems in liaison with the troops. The idea is to have them advance and meet with all the possible difficulties and annoyances of a regular fight and then, about that time, the airplane comes along and shoots off its rockets. The first rocket identifies the plane as being qualified to carry on business. The second rocket calls for the line [message], whereupon the doughboys put out their individual panels of white cloth, and those in the woods light flares.

Having got the line, the observer shoots a third rocket, meaning "I've got you! Pull in your panels before the Boche also gets you!" Then the observer lets loose another "compris" [message understood] and beats it back to headquarters with his information, and so on until the problem is ended. The weather has been favorable so far.

Affectionately,

George

GEORGE HUGHES TO LUCY HUGHES
Saturday, 12 October 1918
Dear Mother:

We ran off a couple more problems today. I gave one of the infantry officers a chance to see the fun from the air during the morning. We stayed up just about a half an hour, when my motor began to go on the fritz, and then came home. This afternoon I took the car [Cadillac] and went on a little visiting trip with a French captain. We stopped at several French fields; had quite an interesting time.

The Major went away some this afternoon in one of my Dodges. That's the reason I took off with the Cadillac. I knew ahead of time that he was planning to leave. He hasn't any transportation of his own, strange to say, and I don't want him to get away with my best. It's a great war, and—as the doughboys say—it's the only one we've got, so we might as well make the most of it. The recent frosts have turned the foliage and the scenery is beginning to remind me of New Hampshire.

Affectionately,

George

GEORGE HUGHES TO LUCY HUGHES
Sunday, 13 October 1918
Dear Mother:

Bad weather held up our program today, so we turned the men loose and let them go up to town to the baths. That's one good thing about this place; they have some fine public baths where the men can go and get cleaned up for the grand sum of nine cents.

This afternoon I went out to find a lake for target practice from the air. I found a peach of a one a couple miles from camp, buried deep in the woods. There was the biggest flock of wild duck on it that you ever saw, at least two hundred. One of these days I'm going to go down there with a shotgun and clean up on them.

The thing now is to get permission from the French to place a target on the lake so we can fire at it from our planes. There are no houses within several miles and the woods are quite thick, so we ought to have no trouble with ricochets. The French are awfully fussy about this aerial shooting, for some reason or other.

The Englishmen, on the other hand, don't give a hurrah for anyone. They hardly get off the ground before they let loose with their machine guns. They generally stick a target out on the home field and blaze away regardless. With them it's "win the war, and the devil take the hindmost." The latest rumor is that Germany has accepted the President's terms, but it's not official—and doesn't hardly seem possible.

Affectionately,

George

GEORGE HUGHES TO LUCY HUGHES
Monday, 14 October 1918
Dear Mother:

The bad weather still holds—drizzle and heavy ground mist. I spent the morning chasing around various headquarters trying to obtain permission to use a local lake for target practice. Finally I arrived at the big mogul's office—Commander of Air Forces for the Army! He's no small bug, now, take it from me. He [General Mitchell] was most affable and obliging. He fixed everything up to suit in all respects; had the intermediate hoboes notified by phone, so I had nothing to do but come on home in peace.

That's the only way to get what you want. The little bugs always stand in your way, just to show their authority—which they haven't got—while the top notches always listen to reason and will give you almost everything. The thing to do now is build some targets and get a raft of some sort in order to tow them out into the middle of the lake. Then we will be all set to blaze away.

Every time I go away from this place someone always gets something balled up. Although the weather was almost impossible, my adjutant [an executive assistant to the commander, usually non-rated (not a pilot)] informed a certain colonel that we would send up two planes for a maneuver twenty miles away. Well, the colonel goes ahead and orders out some fifteen thousand men, but at the crucial point the pilots refuse to leave the ground [because the weather was bad]! I surely told that adjutant to climb down off the band wagon. Of all the nerve, that surely is going some for a ground officer. I don't expect to hear the end of this as long as I work with this outfit of infantry!

They had us all stirred up with rumors of peace, but the war seems to be on again now. That the war will end before next winter hardly seems possible.

Affectionately,

George

GEORGE HUGHES TO LUCY HUGHES

Tuesday, 15 October 1918

Dear Mother:

Rain, drizzle, fog, and bad weather in general still continues. I spent this morning showing the new bunch of infantry officers over the post and introduced some of them to the latest types of planes. This afternoon a French captain took a couple of us around to see the war dogs at work. It was raining buckets but they carried on just the same.

The dogs are trained principally to carry messages. A patrol going out into "no man's land" takes along two or three dogs, and when the occasion requires sending back a message, they put it into a tin tube that can be fastened on to a dog's neck, and away he goes. The dog beats it back to the starting place and as soon as he is again released, he will go out and find the patrol. If it is desired to send the patrol any message, the dogs are trained to go out and hunt them out without having previously been with the patrol.

They are also trained to attack a man, but in my opinion, they aren't half ferocious enough. If I had anything to do with it, I'd teach them to dive for a man's throat instead of his arms and legs. The man who battles with the dogs in practice wears the darnedest-looking uniform—heavy padding all over him so the dog's teeth won't penetrate his skin.

They hold the dogs on a leash some ten or fifteen yards away so they can get a good running start, and at the word they go like a flash and grab the guy at the first place that comes handy. Some of the dogs certainly have vice-like jaws; they have to take a board or a piece of iron to try to pry their jaws open. If they would just spring for a man's throat every time, they would be dangerous critters to run into.

Affectionately,

George

GEORGE HUGHES TO LUCY HUGHES

Wednesday, 16 October 1918

Dear Mother:

The clouds were pretty low but we managed to run off a maneuver this morning. The ground was flooded to a depth of four to five inches of water. The poor doughboys had to wade through it. I am going to look for another training ground at a higher elevation. It seems like damned foolishness to have them get soaked as long as it can be avoided. This afternoon we got all the officers up for a ride, and a few of the men. After that we went down to the lake and constructed a floating target and a raft. Just as soon as the hours can be arranged, I want to start them shooting. The observers can't get any too much practice, and the better they are, the longer they'll live. All peace talk is off and the war goes on just as hot as ever.

Affectionately,
George

GEORGE HUGHES TO LUCY HUGHES
Thursday, 17 October 1918
Dear Mother:

The weather still continues doubtful, but we changed our maneuver ground to a hillside, and everything went off okay both this morning and afternoon. I flew for the morning exercise, and was in the air for about an hour. This afternoon we paid the men of the squadron. Some of them hadn't been paid for two months, and had quite a bit coming to them. Still, two months [pay] isn't much for a man to lose out on [considering the delays that could occur], especially when transferring from the States to France.

This evening we celebrated by opening a bar. A couple of energetic young pilots conceived the idea of making life more home-like, and built a bar with a rail and all the other accessories, over which they are proceeding to dispense the liquors of France. It's quite a live gang we've got, and they are continually up to some deviltry or other. This bar idea was a great success.

Ten of them formed an association with a tax of 100 francs per man, thus getting capital. Now they are proceeding to exploit their trade and make a big profit on the rest of the gang. They decorated the room with autumn leaves; hung up flags; swiped the YMCA piano; and in general made the place most inviting. Now they are talking of building an open-hearth fireplace, so as to have all the comforts of home.

Affectionately,
George

GEORGE HUGHES TO LUCY HUGHES
Friday, 18 October 1918
Dear Mother:

Your letter and one from Gerard written on board ship to be mailed on arrival came in today. It was quite a shock! I had no idea that he was liable to be coming across. It was the very first intimation I had of it. Damn it! There was a whole bunch of junk I could have had him bring along. I am making strenuous efforts to get in touch with him and hope to arrange a meeting at some place or other. Everything is going okay. I expect you folks back home hear more about the war than we do.

Affectionately,

George

JERRY'S COMMENTS

As George's last letter indicates, he had not heard that I had finally been released from my instructor duties at Rich Field and had received orders for France. About the time he first learned of my arrival in France, I was just about to complete my training course at Issoudun. I was trying to get through training as fast as I could, so that I might join an operational squadron and fly at the front before the war ended. I almost made it.

8

Jerry Hughes in Training in France

On August 25 Jerry was released from Rich Field to travel to France. With his Rich Field fellow instructor Russell Klyver as his companion, he departed New York on September 8. From October 1 through the 31 he was in training at the 3rd Aviation Instruction Center at Issoudun, France. The training complex at Issoudun was one of the largest in France; it consisted of one central field and seven other satellite fields where specialized flight training was conducted. As an experienced instructor pilot with many hours of flying time, he hoped to move through the training program at a rapid rate. Unfortunately, rainy weather set in for almost two weeks, nearly doubling the amount of time needed to complete his training requirements. Once through, however, he proceeded directly to the American-run gunnery school at St. Jean de Monts, on the west coast of France. Once again, he was able to move through that school quickly and successfully; he entered training at St. Jean on November 1 and concluded on November 8. He then hurried as quickly as he could to the reassignment center at Toul, for every day brought more news of the war's impending end.

JERRY'S COMMENTS

I had a long and rugged road to travel before I finally caught up with my brother in France. I sold the faithful Dodge back to the dealer from whom I had bought it, and surprisingly enough he gave me more than I had originally paid for it. Automobiles were at a great premium on the home front because production was limited or even shut down. The same thing happened during World War II.

Klyver and I lost no time entraining for New York. We spent a night or two at a hotel and then hailed some transportation to take us down to the ferry which would carry us across to Hoboken, New Jersey. Our boat was the *S. S. Minnekada*. She had been rushed into the water before she was completely built and placed into service without a super-structure. We sailed into the ocean in a convoy of about twelve vessels. For several hundred miles, small destroyers and a cruiser kept us company. Then they left us and we continued zig-zagging our way across the ocean until we neared the Irish coast, where other destroyers joined us and escorted us into the harbor at Liverpool.

We immediately took a train down to London and spent the night sleeping on the benches in Waterloo Station. In the morning we were on a ferry boat crossing the English Channel to Le Havre. We were traveling in a group of what were known as "casuals." We were sort of "nonpersons," having no special privileges or standing, or even rank of any sort. We had to find whatever transportation we could, and we would get our rank back when we reached our final destination.

We finally made it to Saint Maixent, and then moved on to Tours for a few days. Then we traveled down to the flying field at Issoudun, where we were to receive further training [See Fig. 12]. Issoudun was a tremendous complex which offered facilities for some eight stages of training. Here we engaged in formation flying, cross-country flying, and finally acrobatics and mock combat.

GERARD HUGHES TO LUCY HUGHES
Saturday, 5 October 1918
Dear Mother:

Pershing's army is not the American army of the States. Things move over here and there is no horseplay. This [Issoudun] is the biggest aviation field in the world, where men are taught to fly in rush time, and go to the front with less than one hundred hours. Those graduates from here are giving a splendid account of themselves. In fact, they say the graduates from here are the best-trained pilots on the front.

Production is beginning to tell at last, and the need is now not for machines, but for pilots, and things look pretty fine. They use to rave back in the States when a man was killed, but here it is nothing. They have a funeral every day. I was Commander of the Guard two days ago and nearly broke my arm standing at salute while four trucks rolled by— each with some poor fellow going to Field No. 13 [the students' name for the Issoudun cemetery]. They were not all killed in training. Some of them died from natural causes. There is quite a bit of disease over here. Many men die from pneumonia.

Klyver and I have been exceptionally well since leaving. Our only complaint is lack of water. It is very scarce around here and, as far as I can see, all over France. Wine is drunk instead and people don't bathe. The food we get is good—and cheap. In fact we have very little to complain of.

Affectionately,
Gerard

GERARD HUGHES TO LUCY HUGHES
Sunday, 6 October 1918
Dear Mother:

We are being shoved through this school with great rapidity. A bunch of us, all with over 300 hours in the air, are being given a clear track, and we are surely going through! We started flying last Thursday (3 October) and have moved through four stages as of today—i.e., in three days. Many of the instructors here are old time Rich Field cadets whom we instructed.

We are going into pursuit work. Tomorrow we start flying the 15-meter Nieuports. They are nice ships—fast and easily handled. All our work from now on will be with them. When we go to the front we will get SPADs. The latter are much the same, expect that they do not handle as nicely, I understand. Several men have told me George is in command of a squadron at the front. That means he is doing a little fighting. He has done his bit in a fighting way by now, I guess.

Yesterday I took two cross-country flights. The first was just a local one. The second, however, took me some distance from the field. I was lost the whole time. I never saw such country. It is covered with little towns which all look alike. Also the forests and roads are just the same everywhere. Coming back I was lost and landed at a little town to find out where I was. The peasants drove me crazy—offering me champagne, beer, and bread, trying to talk to me. I found out where I was, but then I couldn't start my motor. I worked for a couple of hours on it, then stopped and telephoned in.

I spent several more hours awaiting assistance which never came. Two American mechanics, however, happened along, and they started my motor. I landed back at the field at dusk. I had started at 7:15 AM and was hungry by the time I got back. The country is very beautiful from the air, even though it is very confusing.
Affectionately,
Gerard

GERARD HUGHES TO LUCY HUGHES
Monday, 7 October 1918
Dear Mother:

Today we received news that Germany wants an armistice, which is good news. But peace, of course, is still a long way off. I suppose the Boche will fight all the harder and so will the Allies, for that matter. We haven't received any mail as yet, but it will come some day. We surely are living years in a few weeks. Seems like two years ago that we left.

We have crossed the Atlantic, been in England, through quite a bit of France, half way through this school, met all sorts of characters, and a thousand other things. McMullen is just about through and seems to be in Seventh Heaven. Those little Nieuports are just made for him and he is having the time of his life.

All that has been said about what the Americans have been doing over here is true. Everywhere you see evidence of it—enormous assemblage plants for aeroplanes, for cars, for engines, covering acres. A big train thunders by drawn by American locomotives, dragging a big train of freight cars, of all which are four or five times the size of the French trains. Everywhere you hear about the American doughboy at the front. It is always the same. The Boche can't stop him, and neither can his officers. He just keeps going until he gets hungry, and then he waits for the provisions to come up. The same spirit is found in the Air Service and everywhere else. Germany is out of luck all right.

Affectionately,
Gerard

GERARD HUGHES TO LUCY HUGHES
Tuesday, 8 October 1918
Dear Mother:

We continue our rapid rush through this school. We are flying the small Nieuports and they are wonderful little ships. Having had so many hours in the air, we don't spend any time in the different stages; just twenty or thirty minutes of flying time and then we graduate to the next stage. After finishing here, we will go to Gunnery School and then be ready for the front. Since arriving here over a week ago, neither Klyver nor I have left the field. We don't get the time. All we spend money for is food. Meals cost about two and a half or three francs—a franc being about 18 cents.

The Air Service is coming into its own over here at last. The work of the squadrons at the front lately has done it. Colonel [Hiram] Bingham*—an old Yale professor—is the commanding officer of this field, and he is very efficient and well-liked. He combines the college spirit with necessary military spirit, a thing which the West Pointers seem unable to do. We understand that pilots are in great demand at the front now, in that aircraft production is at last hitting its stride. We are all set to go, just so the war doesn't end. It may end soon, according to the latest news, although it hardly seems possible.

Sure do miss water over here. All drinking water has to be chlorinated before using. Washing water has to be carried to the different fields in tanks—like old Texas days. I was pretty lucky as regards my

baggage—have it all with me. Many lost one or two pieces. Klyver lost his clothing roll in England. No mail as yet.
Affectionately,
Gerard

JERRY'S COMMENTS

All of the flying at Issoudun was pretty much "old hat" for Klyver and me, except that the latter portions of our training were done in tiny little 15-meter Nieuports. These were the first fighters which the French used over the front earlier in war. Of course, I couldn't wait to take up one of these tiny ships and spin it. My opportunity came, and I went to about two thousand feet. As it turned out, I made a number of mistakes in deciding to spin this aircraft. In the first place, I failed to take into account the fact that these planes had rotary motors and that the engine, which whirl around as one unit with the propeller, developed tremendous torque and thrust toward the right. Any turn in that direction, which was the direction I foolishly chose to spin, would be heavily speeded up by that torque. This fact combined with the smallness of the aircraft itself, meant that the rate of spin would be many times faster that the rate I was used to in the old Standard.

My second mistake was failing to strap myself tightly. The man who had flown the plane ahead of me must have been a very big fellow. The seat belt and shoulder harness had been loosened quite a bit. I should have tightened them up to fit me before I took off. As I started down into the spin, I was startled at the rapid rate at which the plane was spinning, and at the same time, the centrifugal force threw me up against the loose seat belt and the straps. Before I knew it, I was half out of the cockpit, and my feet were pulled off the rudder pedals. And, to get out of a spin, you needed to reach the rudders. You can only get out of the spin by a hard reversal of the rudder and thrusting the stick well forward. After a brief but frantic struggle, I was able to pull myself back into the cockpit and get the plane out of the spin, That little adventure scared the daylights out of me and gave me a valuable lesson. It was the last time I ever spun a plane!

GERARD HUGHES TO LUCY HUGHES
Friday, 11 October 1918
Dear Mother:

We are ready for the last stage at this field. Our progress has been very rapid indeed and instead of spending a week at each stage, we have only spent one or two days. The last stage will give us training in combat, and we will get three or fours days of it, probably. We just started flying a week ago yesterday. In combat training, two ships go up together and have a mimic battle. Instead of a machine gun, you use a camera gun and take shots with it. When the films are developed, you learn whether your shooting was good enough to have brought down the enemy.

At the Formation Stage I was looking at the names in the arrival book and found Hugh Bridgman's* and Phil Carret's* names. I saw Percy Dodge, who is now a captain and was at Rantoul. He saw George over a month ago. He said George was hale and hearty and was in command of a squadron which was doing training work with the Infantry. The Infantry is being shown how to cooperate with the front but was with the British back of the lines. Dodge said the major under whom George was working was pleased with his work.

These little Nieuports are great ships. They are a little bit of a thing with a 120 horsepower motor. They jump off the ground and climb right up straight. I think they go about 120 miles an hour. The Germans seem to be losing their fighting power. Doesn't seem as though they can last much longer—but guess they will stick long enough to give us a chance at the front. Surprising how many young Americans around here don't want to see the front. They are hoping and praying to see the war end before they get there. They must have a lot of yellow in them. No mail received as yet.

Affectionately,

Gerard

GERARD HUGHES TO LUCY HUGHES
Wednesday, 16 October 1918
Dear Mother:

The rainy season has just set in and caught us; otherwise we would be through this field and gone. As it is, we are sitting around, chomping at the bit and chewing the rag. Three or four days is all we need to finish our combat work and then we will leave for gunnery school.

I received my first mail yesterday. It was all stuff forwarded from Waco. I have had no word from George as yet. Probably he hasn't got any of my letters. This rainy season is disagreeable. Misty all the time—and cold. It clears up for a few minutes, then mists up and rains. If we had only got here a week earlier we would have been gone by now. There are a lot of men coming here from the States whom I know. You remember young Kimball? He breezed through here yesterday. [Alton B. Kimball, from Harvard, was killed at Issoudun, shortly after starting training.]

The Red Cross is a great institution over here. At the main camp at this field they run a mess hall for officers and serve sandwiches and

cocoa to the enlisted men practically all day long. They also run a bath house and a barber shop and an officers' club—also a technical library—not to mention many other things. The Germans seem to want peace, but apparently they won't get it for some time.
Affectionately,
Gerard

GERARD HUGHES TO LUCY HUGHES
Thursday, 17 October 1918
Dear Mother:

It still rains—and we still sit and fret, unable to get into the air. France is a strange country. It has no fences. Fields spread over the rolling country for miles, interrupted here and there by a tree. Here and there a small section is plowed, but mostly all of it is just grass and stones. There are no big stones, just a lot of hen's eggs. Worse than any of New Hampshire's worst. The woods are mostly hard pine, and they are planted and thinned out like so much corn. It's just one row after another, all the same distance apart, and all running straight as a bee-line. From the air the land takes on a wonderfully uniform aspect. The forests are trimmed and squared off, and the fields just roll on and on. The plowed patches make it look like a dish of green and brown rhubarb.
Affectionately,
Gerard

JERRY'S COMMENTS

The weather was bad through most of the month of October. During one bad spell of rain, I caught up on my correspondence with the Brooks family, back in Illinois. In my letter to Mrs. Brooks, I filled them in on the details of my trip across to France.

GERARD HUGHES TO MRS. MORGAN BROOKS
Urbana, Illinois, Friday, 18 October 1918
Dear Mrs. Brooks:

It seems that most people who cross the ocean at the present time have thrilling experiences with submarines and collisions—but alas! In spite of all our earnest desires and eager anticipations no "tin fish" arose from the deep to interrupt our slow and majestic course. Nor did any heedless cruiser or galloping "sub chaser" run into us in the middle of the night. In short, we crossed the ocean peacefully, and without sickness.

Then we landed in solemn England. That is the most noticeable thing in that country—the solemnness. In the hotels, on the streets, in the cars, everybody is silent or talking seriously and earnestly. If you laugh you feel guilty—feel as though you had laughed out loud in church. There is no dancing. Perhaps a little music in the hotel lobby—advertised as "jazz"—but resembling a symphony orchestra more than an American jazz band. Most of the women smoke. Saw one twirling an exceptionally long cigarette holder. It looked rather startling. You see women doing everything: see them running the trams, cleaning locomotives, in fact doing everything. And they seem much healthier than American women—more rugged and with wonderful color in their cheeks.

We saw fresh English companies of soldiers marching off to the boats—on their way to the front. It was like seeing scenes from "The First Hundred Thousand" or "A Student at Arms" acted out before your eyes. The companies, however, are now made up of older men and boys. They march with firm step and eyes straight to the front—but they do not smile. Nor do the children smile or laugh—the way American children would—as they stand in the streets and grasp the soldiers' hands as they swing by. The war is a real, a terrible thing to them.

What a contrast to the Americans! As we marched to the pier from our rest camp we straggled along (we traveled as a detachment of casual officers not assigned to a particular unit) laughing and joking, and throwing pennies to watch the children scramble for them in the gutter. The English can't understand us, and I don't wonder. One little incident that tickled us took place in London. We had been traveling all night and had to wait from 4 A.M. until 8:30 A.M. before we could continue our journey. Three of us betook ourselves to the Charing Cross Hotel and demanded of the night clerk when we could get breakfast. The startled clerk looked at us in amazement for we were tired and wet and resembled so many tramps. He told us the breakfast hour, and then still more to his amazement and dismay we curled up on the sofas in the lobby and went to sleep.

France reminds one of a big factory closed down. Everything seems dead. A peculiar stillness reigns everywhere, both in the city and in the country. A man not in uniform is a rarity, and the women, as in England, are doing the work. In sanitation and engineering and, in fact, nearly everything France seems almost primitive compared with the United States. And I know of nothing that has thrilled me more over here than the sudden appearance along the railroad track of some enormous American assemblage plant. There are many of them and they cover acres. They have sprung up over night and are a constant source of astonishment to the French. Another pleasant sight is a big American locomotive tearing along with a train of cars marked U.S.A. Our railroad rolling stock is three or four times the size of the French.

After spending one night in a rest camp and another at a concentration camp, we finally arrived at the Third Aviation Instruction Center—where we are at present. We started right off in our training as pursuit pilots and would have been gone by now had it not rained. As it is, we will only need three or four good days to finish us up. We are flying 15 meter Nieuports. They are very small indeed and handle wonderfully. They are a revelation compared to the old Curtiss. After finishing our course here we go on to a gunnery school—to stay there ten days or so, and then go right to the front. It hardly seems possible that we are on the eve of getting there—and to think that two months ago we were without hope. Even now we are fearful lest they take it into their heads to detain us here. Only last night I found myself "detailed" to go into night flying—to be one of six to remain at this field and instruct in night flying. Good luck (or rather human nature) was with me, however, for six men volunteered.

The "peace scare" does not seem to have upset anyone. Things are going on just the same. We get the Paris edition of the *New York Herald* and *Chicago Tribune* which keep us pretty well informed. Our mail, too, is starting to arrive, and all the stories of how welcome it is are true.

The Red Cross is doing wonderful work over here—much more than the YMCA. Take this field, for instance. At the main camp it operates the following: Officers' Mess Hall (regular meals and tea); Officers' Club Room (reading matter etc); Technical Library (all about aviation etc); Enlisted Men's Mess (only sandwiches and coffee); Enlisted Men's Reading Room; Barber Shop (four French barbers); Mending and Cleansing Shop (French women employed); and Bath House (showers).

The field, as you may imagine, is the biggest operated by us—and is said to be the largest in the world. Besides the main camp there are seven active flying fields each representing a different stage in training, and each a unit in itself just like Chanute or any other single unit field. Each has its own C.O. and staff and YMCA etc, but it is directly responsible to the C.O. back at the main camp (who by the way is Colonel Hiram Bingham*—once a professor at Yale).

About four miles separate each unit from the center, and the country is so open that one can land almost anywhere. From the air, the earth is really beautiful; there is such a blending of colors due to the different stages of cultivation and different types of soil. Everything looks so fresh and green and moist that it is a great relief from Texas. Please give my regards to everyone. When next I write I hope it will be from some point on the front.

Sincerely yours,

Gerard H. Hughes

GERARD HUGHES TO LUCY HUGHES
Sunday, 20 October 1918
Dear Mother:

The rain continues to hold us up. We have been here just three weeks tomorrow. If we had had fair weather, we would have graduated by now. We haven't spent a cent—except for food—since we got here, for we haven't been away from the camp. I haven't heard from George yet, nor from anyone except through the letters forwarded from Waco.

A few days ago they tried to inveigle me into night pursuit work. In fact, they told me that I was "detailed" to go into it. I found out later that they only wanted men who wanted to go into it. An English captain is here to train six men who will then take up the instruction work at this field when he is through with them. The captain gave me a talk about the work. Told us it was soft, cushy, and safe, and that we would be the first in the American army to take it up. There were some twelve men at the lecture and when volunteers were called for they had no trouble in getting six men, and I escaped.

Klyver told the officer in charge of training that the appeal made for the instructors was a "damned insult to the American flying corps," for they merely appealed to a man with yellow in him. "If you want to see the end of the war" was one sentence used by the captain, and "if you have any personal aims" was the gist of another. The yellow birds begin to show their real colors at this place. They try to get leaves, try to get sick, try to get instructor's jobs, try anything that will delay their going to the front. Those men who, back in the States, talked about how well they could fly are usually the ones who fear the scrap over here.
Affectionately,
Gerard

GERARD HUGHES TO LUCY HUGHES
21 October 1918
Dear Mother:

Every few hours we hear that Germany has surrendered. The last local rumor is that they may snare Klyver and I and others at this field as instructors. They will have a fight on their hands if they do. We don't intend on getting so near the front and then being stopped. We have served our apprenticeship and now are ready for our reward—which is the front. I would feel ashamed to go back to the States if I had not had a shot at a German, let alone not having heard a hostile gun fired. They employ lots of German prisoners around here, making roads and doing similar work. They seem to be content enough. McMullen has graduated from this school and left yesterday for gunnery school. We will follow him in hour or five days.

Affectionately,

Gerard

GERARD HUGHES TO LUCY HUGHES

Thursday, 24 October 1918

Dear Mother:

We finally finished our course here today. Having put in some ten hours of tumbling head over heels trying to shoot an opponent down with a camera gun, we have been declared ready to tackle the Hun. We still have our gunnery course to go through; we will get that at some other place. I put in four and a half hours in the air yesterday, and as most of it was combat work, I was ready for bed.

One's sense of equilibrium is rather befuddled after so much combat, for you turn around and around, up and down, spin and twist and tumble and turn until you feel all inside out. It means keeping in the best of condition to stand it, especially when you are not used to it. I notice that many who don't keep early hours complain of being sick in the air. Klyver and I hit the hay at seven every night. We have orders to get an hour's exercise every day.

Affectionately,

Gerard

JERRY'S COMMENTS

Although the weather was bad for most of October, we managed to fly on eight different days. That was enough flying for us to demonstrate our abilities and pass through all the stages of training which qualified us for pursuit work. The instructor who gave me my combat test at Field 8 wrote in my training report that I was "mediocre and conservative in combat work." He was undoubtedly justified in this reaction to our flight. It was a flight of only about 30 minutes and we were flying the little fifteen-meter Nieuports [fifteen square meters of wing surface]. I didn't like the one I had. It looked a bit shopworn and a little too old for me. These craft were being flown every day by one pilot after another and put through every conceivable maneuver. I figured that I would not be the one to put the final strain on the little aircraft.

We rendezvoused at about three thousand feet. The instructor dove on me to shoot me down [not literally, of course; both aircraft carried gun camera film instead of bullets]. I was supposed to escape death by diving and pulling sharp renversements [a rolling, diving turn] and anything else that might work to escape his sights. The circumstances being

what they were and the plane being untrustworthy in my opinion, I made
a rather mediocre attempt to escape, figuring that if I were going to die
as a result of combat flying, it ought to be at the front and not over Field
Number 8. Fortunately, the instructor recommended that I be assigned to
a pursuit squadron after I completed my training.

After completing our course of instruction at Issoudun, Klyver and I
were given orders to proceed to St. Jean de Monts, down on the French
coast, for gunnery practice. Since the staff at Issoudun wanted to send
two 15-meter Nieuports down to St. Jean, Klyver and I were asked if we
would fly them down. We were delighted to do so, of course, and were
soon headed north to a point on the Loire River near Tours.

We then flew west, close down along that lovely stream and had a
good look at some of the beautiful chateaux along the way. Near Angers
Klyver developed engine trouble and landed on the left bank of the river,
and I came down and joined him in a pretty meadow. After spending the
night in the local hotel, we found a mechanic in town who fixed up the
motor. We took off once again and continued on downstream until we
came to the Atlantic Ocean. Turning south, we soon came to the tiny
hamlet of St. Jean de Monts. The gunnery school was just south of town.
As we swung in over the field, we saw black smoke rising from the
wreck of a DH-4 which had just crashed on take-off.

GERARD HUGHES TO LUCY HUGHES
Thursday, 31 October 1918
Dear Mother:

Terrible thing! I haven't written to you for four or five days; there-
fore there must be an excuse of some sort. The best one I have is that we
have been flying again. We finished our course at the 3rd Aviation
Instruction Center [Issoudun], and then, as luck would have it, we were
assigned the pleasant task of ferrying some planes to this Gunnery
School [St. Jean de Monts]—a distance of perhaps 300 miles.

Eight of us started out (after the usual delays) and flew in a fog for
100 miles or so. We had to fly about 200 feet above the ground, which
made it interesting. At our first stop we had dinner, got some gas, and
started again. The fog had lifted a bit and we were able to go on flying at
500 feet, which gave us a good chance to get a good look at the countryside. And what a country! I felt as though I were in a dream. It was
absolutely beautiful.

The grass over here is the greenest of green and serves as a background for the golden poplars which rise tall and stately along every
highway and byway. Here and there are vineyards of red and brown, and
running through the whole a winding river [the Loire], intensely blue.

Those were the elements of the panorama which passed beneath us. It was simply a marvelous symphony in color—as far beyond description as a musical symphony by Beethoven. I have never seen anything to compare to it, and it surely gave me a thrill.

Along the river bank were small towns, each one built around its ancient church, and everything built of stone—ancient and gray. All the roofs were of gray slate, and as you looked down on them, they blended with the surrounding country and seemed a part of it. Never a sign of a red brick or a tall chimney or black smoke. Nothing to remind one that he lived in the twentieth century and not in the fourteenth century. Off to one side would be a chateau belonging in days gone by to some marquis, a tall building surrounded by well-kept grounds and trees.

Well, after an hour above this fairyland, we came to a city [Tours] sitting placidly beside our river. It was just an enlarged edition of the towns, and when we landed and entered it, we found it was a place of which we had read and heard time and time again in connection with ancient dukes and battles between the French and English. In the center (besides the ancient church) was a big stone fortress. The walls were perfectly solid except for a few little windows. Along the top were little turrets from which the Duke was wont to drop rocks on his enemy's dome. Around the whole was the moat—without any water in it.

We saw a thousand and one other things which were interesting or amusing. One of the craziest was a small boy of seven who, when given a cigarette, proceeded to inhale the smoke and blow it out through his nose—to the unfeigned delight of an older brother of nine. After spending the night in the city, we went back to our planes and got ready to leave. Six got away without trouble. Klyver had a missing motor and I waited for him to get fixed up. We took off together and flew for 45 minutes until we sighted another city. Just then my motor started missing, and we landed, spending the afternoon, night, and next morning in the city.

We had some excellent meals, got twelve hours' sleep, located an American garage which took us all over the city in one of their cars, found an American aviation mechanic, got the motor fixed, started off "toute de suite," and landed here [St. Jean de Monts]. So the trip ended, et vraiment c'est la belle France; or at least, when you are up in the air, it is.

I wish I could remember something about French history. Think how wonderful it would be, while flying over a place, to think about what went on there one, two, three hundred years ago. To look down and see where Napoleon fought—or where Jeanne d'Arc was burned—or where Richard Coeur de Lion was jailed. That would be real sport. By the way, the tower in which Richard was confined is in the town near the 3rd AIC [Issoudun], and we have seen a lot of places where Napoleon had his headquarters or spent the night.

Our gunnery course here will last from six to ten days, and then we will have finished our last step in training for the front. We will go from here to another station where we will be equipped—and then straight to the front! There were about 125 men on that old order of ours and we are leading the bunch. Some of them are just starting in training back at the 3rd AIC. It took us longer to get here than we had hoped—on account of the rainy weather—but here we are and the road is clear. I haven't heard a word from George. I sent him several letters in care of the 183rd Flight Detachment, but he has never answered.

Today's news seems to be that Austria has capitulated. What the result will be, we don't know, of course. That reminds me of story of the poor man who, when his wife died, was forced to ride to the funeral in the same carriage as his mother-in-law: it spoiled his whole day. That's the way Klyver and I feel about this peace stuff. If Germany quits cold now, it will spoil the whole war for us. After training for a year and a half for the big game—and then to be left sitting on the bench.

But we will get there for some of it. We are so close now that they couldn't possibly call it off without our getting just one crack at the Huns. I wrote to Mrs. Brooks the other day—but not to Frona. Also received another letter from Virginia.

Affectionately,
Gerard

GERARD HUGHES TO LUCY HUGHES
Saturday, 2 November 1918
Dear Mother:

Klyver hasn't received any mail yet, not a bit. I have got quite a lot. No word from George as yet. That Spanish Flu which you mentioned has been quite prevalent in our army and quite a number died from it. It has about run its course, I think. It also spread into Germany and is apparently just getting to the States. We have started on our course here and things are going smoothly but not fast enough. Four or five days will see us through, I expect. You mention that George is in the 258th Squadron —but don't say what he is doing. I suppose he is back at the front again.

Murray McConnell, John Baker, and Gaines of our old Mineola class are here at this Gunnery School. Gaines is a tester; he tests ships that have been relined or refitted. McConnell is trying to get orders to go to the front in two-seater work, and John Baker is in charge of a certain phase of flying. As far as I can learn, George and Henry Lindsley* are the only ones of the class who really got to the front. Fuller was reported shot down on his first trip over the lines, but he has since been heard of in Switzerland.

It appears also that only about ten of the class are actively flying now, all the rest having ground jobs of some sort. Henry Lindsley is the son of Judge Lindsley of Dallas, Texas. He is said to be one of the best chasse pilots on the front. He was in my class at Mineola under Wheaton, and he and I were both discouraged at one time about whether we would ever learn to fly.

Affectionately,

Gerard

JERRY'S COMMENTS

Our gunnery practice at St. Jean de Monts was simply to go up in the little Nieuports and chase a bigger plane which was towing a canvas "sleeve." The sleeve was our target and we were supposed to get as close as possible and fire our machine guns at it, always making sure that the bullets went out into the ocean and not inland. They didn't want us to shoot the pilot who flew the tow aircraft or any of the French people who lived along the shore.

GERARD HUGHES TO JEANIE HUGHES

Sunday, 3 November 1918

Dear Jeanie:

Think of us always having to address that brother of ours as Captain! I heard last night that he had received his promotion, and today I received a letter from him to that effect. He certainly deserves it and should have had it long ago—only, sad to relate, they were handing out few promotions on merit alone, up until recently. He wants me to put in a bid to get into his squadron, but I don't think I will. It's a game in which we would not work well together. Also, it would mean my changing from chasse to reconnaissance.

The darned war is nearly over, apparently. We are just in the nick of time if we hope to get there before it's over. We ought to be off for the front this week. Even then we may be too late. And again the war may last a year. This post is a fine one. They make it a point to treat you well. The reason is that you are getting ready to go to the front and they want you to be up there in good spirits. At other places they seem to make it a point to make it disagreeable for the Air Service. Must close now and take some exercise.

Affectionately,

Gerard

GERARD HUGHES TO LUCY HUGHES
Monday, 4 November 1918
Dear Mother:

It is hard to think of George being a captain. The best part of the whole matter is that he won his promotion on the scene of action, and promotions won there are more meaningful than those handed out to chair warmers whose father or mother knows somebody in Washington. Most of the captaincies have been of the latter kind so far, and it is only lately that they have started promoting fliers at the front.

It surely looks like the war were about over. It would be just my luck if it were. I hope you have started getting my letters by now. I have written pretty religiously, I think—although I lose track of when I wrote last. Well—here's hoping the war will last three more months. But the darned war is over, I'm afraid. Klyver says he's going to start praying for it to keep on. I tell him he has a devil of a lot of prayers to run counter to, and he will have to make it strong, or it will get lost in the rush.

Affectionately,
Gerard

GERARD HUGHES TO JEANIE HUGHES
Wednesday, 6 November 1918
Dear Jeanie:

There is a funny doctor on this post. He is a great red-bearded bird from Louisiana. He is affectionately known as "Doc" Fulton and he usually writes a column for the camp paper. He said he was once asked if he was any relation to the Fulton of steamboat fame, and made reply that he didn't know a steamboat home but that he had steered many a schooner home [a reference to drinking beer]. His specialty is stories about the South.

Besides "Doc" Fulton there is another bird around here worthy of mention. His name is [Reginald] Bowles,* and he is a sort of eccentric, globe-trotting adventurer. He is taking the course in Gunnery here. In fact, he is just a couple of sections back of us and was training at the 3rd AIC while we were there. According to him, he has a medal for rescuing several people at the time of the *Eastland* disaster [the steamer *Eastland* sank in the Chicago River on July 24, 1915, with a loss of 852 lives. A young man named Bowles was credited with bringing up 40 bodies from the hold of the submerged ship]. He wears a service stripe for serving with Pershing's Expedition into Mexico.

He joined the Princess Pat [a British Army unit] regiment and fought in the trenches with the Canadians or the British for a year and a half, during which he was wounded three times. Later he became a member of our Air Service and started training. He was slated in the beginning to fly a Liberty Plane, a big two-seater [DH-4]. But he scared his instructors half to death and they recommended that he be trained as a pursuit pilot, for the following reason, viz: "Since said Bowles is crazy and is going to kill himself, it is better that he do it in a single-seater, rather than in a two-seater, where two lives would be involved."

And so it came to pass that Bowles began training as a chasse pilot and we ran across him in the combat stage. We always avoided ships that Bowles had flown—for he never brought one down to the ground but that it was strained and stretched, and otherwise damaged. But he didn't kill himself, and soon he will be on the front, where he undoubtedly will get a bunch of Huns, and eventually fall over a brick and kill himself.

The Officer in Charge of Training at this point is another adventurer and is well-known to the American public. His name is Tracy Richardson, and if I remember correctly, he was given quite a write-up in one of the monthly magazines some months ago. His specialties are machine guns and South American revolutions, several of which he has had a hand in. A person could write a book about the different people one runs across in the AEF [American Expeditionary Forces].

I was wandering through the work shops this morning and the following sign caught my eye: "Say! Let's Work Like Hell and Go Home!" That sign typifies the spirit of this post. It has more pep than any place I have yet seen. Everybody is helping and pulling with everybody else. Then, too, there is a wonderful bunch of enlisted men on the field. Some of them were professional actors before the war, and they've got the deuce of good show which they have given several times.

It is called "The Pink Stocking" and it surely is a rip-snorter from start to finish. It's one of the best burlesques on a musical comedy that I have ever seen. It is also filled with a lot of local flying humor and jabs which carry the house. The man who stood out most conspicuously at the performance I saw is an excellent singer. He sang some of Al Jolson's songs—in the inimitable Al's own style—and got away with it in fine shape. He has a voice very much like New York's pet and though not as active and fervid, yet he imitated him as well as anyone could—which is saying a good deal.

There is one fellow dressed up as a blonde—blue dress trimmed with black fur and everything. If she wasn't the best looking girl you ever saw, I'll eat my hat. Why, she had the crowd crazy! Another big bird dressed up as a fashionable society belle with a falsetto voice like a factory whistle made a big hit. Still a third did some fancy dancing— hula hula and so forth. He put the audience on the floor with spasms. Imagine an attractive Hawaiian girl dancing around trying to vibrate an arm that would grace a Hercules! There were about six "girls" in the chorus (I think all of them work in the machine shop), and when they came loping out like so many camels with evening gowns on—you should have heard the roar that went up!

Everybody around here seems to think the war is as good as over, now that Austria has fallen by the way. If it does end now, there surely will be a lot of rejoicing among the yellow devils who are trying their best to keep away from the front. And there is a lot of them. It is certainly sickening, and if I don't get to the front and get a crack at the Huns, I will be ashamed to admit that I was in the American Air Service.

The more I think of it, the more George is to be congratulated on his promotion. He won it by hard, consistent work, and pure merit and won it at the front. There are few who can boast as much. If it doesn't rain tomorrow, we have a chance of finishing our aerial gunnery, and then we can leave this place and start on our way to the front.
Affectionately,
Gerard

GERARD HUGHES TO LUCY HUGHES
Friday, 8 November 1918
Dear Mother:

I think we are through with our gunnery school here. We raised the devil because they weren't putting us through fast enough. We stormed around so much that we beat the section ahead of us. In fact, they haven't got started yet. We nearly turned their hair gray. Just as it was at Issodun, they say they never had a bunch like us before. We broke all the records they had and showed them what a gang which wanted to get through could do. Rainy weather held us up two days and at that they expected us to get through two days after we did. Well, as they didn't expect us to get through they haven't any orders for us to leave. And so we are still here. It's enough to drive a man crazy.
Affectionately,
Gerard

GERARD HUGHES TO LUCY HUGHES
Saturday, 9 November 1918
Dear Mother:

We leave this Aerial Gunnery School [St. Jean de Monts] this afternoon and start on our way to Paris. From there we will go to a depot where we will be sent to our squadron at the front. On leaving here we become officers once more and cease to be student officers without rank or recognition. I'll be glad to get somewhere where we can get some news about what is going on at the front. The war may be over for all we know.

Affectionately,
Gerard

JERRY'S COMMENTS

After a week at St. Jean, Klyver and I finished with flying colors. The only comment the training staff made on my gunnery report sheet was: "Good pilot—good shot." Klyver and I hightailed it out of there and headed for Paris and hopefully the front. As we traveled we began to hear rumors that an armistice was about to be signed and that the war would soon be over. We didn't like the sound of that, after all the struggle we had had to get there in time to get into the action. We should have rejoiced, of course, but at the time our attitude was understandable.

9

Return to America

In spite of his frantic rush to reach the Air Service assignment center at Toul before the war ended, Jerry was too late: he arrived on the day the Armistice was signed. He consoled himself with the thought that he had made his best effort to get to the front and contribute to the war effort. After being persuaded to join his brother's squadron, he looked forward to flying in Germany as part of the Army of Occupation.

For the first few days after the Armistice, Jerry took advantage of his brother's well-equipped squadron to do some flying and some touring of the country between Toul and Luxeuil. He and Klyver, who had also joined the 258th, were able to enter Metz in time to see General Petain's triumphant entry on November 19. In December, Jerry witnessed Russell Klyver's tragic death, when Klyver flew a friend's SPAD into the ground in cloudy weather. With Klyver's death, Jerry had personally witnessed the deaths of two of his best friends from Waco—Kuhn and Klyver—victims of their own flying errors, not the war. But even before Klyver was killed, Jerry's mood had already begun to darken as a result of the illness of his brother George.

Just when the two Hughes brothers thought that they might enjoy the opportunity to fly together during the weeks after the Armistice, George suffered the onset of what we would today call combat fatigue. The war over, his important responsibilities ended, George was unable to resist the cumulative effects of his leadership responsibilities and the stressful combat experiences he had faced. Jerry discovered George shaking uncontrollably in his bed on November 15, four days after the Armistice had brought the war to an end. Jerry rushed George to a hospital and then remained nearby for the next four weeks while doctors tried to discover what was afflicting his brother.

During his month in the hospital, George attempted to recover his strength, while the doctors ineffectually diagnosed his illness. Eventually George prescribed his own cure—he needed to escape from the hospital, where he saw men dying around him, mostly from the effects of the flu. With Jerry's help, George was able to obtain his release from the hospi-

tal. Jerry knew that their flying days in France were finished, and he determined to help his brother regain his health and return to the United States as soon as possible.

JERRY'S COMMENTS

After leaving St. Jean-de-Mont Klyver and I reached Paris, the "City of Light" (which was in total darkness when we got there), early on the morning of November 10th. The Armistice was signed the next day, at the eleventh hour of the eleventh day of the eleventh month. The war was over!

Klyver and several others elected to remain in Paris that night to join in the celebration. But I said "Not me! I am heading for the advance headquarters of the Air Service at Colombey-les-Belles. Maybe the war isn't really over." It was late that night when I reached headquarters and reported to Captain [Frederick] Zinn,* the man in charge. The first thing he said to me was, "Your brother George has been looking for you. He knew you were coming."

George had flown up from his squadron, which was stationed at Luxeuil, to wait for me. We were mighty happy to see each other after being apart for over a year. I had hopes of joining a pursuit squadron, of course, but George said no, I should join his 258th Aero Squadron, which he was commanding. He was about to take the squadron to Coblenz, Germany, as part of the occupation forces. It would be a lark! It was okay by me, but I wanted my friend Klyver to join, too, if he should ever decide to leave Paris. Klyver arrived the next day and told us of the wild scenes in Paris the night before. Apparently I had missed a good party. Klyver said sure! He would join the 258th, too.

George was good friends with Captain Zinn at headquarters and could get anything he wanted. In foraging around for supplies for the squadron, George had been able to obtain some bottles of a special wine the captain was partial to. In return, Zinn saw to it that the 258th was well equipped with squadron transportation—several motorcycles, extra Dodge motor cars, and even a Cadillac for the squadron commander. Zinn was in complete charge at headquarters and was living the "life of Riley." A French woman served as his housekeeper (and mistress) and he literally had all the comforts of home.

The 258th Aero Squadron probably had more ground equipment than any other outfit on the front. George, nobody's fool, saw to it that his Cadillac was well out of sight whenever he learned that high-ranking officers were coming to make an inspection. Zinn probably tipped him off in advance. A colonel would have grabbed that Cadillac in a hurry. Cars like that were rare at the front.

With an enlisted man at the wheel of the big Caddie, George and Klyver and I headed for Paris. We spent the night there and then continued on to Luxeuil. The 258th was equipped with French Salmson planes. They were big two-place observation craft with a radial motor and plenty of power. Klyver and I enjoyed flying the Salmsons. They were different from anything we had flown earlier, especially the little 15-meter Nieuports.

Two days after we landed at Luxeuil, we found ourselves at the controls of these big planes and heading northwest to the city of Toul and the nearby field of Manonville. The field at Manonville was a sort of hillside pasture. The hangars, which were already in place, were large canvas structures, easy to knock down, transport, and erect again at some other site if the need arose. The other buildings—the barracks, the dining rooms, the administration offices—were quonset huts. These were big half-round metal fabrications set right on the ground. The letter I wrote home after joining the 258th suggests the happy frantic pace of those days after the Armistice.

GERARD HUGHES TO LUCY HUGHES
Saturday, 16 November 1918
Dear Mother:

I have not been able to write during the last week because many things have transpired which have prevented writing. To begin at the beginning: We finished our course at St. Jean-de-Mont on the coast of France and started off for the front. We knew that we were too late [to see action], for already the Germans had asked for terms. After an uncomfortable journey—as usual—we finally reached Paris. Klyver had dropped off at Tours to look for some of his lost luggage. It was Sunday, November 10th.

We looked over Paris a bit and tore around looking after baggage. Went to a play in the evening and saw a lot of wild women. The next morning we took the train for Toul at eight o'clock. We knew that the Armistice would be signed that morning and that Paris would shortly be in a whirl of frenzied joy—but we didn't feel much like celebrating. After traveling all day we reached Toul and snatched a few hours' sleep. Then we took a train for the Air Service Headquarters in the Zone of Advance, where we learned the war was over.

Klyver had not caught up with me in Paris, and at headquarters I found that McMullen was in the 4th Pursuit Group. I asked for that group and was assigned to the 13th Aero Squadron. Left a note for Klyver to join it also. Went back to Toul where the 4th Group was quartered. Found McMullen. Before going out to the aerodrome, I went to the local Air Service headquarters and got the dope on where it [the air-field] was and how to get there. After dinner I went back to the Air Service headquarters and learned that Captain Hughes had been there half an hour before. Back at the aerodrome I walked around—spent the night—and had breakfast with McMullen. Then I went to the headquarters to report and be assigned. There I found your eldest son lying in wait for me. He had been chasing me all over creation.

He proceeded to tell me that the pursuit squadrons would not go with the Army of Occupation to Germany and that the observation squadrons would. Before I knew it, he was tearing off with me in his squadron, having got the permission of Major [Charles] Biddle* [commander of the 4th Pursuit Group]. He tried to get McMullen, too, but Biddle said he wouldn't let him go. But George tore off with Mac and me hell-bent for the Swiss border, where the 258th has its ships. We were to ferry them back to Toul.

On the way we stopped again at the Air Service headquarters and there we found Klyver and also Kieran (another pursuit pilot) and Sewell, a man who came over with us and who was at Issoudun and St. Jean with us. Before we knew it, Klyver and Kieran were out of the 2nd Pursuit Group and Sewell was out of the 1st Army Corps Group and all were headed for the 258th.

Then George went off in his Cadillac, and we followed in a Dodge, which appeared from the Lord knows where. We drove through some wonderful country—about 150 miles—down near Switzerland at a place called Luxeuil, a famous French watering place. The next day George flew up with some of the ships to Toul while we stayed at Luxeuil. He returned that night. We, in the meantime, were taken to one of the most famous eating places in France and also saw the beautiful town of Belfort, which is the most famous watering place in the country.

The next morning we flew up to Toul and came back in the Cadillac, leaving George up there. And here we are. We have covered about 1000 miles the last week and seen most of France. By the way, when we got back to Toul, we found that McMullen had been transferred to the 258th. Mac told George that it couldn't be done, to which George replied that he had got everything he had gone after and guessed he wouldn't be stumped this time. He took another officer out of the 12th earlier in the summer without any orders. The major in the case, Brereton,* threatened him with a court-martial. The officer in question was absent without leave from the 12th for over a month. But George got it straightened out. He says he knows all the colonels in the Air Service up and down the front and doesn't give a damn for the majors. Biddle is mad, I bet.

Well, we are getting ready to move up to the Rhine. What with Klyver and Mac and a Cadillac and three Dodges and George in command, things ought to hum. You will never know that son of yours. He has felt the power of achievement, and has developed into a young dynamo. That's enough for the present.

Affectionately,

Gerard

JERRY'S COMMENTS

Bringing "Mac" McMullen into the 258th was typical of George's ability to get what he wanted. Bryan "Mac" McMullen had been with Klyver and me back at Rich Field. He had come to France ahead of us and had been assigned to the 141st Aero Squadron at Toul. Mac was very unhappy in the 141th; his commanding officer was "Hobey" Baker,* famous as a hockey and football star at Princeton before the war. It seemed that Hobey preferred only Ivy League college men in his outfit. Preferably from Princeton, of course. Hobey had even painted all of his squadron aircraft orange and black, "Old Nassau's" colors. They made a beautiful sight, all lined up in a row.

But Mac was not a college man; he had come into the Signal Corps from the Texas National Guard. He was a fine "spit and polish" type of officer, every inch the gentleman and the soldier. Hobey had apparently gotten the message across to Mac that he didn't fit the image of the other college boys in the squadron. It didn't take us long to persuade Mac that he should join the 258th, an outfit that was composed of common folk. Well, maybe the 258th did have its share of college boys, but we weren't hung up on the fact. Apparently Hobey wasn't unhappy about losing the Texan to the 258th. In December, Hobey received orders to return to the States. He flew one last flight in a SPAD 13. In taking off from the field, he turned, fell into a spin, and was killed.

But before George could enjoy the results of his labors to build a well-equipped, highly motivated squadron, the impact of his months at the front caught up with him. One night, shortly after we had returned from Luxeuil, I was sitting in a YWCA reading room writing letters home. George had left to go to bed in our hotel room in Toul. Suddenly a military policeman appeared at the door and called out, "Is there a Lieutenant Hughes here?" Yes, I was. "Please come with me," he said. "Your brother has taken ill in the hotel."

I ran up to our room and found George lying in his bed shaking violently, as though he had some kind of fever. I said to the military policeman, "We'll have to get Captain Hughes to a hospital right away! See if you can find an ambulance!"

I didn't know what in the world was wrong with George, because he had seemed in good spirits up to that time. I knew he was very tired, but outside of that he appeared to be in good shape. Not knowing what else to do, I thought the hospital was the best place for him. The military policeman finally located an ambulance and we started out for the nearest hospital. When we arrived, I ran in and said that I had an officer outside who needed attention. "Sorry," they said. "We are full. No room. No beds."

I hurried outside and told the driver to head for some other facility. Arriving at the next location, I was given the same story. No room. No beds. I was desperate by this time, and just what I said or did, I don't remember, but they took George in and put him to bed. I headed back to the hotel, taking back all the bedding and blankets which we had used to bundle George up for the trip. I was exhausted by the ordeal.

Every day I journeyed out to that hospital to see how George was doing. The doctors didn't know what was wrong with him and kept giving him tests of one sort and another. One day I went to a clinic with him where he was to be given an examination. The medic had him stepping up and down on a stool. When he started to faint, the doctor gave up, and told me to take him back to the hospital and put him to bed. I was concerned about his health and didn't know what to tell our mother. Finally, George's health improved and he was able to write to her.

GEORGE HUGHES TO LUCY HUGHES
Friday, 6 December 1918
Dear Mother:

I fell down pretty much in my letter writing. The last one, as I remember, was the 10th of November, almost a month ago. But I trust that Gerard has kept you all informed of events in this sector: how that wild gang from Texas joined the 258th in the hopes of going into Germany with the Army of Occupation.

But things didn't turn out as we had planned on at first. In fact, no Air Service unit was taken from around here, and instead of following up the Huns, the squadron has been roosting in the mud on top of a most desolate little old knoll, some ten miles north of Toul at the village of Manonville. The 168th is keeping them company and naturally, having nothing better to do, they are constantly fighting just to keep off the dull times. That gang from Texas is certainly a wild bunch of goats, if there ever was one. For the first week after our arrival up there we did no flying, and the enlisted men of the 168th began to kid our men about their old Salmsons that couldn't get off the ground and their pilots who didn't dare go up, now that the war was over.

Well, one balmy afternoon the Tango Circus from Texas took to the air, chased their mechanics off the field, played hide-and-go-seek in and around the hangars, scraped their wheels on the roofs, looped the loop, allowing but scant clearance with old Mother Earth. And one wild devil came tearing along and pulled a barrel roll, twice to the right and twice to the left, some 200 feet off the ground, so that all on the ground could see the poor observer clinging on in the back. This put the wind up the back of a 168th pilot, who was about to take off, to such an extent, that he got out and walked off the field.

It must have been some show, from all accounts, for I didn't see it myself, for I was in the hospital. But one of my pilots, who went on the front in May in the old 12th, got his nerves so upset when he saw that gang chuckling old Mother Earth under the chin in that insolent manner, that he had to go in and lie down, asking to be called when it was all over.

I have been in this blooming hospital about three weeks now. The first couple of weeks I felt pretty low. If this accursed war hadn't ended when it did, I guess I would have been a nervous wreck by now. The last day or so I have begun to feel pretty good again. Today I have felt the best since coming in here. I hope to be starting home in a week or ten days. It doesn't hardly seem possible; too fine to be possible! But the Disability Board here examined me into Class D (sounds like old school days), and have requested orders to the States for me, and I expect they will come through in a week or so, and by that time I ought to be quite able to travel.

The old fogy of a major who examined me said it was criminal that I should have been flying and that I ought to be put to bed for six weeks. I reckon it will be six weeks before I actually get out of here, but then I knew I had it coming to me when the squadron doctor told me back in June, when I was still with the 12th, that I ought to stop and take a long rest.

All of which makes one speculate as to where all those thirty thousand trained pilots have been hiding themselves all this time—while the poor devils at the front had no one to relieve them from April until the end of the show. Since the cessation of hostilities we have been flooded with hordes of ambitious and striving aviators, come from the Lord knows where, but all alike in their eager desire to see "the front" and to collect some souvenirs. The Lord bless their yellow hides.

Well, McMullen is now the CO of the 258th; the Texas Circus is reigning supreme. Hardly any of the observers dare go up with them, but I don't give a hoot if they knock down all the hangars and chase the Colonel himself off into the woods. They claim they are going to come down to the big field here at Toul and give them a real exhibition as the bunch there isn't much given to stunting, including the chasse pilots. I

only hope I get a chance to see it. If I don't get delayed in making a get-away, perhaps I will be able to beat this letter home. Here's hoping.
Affectionately,
George

JERRY'S COMMENTS

In spite of George's attempts at humor in his letter to our mother, he was still very much a sick man. It was only at a much later date that the medical profession began to realize that a soldier could get wounded, not from bullets, but from over-exposure to danger and the stress and strain of facing death too often. At first they called it "shell shock" and then they spoke of it as "battle fatigue." George had finally broken down from the terrific strain which he endured as a result of his constant flights over the lines. He was suffering from battle fatigue. During World War II a man who suffered from this kind of illness was said to be "flak happy."

For the month that followed George's hospitalization, I alternated between visiting him in the hospital and keeping up with happenings in the squadron. As the month of November progressed, the rains came and never seemed to stop. The field at Manonville turned to mud, and even in our protected hut, when we put our feet out of bed, we stepped into mud. Whenever the weather cleared a bit, we would have the mechanics start the motors on the planes and we would take off and fly around under the low-lying clouds to look over the near-by countryside. We flew over some of the areas of battle where heavy fighting had taken place shortly before. We flew over Pont-a-Mousson and saw the devastated landscape spread out below.

One day we drove one of the squadron's Dodge cars up to Verdun. Great piles of rifles and machine guns and other implements of war were stacked high in one of the town squares. We were not supposed to touch any of it, but I picked up a Springfield rifle and a Browning automatic rifle. I brought these back to the States with me and eventually gave them to the local police department.

Late in November, Captain Zinn's assistant, Lieutenant Brown, knowing we had transportation, suggested that Klyver and I take a car and driver and go for a drive up to Metz, arriving there ahead of the French army, which was on its way there. Lieutenant Brown was to go with us, of course. We headed off in a hurry, spending the first night at Nancy and arriving in Metz the next day. The German army had just pulled out of the city in the morning, and we arrived in the afternoon. In Metz, we managed to get a room in a hotel and began looking around the city. The French army was not supposed to occupy the town until the following day. Night fell, and we were in a café having dinner and watching the excitement. Bill Thaw,* well known for his flying achievements in the original Lafayette Escadrille, came in, looking for something to eat.

Next morning the French army moved in and in the distance we saw General Petain* sitting on a white horse, watching his troops march into the ancient fortress of Metz. It was an impressive sight. As the day progressed, there were wild scenes in the streets. Nungesser,* the great French ace, passed by in an open car, waving to the crowd.

One unhappy incident marred the festivities. During the celebration, French SPADs were circling the city and diving down close to the buildings. Suddenly one pilot came in too low and struck some wires. His plane plunged into the middle of the main town square. We were standing on the edge of the square and saw the plane smash into the crowd. Several people were badly injured. I'm not sure if any were killed. The report was that the pilot, although badly hurt, came out alive. After we had had enough of the excitement at Metz, we decided we should return to the squadron.

The rain kept falling and flying was more or less impossible. The mud made it difficult to take off, and there was the danger of chunks of dirt and mud striking the propeller and breaking it. One day, early in December, a SPAD came winging in under the low-hanging clouds and landed in our pasture. The pilot was a lad named Faulkner, whom Klyver had soloed back at Rich Field. I had given him his first ride. Faulkner had discovered that Klyver and I were stationed at Manonville, and he wanted to show us his brand new ship, his beautiful SPAD. Klyver and I were delighted to have the chance to fly it, as neither one of us had been up in a SPAD before.

Klyver had the first shot at the SPAD. He was soon in the air, darting in and out of the clouds, and diving down over the field. Then he must have pulled a wingover type of maneuver in preparation for coming in to land. Whatever he did (he was out of sight in the clouds), he didn't have the power to pull out. We saw the SPAD diving out of the clouds towards the ground. The SPAD struck the ground and Klyver was killed.

It was a sad day when we buried Klyver, with whom I had flown so often and shared so many adventures. The lifeless body of this fine pilot and wonderful gentleman was placed in an Army truck, carried out in the pouring rain, and buried in a temporary grave in a bleak and barren military cemetery.

During November George lay in that hospital and was getting no better. Finally he said to me, "I've got to get out of here, or I will surely die." He told me that every day men were dying in the ward rooms and their dead bodies were being carried out in the full view of other patients. As this went on day after day, George felt that he would not last long in that environment. Among his several items of clothing he had a handsome Air Service overcoat with a large fur collar. It was a most attractive coat. This garment was much admired by one of the young doctors. One day George said to him, "Do you like that coat?" "I certainly do!" replied the medic. "Then mark me fit for duty and that overcoat is yours," George said. No sooner did George make this statement, than release orders were cut.

With George's release papers in hand, we were off to Colombey-les-Belles and good old Captain Zinn. He arranged for travel orders to be issued to us, and we took off for Paris. I got a room in a hotel and we spent a few days in the city [Fig. 19]. There we ran into Lieutenant Hugh Montgomery,* a pilot who had been with George in the 12th. The day after our arrival, President Woodrow Wilson came to Paris, and the city went wild. I ventured out into the streets and before I knew what was happening, my mouth was full of confetti, and someone had snatched off my cap. I decided I was safer in our hotel room with George. We learned that it might be days or even weeks before we would find our place in the great stream of veterans who were heading for home. We just had to wait our turn.

GERARD HUGHES TO LUCY HUGHES
Friday, 13 December 1918
Dear Mother:

George and Lieutenant [Hugh] Montgomery* and I leave Toul tonight for Tours. We may be held up there for a couple of weeks and then we will really start for home. We shall be as glad to get home as you will be to see us, I guess. George is feeling fine now. He had one of his run-downs shortly after we came to Manonville and has been in the hospital ever since. He wasn't sick—just completely worn out. He will have been in the hospital four weeks this Sunday. We will probably be back in the States by January 15th.
Affectionately,
Gerard

GERARD HUGHES TO LUCY HUGHES
Saturday, 14 December 1918
Dear Mother:

Both George and I hope to be home shortly after you receive this letter. I enclose a picture taken from a French magazine. It shows General Petain reviewing his troops as they marched into Metz. Mac

Fig. 19. George and Jerry Hughes on Leave in Paris. Jerry on the left, George on the right. Photo taken December 1918.

McMullen and I were standing across the road from him. The squadron moves shortly to Le Tracy. My orders to go home should be in today. It continues to rain here and the mud is the same. We shall certainly be glad to get home.

Affectionately,

Gerard

JERRY'S COMMENTS

Lt. Hugh Montgomery suggested that since we had time on our hands we should head south. No point going to Nice, he said; too crowded. So we decided to go down to Toulouse. There was plenty of room in Toulouse—and it was quiet. We arrived in Toulouse in time for Christmas. We spent several days in Toulouse and then journeyed back to Tours.

GERARD HUGHES TO LUCY HUGHES

Tuesday, 24 December 1918

Dear Mother:

We shall be home shortly after this letter reaches you. George sent a cable yesterday—but it may not reach you. On arriving at Tours, we took some leave, as there was no prospect of getting away right off. Everything is tied up. The ports are jammed and the concentration camps [embarkation camps] are full. We may not have to stay in Tours long after our leave is up. We will be glad to get back. All this hanging around with nothing to do gets on one's nerves.

George is well enough now, but should be at home so that he can take a long rest. When we get to Boston he is going to see Dr. Rogers (an osteopath) and then we will travel up to New Hampshire. It's a good thing the war is over, because George was hitting the pace that kills. He had a big reputation in the First Army. He was among the first fliers on the front and got to know all the top officers. He was recommended for the French Croix de Guerre but it never went through. He was also recommended to go back to Issoudun to tell the birds there how things were run on the front. He preferred, however, to take a squadron, and took the 183rd Flight Detachment.

Affectionately,

Gerard

GERARD HUGHES TO LUCY HUGHES

Saturday, 28 December 1918

Dear Mother:

We are doing nothing but amusing ourselves, living in a hotel in Tours and awaiting orders to return from overseas. Today they tell me

that the orders are expected in a day or two. All we can do is sit tight and wait. They have a very nice YMCA Officers' Club here and we usually take supper there and sit around and read in the evening. It's a great life.
Affectionately,
Gerard

GERARD HUGHES TO LUCY HUGHES
Sunday, 29 December 1918
Dear Mother:
    Just a line. Having nothing on earth to do all day long, I find time enough to write you every day now. All I do is think about getting home, and seeing you and Jeanie—and Virginia [his Texas girl friend]. All George does is sleep! I think we will leave Tours this week, but I'm afraid we will have to wait for another week at Angers. It has become a sort of concentration point and the last stop before the boat. We would like to go over to England and see who is over there, but no one at all is allowed to go over. Some time when we all have the money we can come back and visit. I'm sick of France. It rains all the time. It's no place for anything but a duck.
Affectionately,
Gerard

GERARD HUGHES TO LUCY HUGHES
Wednesday, 1 January 1919
Dear Mother:
    Orders are now in our possession which enable us to proceed to Angers, which is a sort of concentration point for casuals going home. Probably we will stay there a week or ten days before we will be sent to the Port of Embarkation. There will be no delay at that port, I understand. All of which means that we will leave before the middle of January, and will arrive in the U.S. sometime after, depending on the speed of the scow which takes us home. The end of the month will see us in the U.S. anyhow.
Affectionately,
Gerard

GERARD HUGHES TO LUCY HUGHES
Saturday, 4 January 1919
Dear Mother:
    Just a line to say we have left Tours and are now at Angers. We are in a big Officers' Casual Camp. We will stay here probably ten days or at the most two weeks, and then go straight to a base port and a ship. That's

my understanding of the situation. We have good barracks here. They are big brick buildings, recently constructed. We are both well, naturally, but we sure would like to be in the U.S. This hanging around gets on a man's nerves.

Affectionately,

Gerard

JERRY'S COMMENTS

Finally we received orders which directed us to proceed by train down to Angers on the Loire. In Angers we were housed in an old French army barracks building. It was winter, and that building had windows with nothing in them—no frames, no glass, nothing—just the cold air coming in. The mattresses on the beds were stuffed with fagots, which were pieces of wood slightly smaller than broom sticks. The concrete floor would probably have been more comfortable. Fortunately, George's bedding roll, containing several blankets, arrived safely from Manonville. My bedding roll, however, never made it. I found it many months later in an Army warehouse in Hoboken, New Jersey. Every morning and every evening during our stay at Angers, an officer appeared and conducted roll call. We lined up outside the barracks and answered when our names were called. George never came out for roll call; he was too ill to come out into the chill winter air. When his name was called, I answered in as deep a voice as I could, "Hoooh!" When my name was called, I yelled in a squeaky tenor, "Heeer!"

They never discovered the deception, although we were fearful they would. If they would have, the result might have been that George would have been sent to another hospital and would have faced the prospect of a trip home in a hospital ship—if he survived. Finally orders came through directing us to travel to Brest to await a ship. What a place Brest was! The rain was falling and the place was a sea of mud. We could walk safely only on the board walks which were laid down everywhere. If we took a misstep, we sank up to our ankles in mud.

GERARD HUGHES TO LUCY HUGHES [POST CARD]
Sunday, 5 January 1919

Maybe the ice has been broken at last. Some 250 go out in the morning.

Gerard

GERARD HUGHES TO LUCY HUGHES [POST CARD]
Wednesday, 8 January 1919
 We will be very lucky if we reach the U.S. by February 1st. We should leave here about the 16th.
Affectionately,
Gerard

JERRY'S COMMENTS
 We sat around those barracks for a week or so. No roll calls to fill our days with excitement. Just boredom. There was one character there, an artist named Otto Cushing, who had apparently been sent over to make sketches at the front. I well remembered his drawings in the old *Life* magazine, when it was a humorous periodical. I always admired his pictures because they were line drawings of gods and goddesses of ancient Greece, done in the classic style that fitted the stories of the *Iliad.* If I remember correctly, he stated that he had left some of his best work on the walls of the leading brothels of Paris. He was a real character.
 Finally a fairly large boat showed up in the harbor. It had no superstructure. Sure enough, it was the old *Minnekada,* the ship that brought Klyver and me over. Now it was here to take George and me back. After we arrived in the New York harbor, officers came on board, and the first thing they barked at us was, "Take off those Sam Browne belts! Nobody is allowed to wear them in the United States!" We were flabbergasted. Every officer in France was wearing them. What a welcome for the returning veterans! We immediately sensed a powerful feeling of hostility toward the returning veterans, at least in the ranks of the commissioned officers. Apparently those who didn't get a chance to get across resented those who had—especially when the veterans wanted to strut around the home front wearing those Sam Browne belts.
 But we were safely home at last. Our final step out the door of the Army was a trip to Mitchel Field and an honorable discharge from the United States Army. On February 5th, 1919, my brother George and I were no longer active members of the Air Service of the United States Army. We had been members of the Air Service for almost two years. Our experiences had broadened our personal perspectives immensely, but we—and certainly George—had paid a price for the hazards we faced.

Conclusion:

Postwar Activities of George and Jerry Hughes

After the war George and Jerry embarked on a career that, while not directly linked to their aviation adventures, nevertheless could be said to have been generated by them. Perhaps because their flying experiences at Mineola had been so valuable to them, they decided to go into business for themselves in the Mineola area. The idea was apparently suggested to them by one of the members of George Hughes's 258th Aero Squadron, Andrew Shiland, the squadron adjutant and in civilian life a prominent Wall Street lawyer. Through his assistance the Hughes brothers were able to borrow $3000, with which they purchased the Garden City Garage, located within five miles of the flying field at Mineola. The garage, situated at 7th Street and Franklin Avenue, near the Garden City Hotel, was in an ideal growth location (Fig. 20).

As a result of their Air Service experience, the Hughes brothers had gained valuable knowledge about operating and maintaining aircraft engines and in overseeing related maintenance activities. Through his determined efforts to enlarge the 258th Aero Squadron's fleet of cars, which included a Dodge and a Cadillac—and to keep them in good running order—George had undoubtedly become something of an expert in car repair. In his letters to Jerry written while he was in France, George often mentions hints for engine repair and maintenance. The Hughes brothers were in an excellent position to take advantage of the quickly growing interest in automobiles that bloomed in America, and especially in the Long Island area, in the years immediately after the war. The Hughes brothers operated the Garden City Garage from 1920 through 1946. During those 26 years they made many improvements to the facility and contributed significantly to the business and cultural life of the Garden City area.

In 1926 Jerry Hughes became one of the founding members of the Garden City Chamber of Commerce. He was the third president of the Garden City Chamber of Commerce, serving three terms. An example of his civic-minded spirit was his initiative, in the mid-1930s, in encouraging other members of the Garden City business community to support the development of over 6,000 accessible parking spaces for Garden

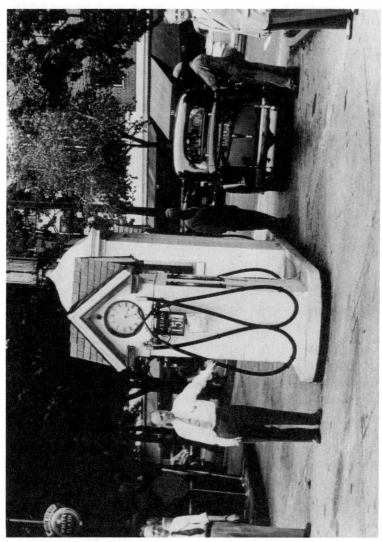

Fig. 20. The Garden City Garage. This photo shows one corner of the building, which took up most of one city block. George (left) and Jerry (second from left) observe as one of their customers fills his car with gasoline, which cost just under 16 cents a gallon in 1940.

City customers. This Chamber-endorsed activity drew national attention, as representatives from states as far away as California came to Garden City to see how such a project could be brought about. In addition to helping found the Chamber of Commerce, Jerry was a founding member of the Mineola Rotary Club and was active in many club activities through the years. In 1977 the Chamber honored Jerry for his many services to the community by naming him "Man of the Year."

Throughout the years, George and Jerry saw the flying field at Mineola evolve from a grass pasture into a thriving commercial airfield. The main center of activity of the original Mineola flying field in 1917 was located near the corner of Old Country Road and Clinton Road. The other two roads which formed the approximate boundaries of the field were Stewart Avenue, which paralleled Old Country Road to the south, and Post Avenue, which paralleled Clinton Road to the east (Fig. 3). The earliest flying hangars had been built along Clinton Road. When the pace of activity began to increase in the summer of 1917, additional hangars were built along Old Country Road. The dual instruction that George and Jerry received was given near the corner of Old Country Road and Clinton Road. Once the students soloed, they flew from a part of the field farther east, called the "Plateau," which extended toward the corner of Old Country Road and Post Avenue.

South of Stewart Avenue was another field, near the corner of Clinton Road and Fulton Avenue, which was used to house Army infantry during World War I and became known as Camp Mills. The east end of that field, near the intersection of Post Avenue and Fulton Avenue, was known initially as the LWF Field, where the Lowe, Willard, and Fowler training aircraft were located. These two areas were separated from the Mineola Field and the "Plateau" by Stewart Avenue. Even before World War I ended, these fields began to be modified and renamed. The original Mineola Field became known as Hazelhurst Field No. 1, and underwent significant new construction, including additional hangars and administrative facilities. The "Plateau" area of the field became known as Hazelhurst Field No. 2, and then, after the war, it was known as Roosevelt Field [named in memory of Quentin Roosevelt]. After the death of John Purroy Mitchel,* former mayor of New York, the old LWF field became known as Mitchel Field.

After World War I, the flying fields at Mineola became increasingly used for commercial aviation and as a jumping-off point for fliers interested in flying across the Atlantic. The Curtiss Aircraft Company took over the old Mineola Field for its commercial flying activities, and the name changed to Curtiss Field. The few times that Jerry flew after the war, he did so through the use of Curtiss aircraft and Curtiss instructors.

A program for an airshow held at the Curtiss Flying Field in April 1922 indicates that both Jerry and George were participants. Other fliers scheduled to fly in that airshow included Bert Acosta, Eddie Rickenbacker, and Charles "Casey" Jones. Jerry flew often in the early 1920s, accumulating a total of over 40 hours from 1922 to 1927.

Those were years of great excitement at Curtiss Field, for by then interest in flying across the Atlantic had grown. One of the best-known aviators involved in the attempt was Richard Byrd, who, along with his copilot, Floyd Bennett, claimed to have flown over the north pole in 1926. Byrd's next goal was to fly the Atlantic, and he gathered his team at Roosevelt Field, the area formerly known as the "Plateau," the northeast corner of the old Mineola flying field. Byrd had a hangar constructed at the west end of the Plateau area. His flying team included Bernt Balchen and Bert Acosta. Many other teams were attempting to cross the Atlantic, using Roosevelt Field as their base. One team, led by Rene Fonck, a World War I French ace, crashed and burned at Roosevelt Field on September 21, 1926, when their three-engine aircraft lost control on takeoff. Two men were killed.

Jerry Hughes said that he had never before seen as much traffic as that which passed through the Garden City Garage during the months of April, May, and June of 1927, when so many well-known aviators were attempting to fly the Atlantic. Members of the press were especially numerous while each team prepared to depart. Jerry was friends with one reporter in particular, John Frogge, a cub reporter for the *New York Times,* who stopped by regularly and gave Jerry and George all the latest details of events happening at the field.

While Byrd, Fonck, and others were preparing for their flights, suddenly there appeared a single individual among them who flew in from St. Louis one day and announced that he was about to fly the Atlantic himself. That was Charles Lindbergh. Richard Byrd allowed Lindbergh to use his hangar while Lindbergh waited for the weather over the Atlantic to improve. When the report came in early on the morning of May 20, 1927, that the weather looked good, Lindbergh had his aircraft moved out of Byrd's hangar and positioned on the end of the makeshift runway that had been prepared. Lindbergh's takeoff run extended from a position near the Old Country Road to the end of the field bordered by Post Avenue. Lindbergh's aircraft barely cleared the telephone wires bordering Post Avenue. But once it got airborne, it flew the rest of the way to Paris, France, without incident. Jerry was not there to see the historic takeoff, however; he and his brother were opening the Garden City Garage for the morning's business. Eventually population growth in the Garden City–Mineola area resulted in the closure of the flying fields.

Today the Mineola Field is the location of a shopping mall, and the area known as the "Plateau" consists of two race tracks.

With the success of the Garden City Garage, the Hughes brothers decided it was time to build families. George married Frona Brooks, whose family had been long-time friends of the Hughes family, in 1927; Jerry married Charlotte Christ in 1928. George and Frona had two children, Octavia and Anita, and Jerry and Charlotte had four children, Anne, Thomas, Jean, and Marian. Although their work kept them productively occupied, Jerry continued to keep a watchful eye on his brother throughout the time of their ownership of the garage; Jerry believed that his brother never fully recovered his old strength and confidence after his illness in November of 1918.

In 1946 the Hughes brothers retired as active owners and operators of the Garden City Garage and leased the property, first to Gulf Oil, and then to Texaco. They continued to live in the Garden City area for the next twenty-five years, and Jerry remained active in community affairs. George Hughes died suddenly, on April 1, 1971, at the age of 79. Jerry and Charlotte remained in the Garden City area for another nine years, and then, in 1980, moved to a new home in New Concord, New Hampshire. Jerry once again became active in local community affairs while continuing to compile the narrative history of his brother's and his own career in the Air Service during World War I. He was a long-time member of the Daedalians, a society of military pilots; as one who flew in World War I, he was a founder member of that organization as well. Jerry was also active in a successful effort to persuade the U.S. Post Office to issue a commemorative stamp in honor of Eddie Rickenbacker: a commemorative stamp was issued in September of 1995.

When Jerry first discussed with me the possibility of writing a book about the experiences of his brother and himself during World War I, he asked how long I thought it would take to produce a book in its final form. I told him that my previous effort had taken five years from the time I sat down in front of the computer until the time the book appeared in print. When he heard this, Jerry began to laugh with great glee. "Oh my," he said, "I hope you can work faster than that. I don't think I've got five years to wait." I was delighted at his sense of humor and amazed that he could find such a thought amusing. When I visited him, I had the sense that he was unstoppable, would live forever. I was sure he would live at least for five years more. I told him I thought he would outlive me.

I was wrong. Jerry's wife, Charlotte, died in September 1995 at the age of 91; she and Jerry had been together for 63 years. Affected by Charlotte's death, Jerry began to suffer physical setbacks, and his own health began to fail. He died on February 28, 1996, just past his 101st birthday. His legacy is represented in the many good works he accomplished for the citizens of Garden City and Mineola throughout the years, and in his efforts and those of his brother, described in this book, which came to fruition primarily as a result of his lifelong dedication and determination.

List of Significant Names

During their years of flying for the United States Air Service, George and Jerry Hughes encountered many people of significant historical importance. These people, whose names are highlighted in the text by an asterisk (*), are briefly profiled below. Additional information about them may be found in sources listed in the bibliography.

Acosta, Bert. Bert Acosta was one of the best-known and most famous of American fliers in the years 1910-1940. He flew across the Atlantic with Richard Byrd and Bernt Balchen in the Fokker tri-motor aircraft *America*, which crash-landed off the coast of France on July 1, 1927.

Angel, Cyril M. A pilot in 12th Aero Squadron, he was killed in action on a mission flown on May 12, 1918, along with his observer, W. K. B. Emerson.

Baker, Hobey. A graduate of Princeton University, "Hobey" Baker was well-known for his prowess in football and hockey. Baker flew with a number of American aero squadrons, the 94th (March-April 1918), the 103rd (April-July), and the 13th (July-August). In August he became commander of the 141st Aero Squadron. He was killed after the Armistice, on December 21, when he decided to take one last ride in one of the squadron aircraft. Apparently it developed engine trouble on take-off, and instead of landing straight ahead, as was the preferred practice, Baker tried to turn back to the field. The aircraft stalled and hit the ground, killing Baker. Baker apparently had a strong preference for ivy-league graduates in his squadron; he painted the aircraft in his squadron with the Princeton colors, orange and black.

Biddle, Charles. At the end of the war, Charles Biddle was in command of the 4th Pursuit Group, which included Hobey Baker's 141st Aero Squadron. Biddle had been a long-time member of the Air Service; he had flown first with SPAD 73 and SPAD 124, French Escadrilles; he commanded the 13th Aero Squadron from June through October of 1918. He was placed in command of the 4th Group at the end of October, shortly before the war ended.

Bingham, Hiram. Before the war Hiram Bingham had been a faculty member at Yale University. He was brought to France as the third commanding officer of the 3rd Aviation Instruction Center at Issoudun, from August 1918 until the Armistice. After the war he served in Congress and continued to be a strong supporter of military and civilian aviation development.

Bowles, Reginald. After a colorful career as a foot soldier, Bowles transferred to the American Air Service. Like Jerry Hughes, he completed training too late to see combat before the war ended. He was assigned briefly to the 147th Aero Squadron (on 19 November 1918) and then to the 138th Aero Squadron (on 21 December 1918). He was apparently the same Bowles who brought up 40 bodies from the hold of the steamer *Eastland* when it sank in the Chicago River in July of 1915.

Brereton, Lewis. A 1911 Naval Academy graduate, Brereton learned to fly in 1912 and went to France with General Benjamin Foulois in 1917. In April of 1918 he was assigned as commanding officer of the 12th Aero Squadron, replacing Major Harry Brown. Brereton was C.O. of the 12th until July 1, when he moved to the staff of 1st Corps of the Air Service. After World War I, Brereton continued to progress in his military career, advancing to the rank of Lieutenant General. He held a variety of command positions in the Pacific, Middle East, and Europe in World War II. After World War II ended, he published *The Brereton Diaries*.

Bridgman, Hugh. Bridgman enlisted in the Air Service in September of 1917, trained at Tours and Issoudun, served for a time with a French Escadrille, Spa 98, then flew with the 49th Aero Squadron from the middle of August until the Armistice.

Brown, Harry. Brown was the first commanding officer of the 12th Aero Squadron, from 1 February to April 1918, when he was reassigned as commanding officer of the newly formed 96th Aero Squadron. On July 10, flying a bombing mission in bad weather, he and several other aircraft of the 96th Aero Squadron were forced to land behind enemy lines, and all men were captured and made prisoner.

Carret, Philip L. Carret enlisted in July 1917, trained at Tours and Issoudun, and was involved primarily in ferrying planes from Orly Field, Paris, to other locations in France.

Christie, Arthur. Christie was the first commanding officer of Wilbur Wright Field, in Dayton, Ohio. Christie joined the army in 1913, learned to fly at North Island in 1915, and flew with the 1st Aero Squadron in Mexico. In February 1918 he left Wright Field and became commanding officer of the 99th Aero Squadron, an observation squadron. By the time of the armistice he was commanding officer of the 5th Observation Corps.

Coffyn, Frank. Frank Coffyn was taught to fly by Orville Wright in May 1910 and was associated with the Wright brothers for the next two years. He is credited with taking the first motion picture film from an aircraft. He served in the U.S. Army during World War I and was supervisor of training at Rich Field, Waco, Texas, from January to July of 1918.

Coyle, Arthur. Coyle learned to fly at Mineola and was assigned to the 1st Aero Squadron, flying with it through the spring of 1918. When Major Royce was reassigned, Coyle was made commanding officer of the 1st, and served in that position from May through most of October. He was assigned as commanding officer of the 1st Corps Observation Group in October.

Dunsworth, James L. Dunsworth received flight training at North Island in October of 1916 and served with the 1st Aero Squadron in New Mexico. He was officer in charge of instruction at Chanute Field for a brief period of time in the fall of 1917, then was sent to France. He took command of the 90th Aero Squadron (an observation squadron) for one month, in April of 1918, and then took command of the 96th Aero Squadron, a bomber squadron, in July, after its commander, Maj. Harry Brown, was captured. On September 10, Dunsworth was placed in command of the newly formed 1st Day Bombardment Group, a position he held for approximately two weeks before he was relieved. It is apparent that Dunsworth was a by-the-rules officer with little sense of the subtleties of leadership.

Emerson, W. K. B. An observer in 12th Aero Squadron, he was killed in action on a mission on May 12, 1918, along with his pilot, Cyril Angel.

Fitzgerald, Shepler W. Fitzgerald learned to fly at North Island, California, in 1914. He traveled to France in the fall of 1917 and was assigned to a staff position. During World War II he served in the Office of the Inspector General.

Flickinger, Harrison William ("H. W."). Flickinger was educated at Massachusetts Institute of Technology, learned to fly in Chicago in 1917, and instructed at Chanute Field and elsewhere. He served in a variety of positions in Republic Aircraft, near Farmingdale, Long Island, eventually becoming president of the company.

Foulois, Benjamin D. Foulois enlisted in the Army in 1898 and was commissioned as 2nd Lt. in 1901. After receiving some flight instruction from Orville Wright, he taught himself how to fly in Army Airplane No. 1 at Ft. Sam Houston Texas, in 1910. As commanding officer of the 1st Aero Squadron, he assisted General Pershing in his Mexican campaign. Foulois sailed for France in 1917 and was assigned as Chief of the Air Service of the 1st Army of the American Expeditionary Force. His office had primary responsibility for overseeing procurement of aircraft and training of aircrew. Foulois later was promoted to the rank of Major General and named Chief of the Army Air Corps. He retired in 1935.

Gilpatric, Guy. Gilpatric learned to fly in Los Angeles in 1912 at the age of 16. During that year he set an altitude record of 4665 feet flying in a Deperdussin monoplane. In 1916 he flew as a civilian instructor in Toronto teaching Canadian cadets to fly. After the United States entered the war, he was commissioned and sent overseas with the 1st Aero Squadron in August of 1917. He served as the Engineering Officer for the 1st Aero Squadron throughout the full period it was in action. Gilpatric later achieved fame as the author of the Glencannon stories, which were published in the *Saturday Evening Post* in the 1930s and 1940s. He also was the author of a collection of flying stories, *Guy Gilpatric's Flying Stories*.

Hanley, Thomas. Hanley graduated from the U.S. Military Academy in 1915 and learned to fly in North Island in 1917. He served briefly as commanding officer of Chanute Field, Rantoul, Illinois, and later as assistant to the commanding officer of Rich Field, Waco, Texas. He served in the Army Air Forces throughout World War II and retired as a Major General in 1952.

Haslett, Elmer. Haslett flew as an observer with the 1st and 12th Aero Squadrons. He was with the 12th from November of 1917 to February of 1918. He then flew as an observer with a French unit. He returned to the 12th and flew as an observer from April to July. Haslett flew at least one mission with George Hughes as pilot. He wrote an account of his experiences in the 1st and 12th, *Luck on the Wing*.

Hinds, Elliott P. ("Pop"). At 45 years of age, "Pop" Hinds was perhaps one of the oldest fliers serving on the front. A pilot in the 12th Aero Squadron, he replaced George Hughes as Engineering Officer. He died in an aircraft accident on June 26, 1918.

Jones, Charles S. ("Casey"). One of George Hughes's first students at Wilbur Wright Field, Jones completed his flight training at Wright Field in October 1917 and traveled to France, where he completed his training at Issoudun and Cazeau. He returned to Issoudun as a flying instructor. He served for a time with a French aero squadron at the front, then returned to Issoudun. After the war he was involved in a number of aviation activities, becoming a senior executive in the Curtiss-Wright Corporation.

Kennedy, John C. ("Jack"). Kennedy flew with the 12th Aero Squadron from the middle of April until the first of August, when he was assigned as commanding officer of the 186th Aero Squadron, an observation squadron. The 186th became combat ready shortly before the end of October, but bad weather kept the squadron from flying many combat missions.

Kennedy, Wilbur. One of the few pilots who remained with the 12th Aero Squadron throughout the time the squadron was in combat, from May through October 1918.

Kilner, Walter G. Kilner, then a captain, was the commanding officer of the Mineola training field in the spring of 1917. He received his Junior Military Aviator rating in 1915 and in 1916 he was a member of the 1st Aero Squadron, which was involved with General Pershing's Mexican Expedition in 1916. Eventually promoted to Colonel, he was assigned as commander of the 3rd Aviation Instruction Center, Issoudun, France, from October 1917 until May 1918, when he was made Chief of Training for the Air Service, Allied Expeditionary Force.

Kirby, Maxwell. Kirby had enlisted in the Army in 1904. He flew with the 1st Aero Squadron in Mexico. He served as officer in charge of training at Wilbur Wright Field before being assigned as commanding officer of Chanute Field, Rantoul, Illinois. Later sent to France, he flew for a short period of time with the 94th Aero Squadron and was credited as being the last pilot to shoot down a German aircraft before the war ended.

Lindsley, Henry. Lindsley trained with the Hughes brothers at Garden City and eventually flew with the 93rd Aero Squadron from the middle of August 1918 until the Armistice.

Lufbery, Raoul. Lufbery, an ace with 17 aircraft to his credit, was one of the original Lafayette Escadrille pilots flying with the French Air Force until America entered the war, when he was transferred to the 94th Aero Squadron, the first of America's pursuit ("chasse") squadrons to be declared combat ready. On May 19, 1918, Lufbery took off in a Nieuport 28 in a hurried attempt to intercept and shoot down a German aircraft that was flying in the vicinity of the airfield. Apparently in his haste to become airborne, Lufbery failed to fasten his seat belt and fell out of his aircraft while he was maneuvering to attack the other aircraft.

Luhr, Frederick J. Luhr traveled to France with George Hughes in December of 1917. He trained and flew with the 12th Aero Squadron until August of 1918. In the middle of September he was assigned as Commanding Officer of another observation squadron, which became operational by the end of October.

Mitchel, John Purroy. Before the war Mitchel was Mayor of New York City. He entered the Air Service and apparently fell out of a training aircraft while doing acrobatics at Gerstner Field, Louisiana. The training portion of the field at Garden City was later named in his honor.

Mitchell, John. Mitchell served in Chaumont, France, on the staff of his older brother, Colonel William Mitchell. He was killed May 27, 1918, in an aircraft accident at Colombey-les-Belles, France (near Toul), while attempting to land.

Mitchell, William ("Billy"). Colonel (later Brigadier General) "Billy" Mitchell was assigned as Chief of the Air Service of the Armies of Advance, located at Chaumont, France. Mitchell's job was to oversee the preparation for combat of all American units serving on the front. He served in this position throughout the war. After the war he advocated the establishment of a separate American air service. He was eventually court-martialed in December 1925 as a result of his comments critical of the American political and military leadership.

Montgomery, Donald H. ("Hugh"). Montgomery, a pilot, flew with the 12th Aero Squadron from the first of May until the middle of August, when he was transferred to the 183rd Flight Detachment. Then, around the first of September, he and the other members of the 183rd were transferred to the 258th Aero Squadron. He remained with the unit until the Armistice. Montgomery was one of the few fliers to accompany George Hughes from the 12th to the 258th Aero Squadron.

Morse, Daniel. Morse was one of the original members of the 1st Aero Squadron in France and flew with the 1st until the middle of June 1918, when he was assigned as commanding officer of the 50th Aero Squadron, another observation squadron. After the war, he was chief author of the 50th Aero Squadron history.

Nungesser, Charles. Nungesser was the third-ranking French ace, with 45 aircraft shot down; his record was exceeded only by Fonck and Guynemer. He was a logical choice to enter Metz with the French entourage. After the war he perished, along with his copilot Francois Coli, in an attempt to fly the Atlantic from east to west in 1927.

Pagé, Victor. Pagé was an aircraft engineering officer and academic instructor initially assigned to Garden City. Later he was sent to France and served on Colonel Hiram Bingham's instructional staff of the 3rd Aviation Instruction Center (AIC) at Issoudun. He authored several important text books and reference books pertaining to aircraft operation and design.

Patterson, John H. John Patterson, one of Dayton's most prominent businessmen, founded the National Cash Register Company (NCR). The "Patterson" portion of Wright-Patterson AFB is named after his nephew, Frank Stuart Patterson, who died in an aircraft accident at Wright Field on June 19, 1918.

Pershing, John. General John Pershing was the head of the American Expeditionary Forces in France. Prior to American entry into the war, he had achieved fame as head of the American Punitive Expedition into Mexico. Pershing was a widely respected military leader, and his arrival in France in the fall of 1917 was hailed as a significant event. Pershing ranks in the top ten listing of important American generals of the twentieth century.

Petain, Henri. General Petain, an important French general, led the French forces into the town of Metz, France, on November 19, 1918. The entry of the French troops was significant in that Metz was the largest and most important French town to be held by the Germans throughout most of the war and the French triumphant entrance signaled the return of the town to French control.

Reynolds, John. Reynolds transferred to the Signal Corps from the Coast Artillery in 1916, learned to fly at Rockwell Field, California, then spent some months with the 1st Aero Squadron in Mexico. In November 1917 he was sent to France and participated in observation pilot and observer training at Amanty, France, along with members of the 1st and 12th Aero Squadrons. He was commanding officer of the 91st Aero Squadron (another observation squadron) from February until early September of 1918.

Rickenbacker, Eddie. Rickenbacker began the war in 1917 as a driver for General Pershing. He went through training at Tours and was one of the original members of the 94th Aero Squadron. He was credited with 27 aircraft shot down and by the end of the war was the commanding officer of the 94th Aero Squadron. He was America's top World War I ace.

Roosevelt, Quentin. Youngest son of President Theodore Roosevelt, Quentin Roosevelt went to France after completing his training at Garden City. He was assigned for a period to the 3rd Aviation Instruction Center at Issoudun, France, then to the 95th Aero Squadron. He was killed in combat on July 14, 1918. He was credited with downing one enemy aircraft.

Royce, Ralph. A 1914 graduate of West Point, Royce learned to fly at North Island in 1915 and was sent to France in August 1917 with the 1st Aero Squadron, to which he was assigned as commanding officer. At their initial location at Amanty, France, he set up an observer training program for the 1st and 12th Aero Squadrons. He remained in command of the 12th until August 1918, when he was assigned to the aviation staff of the 1st Army.

Russell, Clinton W. Russell graduated from West Point in 1913, learned to fly in 1916, and participated in General Pershing's Expedition to Mexico later that year. He served in various capacities at a number of flying fields during World War I, including commanding officer of Rich Field, Waco, Texas, during the spring and summer of 1918. He eventually reached the rank of Brigadier General.

Saunders, William H. Saunders was the senior observer and operations officer for the 12th Aero Squadron. He flew with the squadron from the April 25 until the first of June 1918, when he was replaced as squadron operations officer by Elmer Haslett. Saunders eventually returned to the United States as an instructor in the Air Service Observer School at Ft. Sill, Oklahoma.

Schroeder, Rudolph ("Shorty"). Schroeder learned to fly on his own before the war. He was an instructor at Chanute and Ellington Fields before being assigned in 1918 to Wilbur Wright Field, where he was chief test pilot. At Wilbur Wright Field he set three altitude records, in September 1918 (28,900 feet), in October 1919 (33,500 feet), and February 1920 (over 38,000 feet). He left the military service in 1920, eventually becoming vice president in charge of safety for United Air Lines.

Thaw, William ("Bill"). William Thaw was one of the first members of the Lafayette Escadrille, an all-American volunteer squadron in the French air force. Thaw flew with the unit from April 1916, when the unit first flew in combat, until February 1918. He then was assigned as commanding officer of the 103rd Aero Squadron, the unit that the Lafayette Escadrille became when it joined the American forces. Thaw commanded the 103rd until the middle of August, when he was assigned as 3rd Pursuit Group commander. His younger brother, Blair Thaw, was killed on August 18 while flying a mission with the 135th Aero Squadron, of which he was the commanding officer. Bill Thaw was widely recognized and respected for his many years of experience and leadership with the French and American aviation units.

Thayer, Sigourney ("Sig"). Thayer, a pilot, flew with the 12th Aero Squadron from the beginning of June until the end of September 1918. He then transferred to the 94th Aero Squadron in October, and then, about ten days later, to the 95th Aero Squadron, with whom he was flying when the war ended.

Weaver, George ("Buck"). A civilian instructor at Rich Field, Waco, Texas, George Weaver later moved to Troy, Ohio, north of Dayton, and started the Weaver Aircraft Corporation. WACO aircraft, sturdy biplanes, were immensely popular aircraft in the 1930s.

Zinn, Frederick W. Zinn joined the French Foreign Legion early in the war, then flew as an observer in a French squadron, Esc. F. 24, from December 1916 until October 1917. Working at the American Headquarters at Chaumont, he coordinated the transfer of American personnel flying with the French to American units. He flew for a short period of time with the 135th Aero Squadron in September and then worked as part of the 1st Air Depot at Colombey-les-Belles.

Bibliography

These works provide additional information about the people, units, and actions that George and Jerry Hughes encountered or experienced during their travels in World War I. Each source is followed by a brief explanation of its importance or relevance to the Hughes narrative.

Biddle, Charles. *The Way of the Eagle*. New York: Scribner's, 1919. Biddle was a member of the 13th Aero Squadron before being assigned as Commanding Officer of the 4th Pursuit Group.

Bingham, Hiram. *An Explorer in the Air Service*. New Haven: Yale University Press, 1920. One of the most detailed accounts of Air Service training at the 3rd Aviation Instruction Center at Issoudun, France. Bingham was camp commander from August 1918 until the Armistice.

Codman, Charles. *Contact*. Boston: Little, Brown, 1937. An account of the 96th Aero Squadron, the unit commanded for a period of time by Major Harry Brown, who landed behind German lines with a number of squadron aircraft in bad weather.

Dade, George C., and Frank Strnad. *Picture History of Aviation on Long Island, 1908-1938*. New York: Dover, 1989. Profusely illustrated; very helpful in tracing the evolution and historical development of the Mineola area flying fields.

Hall, James Norman, and Charles Nordhoff. *The Lafayette Flying Corps*. Boston: Houghton Mifflin, 1920. 2 vols. Detailed accounts of several noteworthy Americans who flew for the French before flying in American units, including Raoul Lufbery and William Thaw.

Haslett, Elmer. *Luck on the Wing: Thirteen Stories of a Sky Spy*. New York: Dutton, 1920. Haslett, an observer in the 12th Aero Squadron, devotes most of his book to describing his experiences in the 12th, including two rides with the squadron commander, Major Lewis Brereton. Although Haslett flew with George Hughes on at least two missions, he never mentions him.

Hudson, James J. *Hostile Skies: A Combat History of the American Air Service in World War I*. Syracuse: Syracuse University Press, 1968. One of the best summaries of American Air Service flying experience in World War I.

Lowell, A. Lawrence, and Caroline Ticknor, eds. *New England Aviators, 1914-1918: Their Portraits and Their Records*. Boston: Houghton Mifflin,

1919-1920. 2 vols. A classic reference work, useful for providing bio-graphical information for World War I aviators from the New England area. The entries for George and Gerard Hughes are found on pages 206-10 of Vol. 1.

Maurer, Maurer, ed. *The U. S. Air Service in World War I.* Washington: Office of Air Force History, 1979. 4 vols. Valuable information about the 12th Aero Squadron is contained in Vol. 1.

Norton, T. F., G. W. Stockwell, J. B. Burns, and W. F. Gates. *639th Aero Squadron Book: Being a Record of the Squadron's Activities.* Privately Printed, 1920. The 639th was a support squadron for the 1st and 12th Aero Squadrons during the first weeks they flew in combat.

Pagé, Victor W. *The A-B-C of Aviation.* New York: Henley, 1918. An overview of the principles of aircraft and flying. Volume based on information Pagé provided in his ground school classes during World War I.

——. *Modern Aircraft.* New York: Henley, 1927. Although published well after the end of World War I, this volume and the one that follows contain much information about World War I–era aircraft and engines.

——. *Modern Aviation Engines.* New York: Henley, 1929.

Perry, Garland. *An American Saga: William George Hughes. 1859-1902: A Pioneer Texas Rancher.* Boerne TX: Lebco Graphics, 1994. A biography of George and Jerry Hughes's father.

Rickenbacker, Eddie. *Fighting the Flying Circus.* New York: Stokes, 1919. An account of the activities of the best-known American unit, the 94th Aero Squadron, by America's best-known World War I ace.

Roosevelt, Kermit, ed. *Quentin Roosevelt: A Sketch in Letters.* New York: Scribner's, 1921. Memorial volume for Quentin Roosevelt, who trained with the Hughes brothers at Mineola.

Sloan, James J., Jr. *Wings of Honor: American Airmen in World War I.* Atglen PA: Schiffer Military History, 1994. A complete account of all American airmen who flew in combat in World War I.

Sweetser, Arthur. *The American Air Service: A Record of Its Difficulties, Its Failures, and Its Final Achievements.* New York: Appleton, 1919. An invaluable reference work describing the development of Air Service training and support activities during World War I.

Thayer, Lucien H. *America's First Eagles: The Official History of the U.S. Air Service, A. E. F.* Ed. Donald McGee and Roger Bender. San Jose: Bender, 1983. A useful early summary of Air Service activities.

Vaughan, David K., ed. *An American Pilot in the Skies of France: The Diaries and Letters of Lt. Percival Gates, 1917-1918.* Dayton OH: Wright State University Press, 1992. Gates flew with the 27th and 185th Aero Squadrons in France. Useful for comparing the training and combat experiences of another American aviator.

Walker, Lois E., and Shelby E. Wickham. *From Huffman Prairie to the Moon: The History of Wright-Patterson Air Force Base.* Dayton: 2750th ABW Office of History, 1988. Contains much information on Wilbur Wright Field and many of the pioneers of early flight.

Index

(Italicized items shown in photographs)